A sense of place :
978.83 WIS

Wise, Joe.

a sense of place

A CONVERSATION WITH PERK VICKERS

DATE DUE

© 2003 Joe Wise
All rights reserved in whole or in part.

ISBN 1-890437-78-6

Library of Congress Control Number: 2003107403

Cover and text design by Laurie Goralka Design

First Edition
Printed in the United States of America

Western Reflections Publishing Company®
219 Main Street
Montrose, CO 81401
www.westernreflectionspub.com

PREFACE

When twenty-two year old John Vickers rode into
Lake City, Colorado, on a borrowed horse that summer day in 1888, Grover Cleveland was President and
Colorado had been a state for eleven years. Young
Vickers' arrival in Lake City marked the end of a journey
that had begun seven years earlier when he'd left his
hardscrabble life in Sydney Mines, Nova Scotia, and traveled across Canada to Butte, Montana, and then to
Crested Butte and finally Lake City in search of a better
life. Over a hundred and twelve years and twenty-one
presidents later, his son, Perk Vickers, still lives in the
majestic and hostile land his father came to call home.

"Perk" is the perfect moniker for the youngest son of
John's eight children, for he is, if anything, in spite of his
eighty-eight years, perky. A Leprechaun of a man, his eyes
twinkle with remembered secrets and the lines of his face
bear evidence of his fondness for laughter. He is rarely
seen without his worn silver belly Stetson, and then only
indoors or in the presence of ladies. Perk has a ready wit
and a well-developed sense of irony. He is a student of history and a consumate Irish storyteller. He is a man with
firmly held views and is, as my grandfather would say, "a
good judge of horse flesh." Above all, Perk Vickers has a
love of family, a love of the land and a sense of place.

I have known Perk for fifty years, not as one knows a
personal friend, for our ages never allowed that, but as
a boy knows a true hero such as Babe Ruth or Ben
Hogan. I have never really, completely outgrown wanting his photograph, an admission that would surprise
and, I think, embarass him. I have admired him from
afar, drawn to him by the force of his personality and his

mastery of the mysteries of fishing and hunting and mining and road building, envious of his experiences and fascinated by his stories.

Someone once said there are going-place things and there are staying-place things. Going-place things are long, flat things, like rivers and roads. Staying-place things are tall, thin things, like trees and men. Perk Vickers is a staying-place thing and throughout his life he has fought, against all odds, to stay at home, a place which, as he is fond of saying, is "about as close to heaven as a man can get."

One autumn I rode with him as he drove us through the country he so loves. Using his ranch as a base, we drove north through Lake City and down the Lake Fork of the Gunnison River. We drove west up Henson Creek before weather stopped us at Rose's Cabin. We drove south, above Lake San Cristobal to the summit of Cinnamon Pass. "Tell me everything you know about this place," I said. And he did. What follows is the story of a family, a century and a very special place. It is Perk's story, in his own words — warts and all.

PART ONE

NORTH THROUGH LAKE CITY AND DOWN THE RIVER

"It Wasn't All Pretty"

TO GUNNISON

ALPINE ROAD

ELK CREEK

THOMPSON RANCH

FOURTH OF JULY CREEK

CLINT BUSKIRK'S
RANCH

NORTH OF
LAKE CITY

DEVIL'S CREEK

HIGH BRIDE GULCH

RAILROAD
HIGH BRIDGE

149

INDEPENDENCE GULCH

EATON CREEK

V.C. BAR
RANCH

N
W · E
S

TCM TUNNEL

LARSON CREEK

SPARLING GULCH

B I G   B L U E   W I L D E R N E S S

C A N N I B A L   P L A T E A U

SAN JUAN
RANCH

BALDY
MOUNTAIN
▲

FRIENDS CREEK

CRYSTAL
LAKE

VGARDE GULCH

149

▲ NEOGA
MOUNTAIN

LAKE CITY

▲ STATION ELEVEN

"This is about as close to heaven as a man can get," Perk said, hands in his pockets, rocking with obvious pride and surveying the view before us as we stood together on the front porch of his house looking over his ranch on the Lake Fork.

Beyond the close comfort of the little valley, beyond the weathered ranch buildings, beyond the corrals, beyond the horses grazing in the meadow, beyond the line of pointed river trees, the oversized mountains stood shoulder to shoulder in a protective arc against the sky.

"When we moved down here from the upper ranch in Horse Park we had lived there for years." He pointed out the log building that now serves as the office for the ranch and the tourist cabins along the river. "This house," he patted the porch railing, "was one of our first cabins when Dad went into the tourist business. We remodeled it when we moved in."

When Vickers' father arrived in Lake City in 1888, most of the homes were log cabins. The second local mining boom had begun, fueled by big strikes at the Golden Fleece and the Ute-Ulay Mines. The little city already boasted a new water works, city-wide electric lights, a handsome courthouse, a two-story jail and a one-story school. Rows of newly planted cottonwood trees lined the main streets.

In 1893 President Cleveland repealed the Sherman Silver Purchase Act. The price of silver dropped from $1.29 an ounce to fifty cents and almost immediately the bubble burst.

"When Dad came here in 1888, he went to work in the mines. When he started making a few dollars he bought other mines and started a saloon. In the Senate Saloon,

Dad conducted many of his mining deals. People would partner with him for the value of the grubstake.

"He had a saloon, two bowling alleys and two or three businesses right there in that little block — all on different lots. He had a livery stable just south of where the museum is now, but all that burned down during Prohibition. The city park is on those empty lots now."

"And then, when your dad got enough money, he bought this ranch?"

"Well, that's a little bit premature. See, Dad got a dose of the cyanide. This guy dropped dead in Dad's saloon when somebody put that cyanide in his drink. By God, my dad took a taste of it, and it took all the lining out of his throat. He was sick for a long time after that. While he was recovering he used to go to the Upper Ranch, what they call Horse Park, and hunt grouse. He wanted to homestead it, but he wasn't a U.S. citizen. So when he got a few dollars, just before 1910, he married my mother, Sarah Madison. Dad wasn't a U.S. citizen, so he got the upper ranch in Horse Park in my mother's name.

"They came up here to the Upper Ranch and started raising cattle. Raising big horses. Draft horses. Started raising cattle and sheep. And every two years had another child. Ended up with eight children. That's a lot of children.

"At first we only lived there in the summer. Come winter time, we moved down into town to the house down by the Catholic church. We lived in town during the winter. Up there by the Catholic church is the old Vickers' home. Then finally, my dad bought this place from McLeod, and we moved down here. We sold that dang house in town after all the brothers got married and moved away. During WWII, I was here by myself with my mother and dad. All my brothers were in the service. Money was tight during WWII and that house needed a lot of repair so we sold that house. Sold that house and five lots for five hundred bucks. Can you believe that? That guy that owns it right now put a lot of money in it, of course. He's got it for sale for I think $235,000."

"Who were your brothers?"

"Bob. Joe. They were my partners. My older brother was named Ivan, and then Jack, and two sisters, Ellen and Sarah."

"So the ones who stayed here in town were Bob and Joe and Ivan and you?"

"No. See. It reminds me of what happened. We were all trying to exist. And Ivan was the oldest. We boys was living up at the mine at the time — Jack and Ivan and I. Whenever any of the family got old enough to get married, they knew they had to get the hell out of here. They had to get out of Lake City. They couldn't make a living. So, Ivan got married in 1932, and then Jack. He wanted to get married to a Lake City girl, and then they left. My sisters had left earlier than that — they left when they were quite young. We had an aunt, my dad's sister, in California. She was one of the original sisters that went up to Alaska and made the money and had come down to California. Then my oldest daughter went out there and went to business school while she stayed with her aunt. When she got out of school she had enough money that she could send some home for her sister, Sarah. Sarah went out there and she stayed there, and she married a Californian. So finally, after Ivan got married, and the girls had already gone, and Jack got married, it was Bob and Joe and I. My younger brother, Howard, he got married young and went in the Army and never lived here after that. He died about four or five years ago."

"So you and Bob and Joe were the ones who were around most of the time?"

"That's right. We called our business the Vickers Brothers at that time."

"Where did your mother come from?"

"She was from Iowa."

"And your father met her here in Lake City?"

"He met her here. Yes. My mother and her family, the Madison family, came from Iowa, I guess probably around 1900. Her father left Iowa to come to Colorado to go into the light farming business. He had a team of oxen and came into the state near Eads, Colorado. In eastern Colorado, near Burlington. And he ran a farm there for two or three years 'til the grasshoppers and the drought ate him up. He heard about a place in the Gunnison area where they were building a new railroad into Lake City. So he sold his oxen and bought a team of horses or mules or whatever and came to Savoy (Cebolla) down here and set up a camp right there where the red bridge is today. It was by the hill there. He and his family had three or four kids. He was cutting ties and hauling them down the mountain to the railroad where they would pile 'em up, and the people from the railroad would come and buy those ties to build the railroad.

"One day he was coming down the hill with one son in the wagon. They had rope tied to the brake to stop the wagon. The rope broke and freed the wagon to run down the hill, and it tipped over and killed him. Well, Ray — his son — ran down to the house to tell his mother that his dad was under the wagon, so she went down to the railroad right-of-way, and some of the guys who were working there went up and helped pick him from under the wagon. They buried him right there on that hillside. I never have found the grave. I should have, but I haven't.

"So there she was with three or four kids, and expecting another one with nobody at all to help her. So the train crew and the people up and down the valley helped her get moved into Lake City. That's how she came to Lake City. And she got to be a midwife and got to taking in laundry to support that family. My God, what a physical hardship that must have been, but she raised that family and my mother. Her house was right this side of where my dad's saloon was.

"Well, one day my mother was walking down the alley on her way to school. My dad come out of the saloon there to get a bucket of coal and he met her. She was only about fifteen or sixteen years old. He said right then he fell in love with her. It didn't take long before they got married. God bless her. She was something special. I remember when she died. She helped us deliver most of our kids. Not all of 'em, but she was always there to help with some of them. Grandma Madison. That's what the kids called her. Sweet lady."

"Where is she buried?"

"She's buried down here at the cemetery. All the Vickers that died in Lake City are buried at that cemetery. The rest are up in Nova Scotia. We went back up there this fall. In one of those cemeteries we counted fourteen Vickers graves, and all of them had the same names as my family — John Vickers, Bob, Ivan, Robert. There are Vickers all over that place."

"Now, your father left Sydney Mines, Nova Scotia, and went to Butte, Montana?"

"I'll tell you where he was headed. He had two sisters that married a couple of Bostonians that went to Alaska and settled in the Dawson City area. They made all their money in placer gold mining. When he was just about eleven or twelve years old he heard about how they were making all that money, so he decided he wanted to get away from Nova Scotia. He said he was tired — he was a kid working in the mine and living on codfish and mackerel. That was the main diet.

"When he started out they were building that railroad across Canada. So he somehow, I don't know how, got on that train and decided he was going to Alaska. Well, when he got halfway across Canada, I think his money run out. He only had fifty dollars when he left home. He knew about coal mining and when he heard about a place called Butte, Montana, he got off and worked in a coal mine there. And while he was there, he heard about

Crested Butte, Colorado, an area that was just opening up, and he ended up there.

"See, he had an uncle — A.B. Carey — that had moved from Nova Scotia to Crested Butte some time before. He was the one that got my dad into Crested Butte. While Dad was there, he heard about a gold mining area opening up that was called Lake City, Colorado. So he came to Lake City. When he got to Lake City he heard about the Golden Fleece Mine that was just starting. He worked there for a couple or three years. Then he moved from the Golden Fleece to the Ute-Ulay. That's when he met Charley McKinley. He was always a good friend of Dad's. He helped Dad in every way he could. Dad was lucky. They used to play cards, and Dad got to be a good card player. They called him "Lucky John." It seemed like every time he got a deck of cards he made money. So that's how he got his start."

"Tell him about the ring," Perk's wife Emma Jean hollered at us from inside the house. Perk laughed, remembering.

"That Emma Jean. She likes the ring story. See my dad was what you might call a professional gambler, and he had some good friends who were gamblers. Charley Ward was one of them. Dave Borden another. They always heard about what great gambling there was in Silverton, and it was.

"The train was still running from Animas Forks to Silverton, and Charley Ward and my dad decided they was gonna go over to Silverton and gamble a day or two. So they took that buggy — a two-horse buggy — and they went over Engineer Mountain or Cinnamon Pass, I don't remember which. When they got to Animas Forks they put the horses in the livery stable there. It was a good livery stable. And they was gonna ride the train down to Silverton. It was only twenty miles. That was a long ride, you know, in those days.

"And when they got on that train there were four guys playing cards. One of 'em was a guy by the name of Walsh.

You've heard of the famous Walsh family. Walsh made a lot of money in the mines. They got to playing cards on that train and by the time they got to Silverton the game was going so strong they said, 'Hell, we can play cards. We don't need to go into town. We'll have the railroad park this car and we'll play right here.' And they had food brought into them.

"For two days they played cards. There was a little guy, one of these Cousin Jacks, a little Englishman, who had a diamond ring. When the card game was over, the guy had given my dad that ring as security. He said, 'You keep that ring, and I'll come to Lake City and I'll buy back that ring.' But he never showed up, and I still got the ring. My dad liked to say it was quite an experience — but it was a profitable experience. You know, it's hard to believe people in those days would do that kind of stuff. You can imagine getting on that train in Animas Forks. It's twenty miles down the road to Silverton. That damn little chug-chug train, hauling ore, or whatever it was. It was a freight train but it had passenger cars on it too. Those trains at that time had passenger cars and freight cars all mixed up together. I don't think my dad and those men ever went into town. They said they kept on gambling and had the food catered to them. That Thomas Walsh house is still there in Animas Forks. They rebuilt it. I was by there last year."

"So your father and mother homesteaded this ranch and it's been in the family ever since?"

"Well, by God, it wasn't that easy. See, during the war, when I came back from Tyler, Texas, we found out we didn't own this place. And that's a long story too."

"What were you doing in Tyler?"

"Well, to make a long story short, it was like a big family of us."

Family is an important word for Perk. So is friend.

"Roy Golston, he owned about all the property around. He had Hamden Meadows. He had Child's Park. He had that place where the Moncrief Ranch is now. He had all that. He came up here and bought it for taxes. Bought it and kept improving it. He had all those ranches. Well, I was working on the road up there above his place for the County, and he got to be a friend of ours. He said, 'There's plenty of Vickers. They don't need you here anymore. Why don't you come down to Tyler, Texas, and I'll put you through school and we'll go into the oil business.' He'd already made a million bucks in East Texas over at Kilgore. So, I decided to do that. Well, I'd met Emma here before that, but I thought if I went to Texas I'd get a better claim with her. So I went down there and went to Tyler school. I went to the commercial college before WWII. I had a lot of friends there. Sid Richardson had a home there right next to the guy I was working with, Roy Goldston. That Tyler was a beautiful city then. It's grown now I'm sure. I loved that Tyler. I'd probably stayed if it wasn't for the war starting. My brothers went in the service, but they didn't want me, I guess, because of this short leg. Broke it up in a horse fall when I was a kid. They thought I was gonna lose it.

"So after the brothers left, Mother and Dad were here all by themselves. So I came home. And that was when the events really got going. I had to really start to pushing. We didn't own a thing. We didn't even own this house here. None of it. By God, it's hard to believe it. It's hard to believe how cold-blooded those government guys were. With just a stroke of a pen they could have helped us, see. No sir! They was jealous. They couldn't stand to see us get this land.

"See, when Dad first got this land, he checked it out and found out that Dan McLeod, the man Dad bought it from, had made application under the Homestead Laws, and he would have got the title but he did not complete his requirements. Herman Meyers had it before McLeod. He was one of the jurors in the Alfred Packer trial. Meyers, he picked it up under what they call a declaratory statement in the '80s. On Federal land at that time — it was before they had the Homestead Law — Meyers made application under the declaratory statement. And he sold that to Dan McLeod and McLeod sold it to Dad. Dan McLeod was kicked out because he did not complete it. So after my dad got it, we got to checking into it and found out that this land had been withdrawn under the old government Power of Withdrawal Act for power purposes. The falls down the river was generating power."

"What do you mean withdrawn?"

"It wasn't available for homesteading or anything."

"So, once the government withdrew it, no one could claim it or homestead it?"

"They withdrew it in 1919 and we were already on the land and had made improvements. We couldn't do a thing. It took us ten years with the lawyers and the politicians to get that power withdrawal set aside. There's where we were lucky. Today you couldn't get at that at all. The minute we got that power withdrawal set aside we made application under Color of Title. And they could do that today — withdraw that land. They can withdraw land and all they have to do is add it to the Federal Register. If you don't read the Federal Register you don't know what's going on."

The Federal Register? I couldn't help being surprised. There stood this man, eighty-eight years old, wearing baggy khaki pants, a flannel shirt and an old slouch hat, looking like a simple man of the land and he's telling me he reads the Federal Register?

"So when did you get into the tourist business?"

"The Vickers have been in the tourist business about sixty-seven years. I graduated from high school in 1932 and we started that tourist business in the '30s."

"I know that chicken house you tried to rent to us wasn't the first cabin you ever rented."

Perk laughed. "Oh, I remember that night. You and your folks drove in after dark and asked Dad if he had a cabin for rent."

"That was some night. It was the first time we had been to Lake City, and my father said later when he got to Creede he looked at the map and saw that it was only fifty-six miles to Lake City."

"In those days, that was some fifty-six miles. Fifty-six miles of single lane gravel-road mountain pass." Perk blew his nose and tucked his handkerchief away.

"Well, he didn't know that. It was 6:00, but he figured it would take an hour and a half. We'd be in before dark."

"Hah. An hour and a half! In those days that trip over Slumgullion Pass was a three-hour trip. In good weather."

"And it was raining. Raining hard. We had an old Plymouth and the windshield wipers wouldn't work when the car was pulling uphill, so my father rode with his head out the window trying to see the edge of the road and the drop off. Before long it got dark. My brother and I got down on the floor of the back seat and covered our heads with our Roy Rogers color books. My mother said the lightning flashes that showed us the edge of the road was the only thing that saved us."

"I remember you all looked a little frazzled when you pulled in."

"That trip was so bad that for years after when we came back we always drove the long way around and came down through Gunnison."

"We didn't have any vacancies that night, but Dad had an idea. Hell, two dollars was two dollars. And in those days we needed every penny we could get. 'Let's rent 'em the chicken house,' Dad had said. He told your folks to come back in forty-five minutes and we all got up there and cleaned out that chicken house. The first thing we had to do was catch all those chickens."

He turned to me with a twinkle in his eye. "But you didn't stay. Musta' been all that Lysol smell."

"Mother said later when she went to look in the cabin she saw a mouse run across the floor, and she said, 'I'm not staying in there!'"

"Coulda' been. But you came back every summer after that."

"Every summer."

"And you love it here."

"Kinda like you do."

"Well, I'm sure glad you gave us a second chance. We never did rent that place out. The chickens kept it for years until we finally tore it down."

"I always thought that chicken house was your first tourist cabin."

"The first cabin we ever had was that cabin right next to where my brother is now. Right next to where the old chicken house was. We had that cabin, then we built this one where we're standing. Then we built the one in the middle. This house is part of the second cabin. That room in there, where the living room is now, we built that. My dad had attorneys by the name of Monahan and Lee Niles. They did some work for my dad. They came up to the ranch and said to my dad, 'Now John, if you'll build us a cabin along here somewhere, we'll rent it and help you out in that respect.' They wanted to come up there, see? So he built that cabin. 'Well, then my dad said, 'Hell, we'll build another cabin,' and we built those two cabins right over there. One we tore down later but the other one is where my brother Bob and his wife lived 'til they died. Right next to me—a guy from Texas bought that."

"So you just got into the tourist business a little at a time?"

"Oh, yeah. We built a cabin a year for about twenty years."

"When did you start putting them down by the river?"

Along the far side of the river, beyond the horse pasture and the pond, four old, porched log cabins were spaced under the cottonwoods that shaded them.

"The first one across the river was cabin number 7. We built that one in 1932 or '33. It's the third cabin to the right. We dug a little well there by hand and rocked it up. Had a little chev-wheel and a bucket where we pulled the water up out of the well. Had a two-holer behind the house there. We cut the logs on the upper ranch. Cut 'em by hand. We didn't have a chain saw. Never heard of a chain saw. Stripped the bark off by hand and brought 'em all the way down the mountain by horseback.

"You know, I look back over my books and I can show you family after family that has been coming here for fifty years. Like you. Hard to believe. Some of those youngsters who are now coming back, they came for years, and sooner or later they say, 'I've got to go back.' Always come back." He stood, looking out over the valley, then turned to me. "Come on in. I want to show you something."

I followed him into the house. A fieldstone fireplace covered one end of the room from floor to ceiling. The dark walls were covered with photographs.

"This is a picture of the railroad bridge. Just below VC Bar and in the canyon. At one time that was the highest railroad bridge in the world. Tore it down when the railroad left. Here, I got this last year."

He pointed to a framed plaque.

I read the inscription aloud. "Founding member of the Board of Directors of the Upper Gunnison River Conservancy District. Thirty-four years of continuous service beginning July 9, 1959."

"And this," he pointed to another plaque.

"Colorado River Water Conservation District awarded for thirty-six years of service. For valuable contribution to the Wildlife and the Colorado Division of Wildlife."

"You add those two together and my life is the water business. This a picture of that business block in town before it burned. See, there's a picture of my dad's place — the Senate Saloon."

"Now when do you figure that photograph was taken?"

"That had to be made, I'd say 1908 or 1910. See, that all burned after they passed this ridiculous law called Prohibition."

"You don't suppose somebody set fire to it?"

"Well they did, no doubt. Oh, they burned the whole block. Those guys in the business in those days made lots of enemies."

Here's some of that Golden Wonder gold." He pointed to some ore samples on the shelf. "You can have that piece if you want it. That's worth about $7,000 a ton."

I picked up one of the black rocks.

"Now where's the gold? This black stuff here that looks like soot?"

"That's it. That's what you call tellurides of gold."

I turned the heavy ore in my hand feeling the heft of it.

"So this is what they came for? I thought gold was, well, gold?"

"Not if it's oxidized. That placer gold in California, that gold in the streams, that's gold-colored."

"What's this a picture of?"

"That's the old arrastra out in front of the office," he said stepping to the window. "You can see it from here. That's an antique itself. They had tongues out on the edges and the burros turned it. They turned it and it crushed the rock. On the upper ranch there's an old ox cart. That ox wagon, they broke the axle and they unhooked the oxen and left it. We don't have any idea what year or anything. Nobody knows whose it was. Here's the picture right here. A wagon that was made that way didn't have any nuts on the axle. They had to do it by wedges holding it on. They kept the wheel tight by driving in them wedges."

Emma Jean called from the coffee smells of the kitchen. "What have you men got planned for today?"

"Well," Perk said, walking into the kitchen, "I thought we'd head down below town. Lots of history down there."

"Be sure the car has gas," she said with a wink at me.

"If I run out of gas I'll just have to stop. I'll call you."

"Don't call me," she said, laughing.

Perk leaned over and gave her a kiss on the cheek. "Bye, Sweetie. We'll see you when we get back."

"I'll keep an eye on him," I said as we went out the door, "if you think that will help any."

"Oh, I don't know," she smiled. "I've tried that."

We drove away from the ranch and headed north toward town, two miles away. As we passed the ranch office I asked him about a pile of white bags stacked on the ground.

"Those are the ore bags. Some of those are full, others are just brand new. They take those bags up to the mine, Joe, and they bring the ore out of the mine in a bucket on top there, and they dump the ore right in that ore bag and bring it down. When they got twenty bags they got a truckload. They come in and put them on a truck and tie 'em on so they can't fall off all the way to Helena, Montana. One day when I was sitting out here, a man and his wife came in. They was coming up just this side of the lake, and they wanted to know if they could have those bags to dump their garbage. They thought that was a public garbage dump. I said you don't realize those bags out there are full of gold. I said those bags will run about five or six thousand dollars a ton."

"You know," he said, steering to avoid a dog sleeping in the road, "I'm the oldest native here, except maybe for Joel Swank. When I'm gone, this history goes with me. Boy it's hard to make a living here. Thirteen months of winter. If it weren't for the mines, I couldn't make it. Can't make a living in the tourist business. We've been in the tourist business sixty-seven years. I think that it's the oldest continuously run tourist business in Colorado."

He leaned to look out the car window at the sky.

"The weather's supposed to change, but it's never changed me," he said with a wink, pleased with the joke. "Looks like it's clearing off. We'll get some sun today. Not much, but you'll get a little. You know, they had a hotel in Gunnison during the railroad days. It was one of the fanciest hotels that was ever on the Western Slope. The La Veta Hotel. It's torn down now, but that hotel would advertise that it would give a free meal every day to all its patrons any time that the sun didn't shine in Gunnison. They had a record of it, and it happened very seldom in the whole year."

"Boy it gets cold in Gunnison, doesn't it?"

"It gets much colder there than it does here."

"When we get to town I'd like to see if you can remember what your dad told you Lake City looked like when he first came. I'd like to see how it has changed."

"There was a lot here before he came. Everybody was heading for the hills to find the gold."

"Mining was the big deal."

"That's what they were doing. Looking for the gold, or metal. Mainly gold. Hinsdale County reminded me a lot of the Klondike."

We passed a woman in a jogging suit walking beside the road. Traffic was slowing to pass around her.

"There's a lot people walking now days. Well, I figure instead of walking they ought to be working but I guess I'm old fashioned. I know a couple, both of them working, a housekeeper at home taking care of the kids. And she's probably spending as much money, more than she's making, to keep dressed to meet society. There are the kids at home with a housekeeper, maybe they're at school, but it's no way to raise a family. A man wastes his time talking about it because that's the way it is."

"And if you speak up they say you're just a pig-headed man trying to keep women down."

"Oh, I'm telling you, you go to public meetings, and you got a woman who gets up on the stage, it takes her more goddamn time than all the men you could put up there. As chairman at most of the meetings I've been to in the last fifty years, I allow each one of the candidates to make a nomination of an individual. Women have got a minute and the men have got a minute. Maybe two. Who gives a damn about a candidate who wants to run for office, and they will say he went to Oxford or he went to Harvard or he went to high school. That's all BS. If he's not qualified in the first place, he wouldn't even be up there. They spend hours talking about the history of this guy, how great he is . . . ." Then he was distracted by the river that bowed in here close to the road, flowed quietly beside it for fifty yards then turned away toward the cliffs east of town.

"See what this guy from Ft. Worth does? He bought those cabins there by the river. He bought fish and put them in that river there and lets the people stay there."

"The fish will stay right there?"

"The rainbow will migrate about a mile and a half. If you throw them in fresh, they will stay in here for a month or more. Eventually they will take off and go upstream."

As we approached town, large cottonwoods lined both sides of the road and shaded little houses and small groups of cabins.

"All of this part in here, as far back as you can remember, was settled with houses?"

"Well, as a matter of fact, at one time Tom Griffith had a cobbler shop there. He was a boot maker. He used to fix your shoes. Sew 'em up for you. There weren't many houses. That old house was there," he pointed out a narrow green and white trimmed cottage, "but most of these are new. There were scattered houses here and there. This was Wade's addition. Over there was a big pool right back there by the bluff. It was a mudhole. We used to swim in it when we were kids.

"And that, that's Emma Liska's house. She was an old-time settler here. She was married to a guy by the name of Will Humphrey. He was a mining engineer and a geologist."

"Well, there aren't any places like Lake City. You think what saved it is it's kinda' hard to get to?"

"Oh yeah.

"And then the same thing that makes it hard to make a living keeps the people thinned out a little."

As we neared Henson Creek, Perk pointed out a house on the right, just south of the bridge. "When I was a kid, a guy by the name of Olsen had that old house there. He made the whiskey. That's where he made his whiskey. And up there by the Catholic church, that is the old Vickers' home."

The old Mansard roofed two-story house stands on a hill just up from Henson Creek. Once elegant, it has aged poorly, like an old dowager down on her luck. Its once magnificent view across town and down the valley is marred now by the helter-skelter of a trailer park spread out below it.

"We sold that house and moved to the ranch. That old Vickers' house, that's an old one. That was built by John Mauer. My dad bought it from him. Back then it was a flat one-story house. My dad built the second story. Took it all the way to the top. We sold that house and five lots for 500 bucks. Can you believe that?

"Would that be Larry Ingraham?" I recalled the tow-headed childhood playmate and the days of cowboys-and-Indians in the trees along the river.

"Oh no. He owned it for a while. He's not here any-more.

We crossed the Henson Creek Bridge and headed into down town along Gunnison Avenue. There is barely room enough in the narrow river valley for the painted order of the little wooden town. At its widest point, from the eroded breccia cliffs along the river to the talus slope behind Bluff Street, Lake City's neat rectangular gridwork is only five blocks wide. A walker who didn't stop to talk could travel its length in less than ten minutes. Two main streets lined with old cottonwoods run nearly due north and south along the Lake Fork of the Gunnison River. Henson Creek enters the valley from its canyon to the west, flows through town dividing it into two nearly equal halves, then joins the Lake Fork and is lost.

Lake City was settled in the summer if 1875. It was earlier that spring that the luckless Alfred Packer had wandered out of the little valley to the Indian Agency at Los Pinos. In July surveyors had found the bodies of his five murdered companions and in August, prospectors found the gold.

Within weeks it was a tent city of two thousand people. Cabins and rough shacks were hastily thrown up, and what streets existed were narrow, muddy trails winding among the crude buildings. The town grew so fast that it was said a resident would scarcely recognize the town after a week's absence.

Before the boom ended, there were five thousand people living in the little valley and the newspaper boasted of, among other things, ten assayers, two banks, two pool halls, two breweries, two cigar factories, five stables, fourteen general stores, four Chinese laundries, seven saloons — two open all night — and a red light district.

The durable little town has not so much been preserved as spared. To be sure, many things have changed since it's heyday as the "Queen City of the San Juans." The dirt streets have been paved, running water and indoor plumbing have replaced the wash basin and the thunder jug, and trucks now deliver supplies that once arrived, accompanied by the metallic music of trace chains, in heavily loaded wagons.

But the same cottonwoods still shade the same chinked log cabins and the same porched Victorian houses; and they arch, their upper limbs now almost touching, over those same wide streets. Shoppers, now in Jeeps and Chevy Suburbans, find what they need in the same painted false fronts on the single row of businesses across from the park, and in the evenings after dark, stars still dangle just out of reach and the air is still fragrant with the smoky incense of wood stoves.

"Yeah, that's the oldest house in Lake City," Perk said, pointing out the low shed-like house set back on a lot near the corner of First Street and Gunnison Avenue. "Built in 1874. Old Jakie Richards lived there. I remember when he died. He died in a whore house. They had an inquiry afterwards and the woman, I think her name was Belle, said Jakie came up to see her and they were just having a good time. Suddenly Jakie started shaking all over and she just thought he was having a good time. She said she thought he was just a coming and all the time he was a going."

"We'll just drive through town now. There are some things I want to show you below town. We'll come back through on the way home. That's Carey's old home there. My dad's aunt and uncle. He's gone now. They starve out here pretty fast."

Just beyond town the road made a double curve and climbed a low, wooded hill.

"See this old cemetery, that was probably the first cemetery they had. A guy bought some land that took in the cemetery and he put a sign up on that big tree. He called it Boot Hill. The law got after him and said that you could not put a sign on a cemetery called Boot Hill. So he sold the cemetery and now they got it back."

"These subdivisions out here are putting in a lot of homes."

"Oh, I know. Look at it. I don't like to look at them because it makes me think it's changed a lot, but I guess you got to have 'em. You see there's so many places up and down this valley that have changed hands."

Six miles below town, the canyon walls closed in to leave just enough room for the road and the river.

"That's the site of the old High Bridge," Perk said, pointing out the gap the bridge once spanned. "It carried the Lake City branch of the Denver & Rio Grande. At one time it was the highest railroad bridge in the U.S. It was quite a sight. I've got a picture of it up at the house. It musta been a hundred feet high in the center. Nearly three hundred yards long. They tore it down when the railroad went out in 1933. You know, they sold that whole branch, from Sappinero to Lake City, for four thousand dollars. It's hard to believe."

He turned around in the road. "We'll go back here to the TCM tunnel."

"What does TCM stand for?"

"I never did know what those letters meant. But I do know that Brent Ramsey and Mr. Donneley financed a lot of that stuff. See that big crusty-looking structure?" He pointed up the wooded banking to a rock outcropping. "That is the vein. That comes all the way down from over at Henson Creek. Way down past this area. Now you see right above here, there's that TCM tunnel. A man from Patterson, New Jersey, started that. That tunnel goes in there an estimated five hundred feet. You know in that tunnel I think they penetrated the vein. You can see that fissure of a vein going through the area. It didn't produce anything. They never hit the mother lode, but they sure hit hot water. They discovered a reasonably hot spring. A lot of water come out of there. About twenty years ago the government came and researched this area. They were going to put down some of these deep thermal wells. They never did it. See that dump up there? It is the result of that crosscut tunnel. They never did any mining or stoping."

"What's stoping?"

"Stoping is where you're trying to hit the vein. If you're going up to take the ore out, you're stoping. If you go down, you've got what you call winze. That's an underground shaft."

"So this tunnel starts right here and goes straight back in?"

"Straight in the mountain."

"Anybody own that now?"

"I think it belongs to BLM (Bureau of Land Management), but I'm not sure. I don't think it's on patented land. Pretty sure of that."

"So, if you had a claim and you kept working the claim and improving it like they say, even if BLM comes in, you still get to hold that claim. Or does the BLM take it away from you?"

"You can hold it as long as you do the requirements, which is generally that you have to do five hindred dollars worth of work on each claim. Now they got a new rule that you can rent it for a hundred dollars a year and not do any work on the land at all. The reason for that is — and it makes some sense too — you don't tear up the whole country. If you want to just hold a claim, hoping it might be a mine sometime, you can just pay the rent and then if you want to go underground you can go underground."

"Do you pay rent to the BLM?"

"Every year. I've got four or five of them."

"This is just for claims that existed before BLM came in."

"Exactly."

"Once they came in that was the end of staking new claims."

"Oh, no. You can stake a claim now. All you get is your mineral rights. You can't use it for a home construction.

"This is the ranch Ed Cox bought. He bought this for two million dollars cash. He's put a million in it. He's a good friend of mine."

"Does this connect with VC Bar?"

"Yes. Part of it. See Dan Baker started that ranch originally. The VC Bar Ranch. He had three sons. Each one of those sons got their own ranch next to the home headquarters."

"Now who owns the San Juan Ranch?"

"It's all subdivided now. All different people."

"And that old place down there by the river?" A sun-browned *log house and barn stood in a grove of cottonwoods at the edge of a pasture*

"Yeah, its one of the old ones. Used to be owned by J.R. Greenleese. He had a dairy farm for years, and grew potatoes."

Behind the house and barn, beyond the river, the wooded hill rose to a high, bare flat-topped mountain.

"Is that Cannibal Plateau?"

"That's Cannibal Plateau, all the way to the top of Slumgullion Pass. We'll have hay in every direction out here."

"They get one cut or two?"

"One. We only get one cut out here. The growing season is short. That stream coming in from the west, that's called Larson Creek. Up Larson Creek two men by the name of Barry James and Walter Wagner had a real good mining prospect there. They put through these tunnels, but they never found the ore."

"What made them think it was there?"

"Well, the big vein. That vein comes all the way from Henson Creek down here past the TCM tunnel."

"How do you tell that? Can you see that on the surface?"

"I'll point it out to you. The veins outcrop. Most of the veins in the San Juans outcrop on the surface. This is Larson Creek. An old wagon road goes up there for about a mile. Walter Wagner and Barry James and others also had a saw mill way up there. You know it would surprise you, up here in this high country to see how those guys cut those select timbers, hauled 'em down to a saw mill, and made lumber and then hauled it out. They were at the first gulch coming this way up from TCM. Wagner and Jim Hardeston — they called him Bear Jim — they were on that same vein as TCM. They built two little cabins in there, one for each of them. And they run that tunnel in there for, I don't know how far. From the size of the dump, it looks like it must go in there five hundred feet at least. We just got a new topping on this road. They did a good job."

"You remember how rough this road to Gunnison used to be?"

"Yeah, used to be an all day job to go to Gunnison. And we generally had to fix a flat tire on the way down . . . and back."

"Is this about as far north of town as the mining went?"

"That's right. Now over there, across the river on Sparling's Gulch, the same guy, Walter Wagner, did some development mining on some structures that supposed to cut clear through from the Golden Wonder Mine right straight through to the head of Sparling's. As a matter of fact in Sparling's Gulch they had a sluice box way up that gulch."

"So there wasn't much mining on this side of the river down here."

"Not 'til you get up above Lake City."

"So that outcroping that you see up above the lake where the Golden Fleece is . . . ."

"That's what we call the Pinnacles. That's just country rock. That's not mineralized. The Golden Fleece Mine is right below that pinnacle."

"So that rock looks different to you. I can't tell it."

"You can if you look close enough. It's kind of a yellow rusty formation. Right across here is the old VC Bar Ranch. When I was a kid, the railroad was still coming. It came right up through the canyon here. The only place you could load cattle on the Lake Fork was down here at the old VC Bar Ranch. Every year, after all the hay was up in the fall, we rounded up the sheep and the cattle and said we were gonna ship so many steers and so many sheep. My dad would have to make an arrangement with the railroad. So you'd order the cars and you'd get your cattle ready to ship, and your sheep. Dad and Ivan was there. He was the older son so he was the boss. Well, we used to drive those cattle and those sheep over the ridge from the upper ranch and then we would head north and trail down across Baldy across Velardes Gulch and Friend's Gulch to Ugarde Gulch to Sparling to the VC Bar. They had a railroad terminal there.

"When we got to the railroad junction, then we put them on the railroad. That was a long drive for us. Took most of a long day.

All the people, everybody in the valley, had to use that same terminal because there wasn't any other stockyard.

"We came over that saddle right across the mountain 'til we got to the railroad terminal. Then we'd have to wait 'til the train came that night. We'd sit down there. Mrs. Baker was wonderful. She'd feed us. 'Bout half starved, I suppose. She fed all the ranchers that brought cattle down there. She always fed them a meal.

"The trains were always late. We'd be all ready to roll and we'd sit down there and wait. We'd wait for the train and pretty soon we'd get down and put our ear on that railroad track and hear that train comin' ten miles up that track. The train would come through with a big light and go right on past us. They had to go up to Lake City to eat or change crews or something. Then they would come back down the road to where they'd help us load the cattle.

"And then we'd watch, and it got to comin' back down the canyon, and we knew they was gonna start loading. It was an interesting process. Everybody had their own cattle and sheep and everything in different pens. Those railroad guys loaded those cattle with nothing but these little lanterns. Pitch dark night. I could never understand how they could see just exactly what they were doing. How in the world could they load those things with no more light than they had? So many of them cattle and sheep, and they got it just right."

"You didn't have to load em? They did it for you?"

"Oh they were there, but we did the biggest part of it. We'd always stop at Clint Buskirk's ranch and spend the night. Ol' Clint Buskirk. He'd give us homemade beer. I'll tell you more about that guy. He was a freighter. He was a great freighter. He'd haul logs, he'd haul any kind of supplies up and down Henson Creek from here clear to Engineer Mountain and probably into Silverton and Ouray. He had a livery stable up at Capitol City. That's where he kept most of his horses, his sleds and stuff.

"He met a lady that was running the boarding house by the the name of Witherite. She had a husband and a son. Well, she and Buskirk got to going together and they got very fond of each other. Meanwhile, he homesteaded a ranch, the old Buskirk Ranch, that's now the High Bridge Ranch. Anyway, when those mines up Henson Creek shut down, he'd pick up a lot of material 'cause he knew he'd need it to build that barn and that house.

"He was a really short guy and he always had a big chew of tobacco, spitting that juice. And he got to having a lot of problems. So, meanwhile, he talked that Mrs. Witherite into quitting her husband and moving down to the ranch with him. This Mrs. Witherite had a great big 'ol son called Thornton. He came down and beat up Buskirk. He beat that ol' man 'til it was pitiful. He damn near killed him.

"So Buskirk was telling us boys about it one night after a few beers. He said, "You see that barn? I built that barn. I brought those logs down from the Empire Mine. Even this house. All this material came out of those materials I brought down from the mines when the mines started shutting down. I just picked up some of it and brought it home. I guess it would be safe to say I stole all the stuff and built this house and barn. I have no regrets about that. But the worst thing I do have to regret is when I stole that son-of-a-bitch's wife! It was the biggest mistake I ever made.

"Near Buskirk's place, John Thompson had a ranch, down at the Elk Creek. Ol' Thompson had a guy working for him who was applying for a homestead just a little bit west of Thompson's home, on some land just above him. Yeager was his name. And Yeager got a patent on that homestead and he got a permit to dig a ditch out of Elk Creek. Ol' Yeager kept turning Thompson's ditch off and his own ditch on. Once, when Yeager went out to open up his ditch, ol' John Thompson shot him right in the guts with a shotgun and killed him and left him lying in the ditch. Thompson hired a guy by the name of Charles Monahan, a criminal lawyer. A very prominent attorney — one of my dad's attorneys. Ol' Thompson never went to jail at all. He never spent a day in jail. That was about 1920. Yes sir. It wasn't all pretty."

"And when the railroad went out . . . ?"

"When the railroad went out we used to drive the cattle and the sheep all the way to Sappinero. Drive 'em on horseback. We didn't have no trucks. All the ranches in the valley from Lake City clear to Sappinero had to drive those cattle down the old road. We used to walk 'em right down the railroad right-of-way. We had nothing else to do. We'd trail them all the way to Sappinero. It was a hard three-day drive. So Bob and Joe and I, we'd drive those cows.

"It's hard for the younger generation of people to realize the physical hardships people here had then. Living here, when the mines started shutting down, and the railroad went out. There was no such thing as tourists. It was just about impossible to make a living. And the growing season was so short you couldn't raise anything but enough hay to feed the horses. We had horses and stuff all the way to Sherman and Capitol City and clear back down the valley, trying to find them pasture. Horses and cattle. And sheep. Anything that might make us a little money."

"Was the water that Yeager was trying to control coming down this side from Water Dog Lake?"

"No. The water from Water Dog Lake, it comes down what they call Horse Creek, through Horse Park."

"Where's that?"

"Horse Creek comes right down by our cabins on the other side of the river. That's part of our lake water. One guy had a water right where it comes around the hill, but we bought that away back. That's always been a beautiful situation there too. Another guy bought that Ball Flats land there and thought he had the water right and was going to bring it around Station Eleven. We bought that during the World War. He sold his water right to us. That's where he made his mistake. It would have been a valuable asset to that subdivision."

"Alpine Gulch goes right up that way, to the south behind town?"

"Right. Just over the ridge. That Red Mountain, there's been a lot of core drilling on that. The Department of Interior gave a permit to an outfit out of Golden, Colorado to core drill it. They core drilled that and according to the report they say that it is the biggest known deposit of bauxite in the free world. The company tried to produce it but they got a lot of opposition from the local people here. But someday you got to believe that it will be produced."

"I heard they planned to take the ore out by going up Henson Creek?"

"Clear over to Ridgway. They were going to use some kind of a pipe system. One pipe carrying the load over and the other pipe bringing the empty buckets back. It's being done around the world in some places."

"It's amazing what mining companies will spend on that."

"Oh yeah. There, that's the Ball Flats over there. You could have bought that whole thing at one time. As a matter of fact when I was on the Board of Commissioners before WWII we tried to get some of that land back on the tax rolls. We advertised around the country that we would sell those city lots over there to anybody that would give us a fair price because there was no tax coming in at all. We sold about four hundred of those lots for five dollars a lot."

"Now, Joe, you look up here and you can see the difference in the color of those formations." Perk pointed to the hill behind town. A rusty brown ridge slanted down across the darker rock of the cliff face.

"You see that tunnel up on the hill there? That's the Red Bird Tunnel right there and that's the formation right there. You can see up on the cliffs above that tunnel that the vein runs that way. That tunnel goes in there about eight hundred fifty feet. They went right straight in. When they cut the vein I don't think they did any stoping. They may have cut that vein and then drifted in both directions. Whether or not they did, I couldn't say. It's got the mineralization there. When we go up Henson Creek you can see those veins much easier there."

"How do you spell Ulay?"

"U-l-a-y. Ute and Ulay."

"The Ute-Ulay was one of the first mines?"

"Oh no, the Golden Fleece was probably the first one. Up by the lake. The Ute-Ulay was the first one on Henson Creek. Probably the oldest. That went in to penetrate the other end of this same vein. You can follow that vein from Henson Creek clear across down to here."

"It has a little bit of color to it."

"You can see it's just a little brown color."

"Not much though."

"No, not much. No significant amount. But you go up Henson Creek and you can see those veins easy."

"It would take me a little practice."

"Oh you'd make a good miner in no time. You'd be a mining son-of-a-gun. Boy, a lot of things have changed. As a matter of fact, that land you're looking at right out there, years ago when you first came here, it was nothing but swamps. And today, if they had it set like it used to be, the Government would call it wetlands."

"That ridge there behind the wetlands. Didn't the horse trail to Crystal Lake go right up from there?"

"Still does. You can see the trail going right up there now."

"Where is Slaughter House Gulch?"

"That gulch going up just to the left of the wetlands. That is Slaughter House Gulch. Up Slaughter House Gulch about a half a mile, a couple of guys had a prospect up there for a good many years. Joe Wenton and the Hunt family did a lot of exploration work on that structure. It was right around the corner, you can't quite see the tunnel. They were on the other side of that vein, but they were coming this way with the tunnel."

"When was that?"

"Oh, it was when I was a kid. They did that 'til they all died off. Now here in the '50s they had me take my dozer — in those days you could do it — up there by the cemetery, come right in around the hill by that gulch and put a road into that mine. The road's still there. The government would not recognize it as a road any more."

We drove back up Gunnison Avenue and into town. Under the cottonwoods that shaded the street, neat log cabins and gingerbread-trimmed Victorian houses sat on clipped and fenced lawns, property of the new breed of prospectors who came, not for boom town gold, but for the town itself. Along both sides of the street, ditches, once filled with running water for firemen to pump from and boys to play boats in, were now dry and grassed.

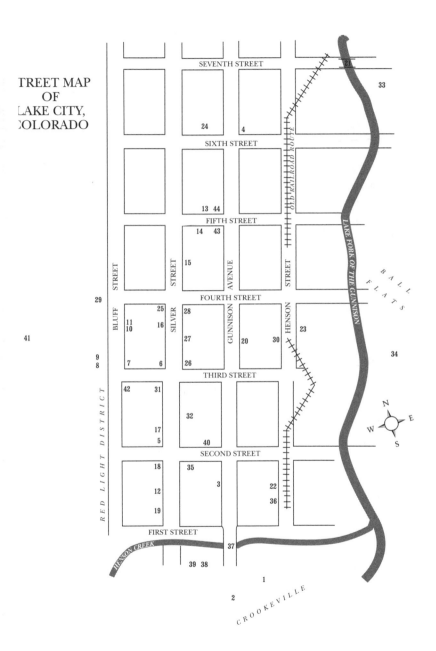

STREET MAP
OF
LAKE CITY,
COLORADO

SEVENTH STREET

SIXTH STREET

FIFTH STREET

FOURTH STREET

THIRD STREET

SECOND STREET

FIRST STREET

Legend for Street Map of Lake City, Colorado

1. Tom Griffith Cobbler Shop
2. Emma Liska's House
3. Richard House (oldest house in Lake City)
4. Carey House
5. Mason Hall
6. Hardy House
7. Soderholm House
8. Hoffman House
9. Doc Lemming's House
10. Bill Hardy Stable
11. First Jail (tunnel)
12. Johnny Atkins House
13. Avery House/Assay Office
14. Dad's Log Cabin
15. Harry Steward House
16. Brent Ramsey Theatre/Bowling Alley
17. Drugstore
18. Pastime
19. Snyders Shop
20. Tom Beam
21. Hangman's Bridge (Ocean Wave Bridge)
22. New Fire Station
23. Golconda Mine Livery
24. Lake City School
25. Silver World Building
26. Hough Bank
27. Pueblo House Hotel
28. Site of Occidental Hotel
29. Baptist Church
30. Hinsdale County Courthouse
31. First National Bank
32. Lake City Park
33. Ocean Wave Smelter
34. Ball Flats (Baseball)
35. Odd Fellows Hall (Museum)
36. Site of Denver & Rio Grande Railroad Depot
37. Henson Creek Bridge
38. Vicker's Home
39. Saint Rose of Lima Catholic Church
40. Ramsey-Brown House
41. Red Bird Tunnel
42. Armory
43. Presbyterian Church
44. Episcopal Church

"Now let's see, the old courthouse there, that is the same."

And it was. The raised green numbers between the upstairs windows testified that the work had been completed in 1877. Two full stories high and sixty feet long, the sturdy wooden courthouse is the largest building left in Lake City and, except for the Episcopal church, the only one which was white. It stands on a double lot at the corner of Gunnison Avenue and Third Street, a steadfast white magistrate, shoulders square, arms folded, feet firmly planted as if it had come to stay.

During its long term the durable old courthouse has been the official community headquarters not only for local government business, but also for the varied day-to-day civic affairs, both commonplace and grand. It was archives and auditorium, jailhouse and playhouse, assembly hall and ballroom. It was there births were recorded, taxes filed, disputes settled. It was there Shakespeare was played out. It was there that Carrie Nation praised Prohibition and where politicians waged their campaigns. And it was there one August afternoon in 1884 that Alfred G. Packer, the Cannibal of Colorado, was sentenced to hang by the neck until he was dead.

We parked a while, admiring the courthouse, then turned west on Third Street to its corner with Silver Street.

"That's where the old bank was," Perk said, pointing to the two-story, gray stone building that anchored the block of painted false front businesses along the boardwalk. "The original bank shut down the year I was born, 1914. It belonged to a man named Patterson from Pueblo, Colorado. Old man J.S. Hough founded that bank. He was a cousin of Ulysses Grant. Hough mined up Henson Creek. There is a mine up there called the Frank Hough. For a while after it closed, there was a bar in there. Then they reopened that bank about twelve years ago.

"That bank is an old building."

"Oh, gosh yes. It was built in 1876, or so. The rocks for that building were cut right here to the north down by the cemetery in what they call the blue cut. Hand cut. Those rocks were never shipped in. Some of the monuments in the cemetery are the same rock. Just down the street there, there's the Mason Hall. That's built out of the same rock."

Across the street from the bank, a grassy park marked the lots where the once-thriving business block burned, empty now except for one bench near the deserted swings where three identical old men sat facing the sun, napping in what was left of the day like gray birds turned to the wind.

"That's where the bars used to be, there where the park is. My dad had two bars there and two cafes. He had five of those lots. He donated them to the city in the late '30s. There was a guy come in by the name of Finney who got with the county commission and said he wanted to do all kinds of beautiful things for Lake City. So my dad donated those lots."

"You remember when the buildings burned?" I tried to imagine how they must have been, well-lit and noisy with loud talk and music.

"They burned in 1915, I was just a kid. My dad eventually donated those lots to the county, and the county turned it over to the Woman's Club to make a park out of it. After a great many years, we tried to get them to give the lots back to the Vickers. They weren't doing anything with them. They just sat there for a great many years, but they didn't give 'em back. Mr. Carey, my dad's uncle, had the corner lot and he didn't donate it. The Pavich brothers ended up with that lot and I noticed here in the paper about a year ago that the city bought that lot for $50,000.

"That little bank building there on Third Street across from the main bank, by the café — that's probably the oldest house in the valley. The Hardy house. It was built in 1876. Look how those logs are notched in there. Its the loan office now. That building has been sitting there well over a hundred years."

We turned right onto Bluff Street.

"That house there on the corner used to belong to old Judge Soderholm. For a while I was on the Board of County Commissioners, during WWII, just before my son

Larry was born. I was running for re-election and I went over to the courthouse the day after the election at about 9 o'clock. They had counted the votes and I got defeated by five votes for county commissioner.

"So I was walking back across the street to where old Bessie had a telephone office and Bessie called out 'Perk, I got a message for you.' It was message from Emma Jean's brother saying that my son Larry was born in the hospital there in Ft. Worth, Texas, where she had gone to be near her folks.

"That cheered me up a little bit. I was walking across the street and there was old Soderholm. He was walking over this way from his store; he had a store around the corner. He said, 'Hey Perk I heard you got defeated for county commissioner.' I said I did. He said 'Forget it. I got a better proposition for you. I want you to take over as Chairman of the Republican Party.' That's how come I got started in the party. That had to be 1945 or '46.

"That's why I got that medal hanging in the office. From the Republican headquarters. After they researched the history of the Republican Party they found out that I was the only person living today that had been county chairman for fifty consecutive years."

"You know, Perk. I remember Mr. Soderholm. By the time I knew him he had white hair and a white walrus mustache. He always wore a tweed suit. With a vest. Even in the summer. When I was a kid, my mother bought an old drop octagon school clock from Mrs. Soderholm. Had 1866 stamped on the back of it. She paid twenty-four dollars for it. I had to carry it in my lap all the way back to Ft. Worth. I told Mother that when she died I wanted that clock. I figured I had earned it. I've got it in the house now."

"Well, you did earn it."

"I guess I did. Somehow Mr. Soderholm knew I was interested in the history of Lake City so, when I was about twelve, or so, he gave me a history of Lake City he had typed up. I found it last month when I was looking through some stuff. The paper has yellowed and the type is barely readable."

I took the papers from their folder, handed them to Perk and waited as he read.

Copy of property of
E. W. Soderholm, Lake City, Colorado

The Growth of Lake City
During the Year 1877

The discovery by Enos T. Hotchkiss, of the mine (later the Golden Fleece) led to the location of the town. The mine was discovered in August 1874 by Mr. Hotchkiss, who was at that time engaged in building the Saguache and San Juan toll road through this valley to the Animas River.

The first cabins were erected by Mr. E.T. Hotchkiss during that year. The Bartholfs, B.A. Sherman, the Lee brothers, Finley Sparling, Brockett and others followed and the foundation of the town was laid. The town company was organized as follows: President, Henry Finley; Secretary, P. Newton Bogue; Treasurer, W.T. Ring. These (men) with Otto Mears, Issac Gotthelff, E.T. Hotchkiss and H.M. Woods constituted the first board of trustees. The townsite was entered in the U.S. Land Office at Del Norte, in October 1875.

When the Spring of 1875 opened, the town was comprised of thirteen log cabins. At the spring election, April 3rd, 1875 Henry Finley, J.H. Haines, D.M. Watson, C.P. Foster and Issac Waldron were elected trustees of the town; Frank Curtis, Clerk; Oscar Downtain, constable and J.W. Cline, street supervisor.

The first wedding was that of D.T. Hughes and Kitty Eastman, May 14, 1875. The first sawmill was erected in May 1875 by Finley & Church. The Presbyterian Society was organized June 18th, 1875, by Rev. Alex M. Darley, being the first religious organization. The first issue of the Silver World *was June 19,*

1875. The first child born in the town was July 8, 1875, to the wife of S.W. Hoyt. The first coach of the Barlow and Sanderson's stage line arrived from Saguache July 11, 1875. Barlow and Sanderson's coaches began making regular tri-weekly trips between this place and Saguache, carrying the mail. The Lake City & Antelope Park toll road was completed Nov 2nd, 1875, contract for building the road was let July 19th.

November 1st, 1875, the town contained sixty-seven buildings and about 400 inhabitants. Crooks concentration works was completed July 4, 1876, Van Gisson's lixivation works, completed in Dec. 1876.

The Ute-Ulay Mine sold for $135,000, in 1876, also the sale of eleven-twelfth of the Ocean Wave Mine.

On the first of November, 1876, the population of the town was estimated at from 800 to 1,000, and contained two assayers, Two banks, three bakeries, three barber shops, two billiard halls, five blacksmith shops, three boot & shoe stores, two brick yards, two breweries, two cigar factories, one clothing house, five corrals & feed stables, two drug stores, one furniture store, fourteen stores dealing in general merchandise, four hardware stores, four hotels, two jewelry establishments, four chines (sic) laundries, fifteen lawyers, four meat markets, one newspaper, The Silver World, *three newsdealers, three painters, one planning mill, six restaurants (two open all night), seven saloons, four sawmills, one shingle mill, nine surveyors.*

By the first of February, 1877, building was recommended and by March first, a large number of business houses and residences were in process of construction. Lots which on the first of December or January could not find purchasers at $250 or $300 on the first of March readily commanded $500 & $600.

From actual count the number of buildings erected during the year 1877 was 136, costing $212,680.

> *The immigration began with the opening of the year
> 1877, the coaches first coming in loaded, compelling the
> line to put on daily service as early as April 10th. The
> real rush came later when teams poured in loaded with
> human freight. During April, May and June, the roads
> leading into town were perfectly lined with newcomers,
> pedestrians with packs on their backs, or on burros and
> Jacks, men on horseback and in wagons — a constant
> stream of humanity pouring into San Juan through this,
> the metropolis. The legitimate population is fully 2,000;
> many good judges place it at 2,500.*
>
> *The first train came into Lake City, August 15th,
> 1889, Pete Ready, Engineer.*

"That Soderholm was a character," Perk said handing
me back the papers. "Soderholm, he was a Swede, you
know. That's the old armory right back there across from
Soderholm's house. Always in the winter time they had
the biggest event of the year here in Lake City — the
Fireman's Masquerade Ball. They had special tickets and
they had to even bring an orchestra in here from Grand
Junction. On the railroad. As young guys, course we
couldn't get in. We'd be hanging around here in the alley
and stuff.

"Over on the other side of the river, that was called
Crookeville. It still is. We lived on the edge of Crookeville.
The people on the south side of the bridge, in
Crookeville, the Irish and the shanty Irish, everybody said
they didn't deserve the same credit as the rest of the people. They looked down on us. Well, every masquerade ball
those guys would come down and get a fight started in the
street. The Irish, they would fight among themselves,
even. One time Soderholm went out there, and he was
trying to quiet 'em down, you know. He lived right there
across the street. The quiet, peace loving gentleman that
he was, he got out there and somebody knocks him flat
on his ass. He came walking in the building and some-

body said to him, 'Why didn't you stop it?' He said, ' I'll tell you, a Swede doesn't have any use in getting mixed up in an Irish fight.' The blood was running down his eyes. He didn't even know who hit him.

"Another time, when the bootleg days were on, most of the whisky came in from Creede to start with. A guy came over here one night; one of those Creede guys. They were partying and drinking and that guy, I was about sixteen or seventeen, I guess. He motioned for me to come outside, you know. And I thought he was gonna give me a drink. My older brother Ivan, he knew ol' Perk was getting into something. I walked out there and that guy turned around in the alley and he said, 'Now, you got your gun and I've got my gun, let's see whoever is the quickest to the draw.' And I said, 'Ho, heh, heh,' I turned around and started running, and he fired one shot right down behind my ass, and he emptied his gun as I ran up that alley. When I got to the end of the alley, Ivan come up behind him and grabbed him behind the neck. My two brothers beat that son-of-a-bitch 'til you could hardly recognize him. The guy thought I had a gun and he had a gun and he was trying to get it straightened out, but he was trying to kill me. Damn near scared me to death."

"So they made the whiskey in Creede and brought it over here."

"Oh yeah. Course my dad got into some of that after that. I'm not ashamed to say that my dad made the whiskey. He never did sell any of it direct. It's ridiculous to tell people you can't drink whisky. It's crazy."

"When did Prohibition start?"

"In 1914 Colorado passed that law and it went into effect immediately."

"Now do you remember hearing about Carrie Nation? She came here and gave a talk."

"Oh hell, yes, they had tickets and everything else. She was famous. That was before my time. There was another thing that happened. The woman who started women's suffrage, what was her name? Susan B. Anthony. She was here and had a big public meeting. That was in my time. Started equal women's rights. She came to Lake City, of all places. That was probably one of the biggest mistakes in the history of the United States when they gave women equal rights.

"Down that way," Perk pointed south toward several wooden houses on weedy lots, "on Bluff Street, that's where the red light district was. The Baptist church was up there to the right. They had the Baptist church and the red light district right next to each other. Now Henry Hoffman had that house right there where that house is at the end of Third Street. Doc Cummings had a house right next to him. One day after he retired, he was out there cleaning up the grass and burning the grass and it caught fire and burned the whole works. Just cleaning up and that's it. This here on the right is the lumber yard now. Bill Hardy had a livery stable and a big hay barn right here where this building is. Right here under that duplex there was an underground tunnel, that's where the first jail was. There's the foundation. On the corner there is the new Baptist house. They spent a lot of money in here."

"A lot of these houses are fixed up now."

"Oh, there are new people coming in with money and they buy these old places and put a lot of money in them. That house there used to belong to Johnny Atkins. He had a race horse. Slaughter House Gulch comes in right at the end of the lane there — the trail head to Crystal Lake."

"When were all these cottonwood trees planted?"

"I'm not sure. When I was a kid, these trees were about half grown. Cottonwood trees grow to be big and they grow fast."

We turned on Sixth Street and headed back north down Silver Street.

"There's the new schoolhouse we just passed."

"I miss the old one."

"We sure had an Indian uprising over that damn thing."

"That was a great building."

"It was, for a fact. We could have fixed that up to serve the same purpose. These new people don't go for that stuff.

"Mr. Avery had that house. That log cabin on the corner there of Fifth and Silver Street. I can tell you a little bit about that house. You know when we would round up our cattle in October, my dad would say we got to make a shipment to buy groceries for the winter. We'd round up the cattle and the sheep and pick out what we wanted to sell, separate them up there, and he'd order the car from the D&RG Railroad. So he rounded up the sheep and the cattle and two of the brothers took the cattle and went on down ahead of us.

"One day Bob and Joe and I were coming behind with the sheep. We had about 150 head. We got down here across from the foot of the hill in front of Baldy and the sheriff came over there and stopped us. We said, 'What's going on?' We got a big argument going. The county treasurer and one of the commissioners told the sheriff to pick up Vickers' sheep and not let him ship them cause he was behind in his taxes on the livestock. But we were so proud we kept going on. We said, 'To hell with you sons-of-bitches, we'll kill somebody first.'

"My dad come back to town and looked up Mr. Heath — the principal of the schools — and told him what the problem was. Mr. Heath was a good friend of the county treasurer. So my dad said, 'I'll tell you what I'll do. If you'll give me $500 so I can pay my taxes and sell my sheep, I'll give you that house and five lots.'

"See that log house there. That's it. My dad owned it for years. He didn't live in it. He just owned it. That's a valuable house. All hand-hewed, notched. I think it's for sale now, for $75 or $80,000.

"Over here on the corner of Silver Street and Fourth Street, on the east side, The Occidental was there. It was one of the old ones. That hotel must have had, I'd say twenty rooms. Two-story. It burned.

"A man by the name of Gregg came in here with an insurance company out of Denver. He was from Oklahoma. He bought that hotel and rehabilitated it and put it back into operation. And after nearly three years of that, all of a sudden it burned to the ground. Well, nobody could prove it, but everybody thought Gregg burned it for the insurance.

"Then right up the street about a block, between the Occidental Hotel and the Pueblo House Hotel, there on the right, a man by the name of John Clay had a bakery. All those buildings that were there are all gone. In the middle of that block, where the jewelry store is now, that was the Pueblo House Hotel. A man by the name of Jack Hammond built that hotel and run it. He's the one that had that big ranch up above the lake. That little brick building. That was the assayer's office. H.A. Avery, who was a very prominent attorney, had an office there, too.

"My dad's uncle, A.B. Carey had that building right there on the east side, between Fourth and Third Streets. He had a store in there. Right by the old Pueblo House Hotel.

"Now the *Silver World* was right here on the corner. Now a man by the name of Harold Stewart, from Oklahoma City, bought that *Silver World* equipment. It's all in the museum there in Oklahoma City. Isn't it a shame some of us didn't have enough sense to buy that old *Silver World* equipment? Shipping it back to a museum in Oklahoma City, it don't mean a thing.

"That house right there was the house Harry Stewart bought and fixed up. It belongs to some of the family now. Brent Ramsey had a theater right there in that very spot, where that yellow false front building is."

"I remember there was a bowling alley there. I used to set pins in there every summer when I was a kid."

"You're right. After Ramsey quit it, some fella by the name of Adams came here and made a bowling alley out of that. Small balls."

"Didn't the drug store use to be here on the right?"

"Well, they called it a drugstore. Actually a fella by the name of Craig fixed it up and made it into a drugstore. Now they call that building up by the bank the drugstore."

"The soda fountain that's in the drugstore now was down here before?"

"Yep. Same one. They moved it up there. There was always all kinds of businesses up and down the street. My dad's was over there on the corner where the park is. If you could dig up that whole park you would find antiques and guns. And we would come along and say some of that stuff ought to be ours, but they wouldn't let you touch a thing."

"Mrs. Soderholm had a hat shop or a clothing store along here somewhere didn't she?"

"She had that right next to the drug store. Had that for years. South of the park, there. That stone building. That's the old Odd Fellows Hall. It's been there for years and years. Now a bunch of civic-minded people got together and bought that building and made it into a museum. These old buildings right here, across from the museum were here when I was a kid. I used to walk down here on my way to school every day. They used to have a bridge across the river (Henson) right here at the end of Silver Street. This bridge washed out. I can remember it."

"What do people do here now to make a living?"

"Every carpenter that wants to work is working. There's a lot of work going on. They got enough work to last the whole year. I got a guy down here who wants to build a house. He's been waiting three years to build a house. He's gonna bring up his own crew from Lubbock. That's gonna cost him a fortune. Bring up a crew from Lubbock and have to find them a place to stay."

"So most of the young people are working?"

"I don't think there's an idle man in the valley."

"Even in the winter?"

"Well, the winter time shuts them down for a while, a few weeks at a time. The cold and the snow, but they build all winter."

"So the major economy now is building houses?"

"I would say so, and road work. The town road work is steady work. They work all winter. They work four ten-hour shifts and then they got three days off."

"They keep the pass open all winter?"

"The Highway Department does. See, years ago Hinsdale County used to do it. But now, the state of Colorado has their own maintenance. That shed at the foot of the pass is where they keep their own equipment. They keep the road all the way from Powderhorn to Creede open all the time."

We parked by the stream and rolled the window down so we could hear the sound of the water over the rocks.

"How many people live here now, you figure?"

"Lake City now? I think probably around 500. There's about 600 registered voters and part of them vote by absentee ballot. I don't like that. I think you ought to live here to vote. You can't live in Colorado Springs and register here and vote. They don't know a damn thing about what they're voting for. A lot of times, our absentee ballots have controlled the election. I don't like that."

"So there is no ranching going on now, really. No mining going on."

"Ranching is dead. I've seen the land go back from federal land to private property. Lots of ranches have been turned into dude ranches, guest ranches. But now you can't make a living in the tourist business, so they are selling off the property as house lots, or selling the individual cabins. The ranchers that are in existence are, in fact, doing the same. Cutting the hay and bailing it and feeding their stock. They don't exactly support themselves. They got a cabin or two and they take out hunters and stuff. The ranches here now are owned by people who've got lots of money, and it don't make any difference whether they make any money or not.

Perk turned in his seat and pointed back toward Bluff Street, "Most of the red light district was up here on this end of Bluff Street. They called it 'The Passtime.' Most of that area between here and the museum was, in fact, the red light district. My dad said when he had the saloon here in town, a lot of these girls would come down to the bar and have a drink and visit with the guys. They were real nice people.

"This was once called Main Street. Snyder had a shop right here. He was a machinist. He fixed wagons and whatever. And out here in Henson Creek he had a water wheel. That's the way he got his power."

"You know in this whole country, there isn't much rainfall, but the whole country runs on water doesn't it?"

"That's right."

"When you get right down to it, you've got to irrigate it, you need it for power."

"Water is the most important resource you got on earth, there's no question about it."

"You own rights on some water running out of the mountains above your place."

"That's Silver Coin Gulch. Up near the lake. We own that water right."

"That must be over a mile from your place. How would you make use of that water?"

"Well, for years we had a ditch come right out of Silver Coin Gulch and we run it behind where Crystal Lodge is now. But they complained that it swamped the ground there. So to hold that water right, we let it come on down into the Lake Fork River and we changed the point of entry. We picked it up out of the river in our irrigation ditches to fill up our fish ponds. See, if you know how much runs into the river, you can take out that much. We just let the river do the transporting. It comes down the river, and we got what they call a coffer dam in the river and it puts it into our ditch and we run it through the meadows."

"How can you buy water rights? Who do you buy water rights from?"

"If a guy's got a water right, say on the Colorado River, or anywhere, you can sell that water right and the other person can take it and pick it up someplace else."

"But like this Silver Coin. How would you get the rights to that."

"Well, you have to go to court to prove what you were using it for and that nobody else was using it. Then you get a decree from the court. We got that decree years before I was born.

"Herman Meyers took that ranch where Vickers is. He moved in on that ranch. There wasn't any homestead laws then. All you had to do in those days, if you wanted a piece of federal land, you'd go in there and take say a 120 acres, and you'd file what they called a declaratory statement. Which he did. He declared that he was so-and-so using this land for so-and-so purposes and that would be on record. Then he sold the land to Dan McLeod, but by that time the Homestead Law had come in and gone into effect, replacing the Declaratory Statement Act. Dan McLeod got all the things necessary to file a homestead, but he never finished it. So it was never completed."

"So he went way up there to to Silver Coin Gulch to get his water."

"Well, it's the same as Waterdog Lake up on the Upper Ranch. We got a storage permit on Waterdog Lake in 1908. Then we put a cement dam on the north end to raise the lake up to where we got it now.

"So then we filed on Waterdog Lake and a guy by the name of Donnelly had a water right to take the water out of Park Creek and bring it around that mountain over here where the Ball Flats is now. Right around that mountain. So we bought that from the guy that had the place named Tom Beam."

"The water came right over that ridge?"

"Come right around the hill. And they made a ditch and they did that by hand, too, and horses, but they didn't get it too steep. They made just the right kind of a ditch. It wouldn't wash. Perfect ditch."

"Now, Henson Creek used to cut across this corner of town so all this land on this end of town was swampy."

"Before they lowered the river level that was an ongoing emerceny every year. Henson Creek would flood Lake City. I've seen Henson Creek come right between the railroad house and the railroad station.

"Down here by the end of town, about thirty years ago, there wasn't no running water. Everybody had their own wells. To try to prevent the flooding, the city went down to where the Hangman's Bridge is. Solid rock. So they took an air compressor and drilled down there about fifteen feet and blasted that out and cleaned it out. When they did, the water table dropped and half the wells in town went dry 'cause it lowered the water table. So they put up a big fight over that. So they go back up for a temporary solution — they knew they was gonna' get a water system — and put some big rocks in Henson Creek to raise the water level up some, so it would feed some of these wells, but not enough so it would flood. Put them rocks right down there where Henson Creek comes into the river. So now you can see what's happened since then, in the last twenty years, heck the water level all through Henson Creek has fallen, it will never flood the town again. Lowered the whole thing."

"You know, it does seem like a smaller stream than it was when I was a kid."

"When you get older everything seems smaller," Perk said with a wink. He started the jeep and drove back to Second Street.

"Right over there, on the corner of Second and Gunnison, is where the livery stable was. Two-story livery stable, big barn, hay loft up on top, and horse corral outside to let the horses out. Across the street, that's the new fire department. We got one of the best fire departments for a little town on the western slope of Colorado."

"When I was a kid, I never did know what these ditches along the roads were, but that's pretty smart to run the water through town so they could pump that if they had a fire."

"This is Henson Street right here. The railroad station set right about where that sign is. The railroad tracks went on both sides and they had a switch. Some of the passenger cars come up on this side and the freight cars go on around the loop. When a passenger train pulled in, they would walk right out into the station. The loop went right round, up the creek and come back down this block and they had another switch down here and the engine, after they unhooked the cars, he would back into what they called the roundhouse. In the roundhouse the janitor would clean the engine up, check the oil and the coal, fill up the coal bin, check the water tanks and they'd be ready to go on the next trip. Had to have that loop to turn it around ...."

"Aw, it's hard for me to tell you what it would be like when we saw that train coming up the canyon. We saw the last train when it went out. We were up on the mountain looking down from Station 11. This street was lined with wagons and horses and everybody was crying and saying it's the end of Lake City. The railroad's gone, we got no highway, we got no transportation. Had to have the railroad. That was what they depended on.

"As a matter of fact, before this train ran, they probably shipped that stuff by wagon in the early days. All that hand selected ore, then they shipped it by railroad. The railroad wasn't going here too many years before '29, when the Crash took.

"So the road to Gunnison didn't amount to much then."

"Oh it was just a wagon road. I remember when I was kid, we made a trip to Montrose maybe once a year to get supplies, and maybe once to Gunnison. That was all. Went by car, but we was hoping to hell we would get on that train.

"I'll tell you, as a matter of fact, it was a rare thing to find any of the Vickers that had money to buy a ticket for the train. No money. You know how I finally got to ride on the train? A horse throwed me and broke my leg, and they brought me out on a blanket and put me in that house up there by the church. Doc Cummings — B.F. Cummings — put on that cast. But the bone split and come through the flesh and the blood was shooting in every direction. So he put that cast on there, but he had no way of x-raying it to tell where the bone was. He did the best he could. He had to leave these two little openings so infection wouldn't get started.

"After about six months of that, they felt my leg. It wasn't healing at all. The bones were just pushing back and forth. They were right along side of each other. So my dad heard about a doctor at the railroad station in Salida. His name was Kokum. Dad put me on the train and we went down to Dr. Kokum. I'll tell you, when I got on that train I was scared. I thought I wasn't coming back. Dr. Kokum took an x-ray, I got a picture of that. It showed the bone like that, (he touched his fingers to show the two ends overlapped) "instead of being like that (he touched the tips of his fingers). He said, 'Well, I'll tell you what, we don't want to break that bone over again, we'll just put it back in a cast'. He said the x-ray showed there was two of these pieces of bone growing up toward each other. In two or three months time, if those bones keep growing, they will grow together. And they did. That's why my leg is two inches short."

"You had what's called an open fracture, where the broken end of the bone comes through the skin. That means infection almost every time. It's a wonder you didn't lose your leg."

"If it hadn't been for my grandmother Madison, who was a midwife, I would have. She took care of that leg. She put iodine on a rag and pulled a string right through that hole in my leg. It come both ways.

"Then further down here they had a big water tank. And that's how they filled the engines."

"Now the railroad wasn't here when your dad came. It came after."

"No, it came about a year after he was here. When the railroad left, this was a street. Henson Street. Later we made this into an airport. They used to fly in the groceries. Land right here on Henson street. Brought the mail in that way. They had a guy that got killed there taking off. That's what shut the airstrip down. Just as they cleared the runway, they failed to see a telephone line going across in front of them. Killed them both instantly.

"I flew out of here three or four times. As a matter of fact, I had Rocky Warren take Emma Jean as far as Montrose close to the time when the twins were born. I called Rocky and said, 'I got to get Emma Jean to Montrose, she's expecting a baby here before too long. She wants to go down for a physical check up.' I got her on that airplane. I saw him a short time later and he said, 'I'll tell you Perk, you've had me fly to Lake City and bring a radiator for that D7 dozer so you could fix your tractor up on Engineer Mountain. I didn't mind that but, by God, don't you ever call me again to tell me your wife's gonna have any babies.' He said, 'I damn near had a heart attack between Lake City and Montrose.'

"On this corner is where the Golconda Mine had their livery stable and horse barn. When we were kids, we would come over here and throw the hay down to the horses. They had mangers on both sides. And with all those livery stables, they always had a corral outside so they could turn the horses out.

We drove down Henson Street, no longer a train track, no longer an airstrip. Travel on this quiet back street was now lim-

ited to cars and trucks running a few errands to and from the few homes.

"There's Hangman's Bridge down there at the north end of town where they hanged those two guys. Just before my dad came here, in the early 1880s, the sheriff was killed by two guys — George Betts and James Browning — who were robbing a house. A posse captured them and put them in the jail. The townspeople were so upset, they broke into the jail and lynched the two men. Hanged them from the bridge below town. That's how it got its name. The next day school was let out and the children were taken down to the bridge to see the men hanging there. To show them what happens to murderers."

Perk turned around slowly in the street wide enough to turn a wagon and team.

"Well, that's the town. On the way back to the ranch, I'll show you the Gold Star and the Gold Pearl and those little claims at the bottom and also I want to show you the Monte Queen. You been in the museum? Boy, they're proud of the museum."

"I have. They've done a great job with that."

"There's a lot of history in there."

We crossed the Henson Creek Bridge and drove south toward the ranch.

"You remember a guy named Lomax who came in here and built that place down here on the left by the river near the Texan cabins?"

"Very well, yeah. Lomax was in the oil business from Texas and Oklahoma, he and his two brothers. They built that lodge down here. They kept it for a long time and then they sold it. They were down in South Texas hunting white-winged dove and an airplane crash killed both of 'em.

"There used to be a lot of homes here. Part of Crookesville. That's what they called it then. These old timers had homes all in here. On both sides of the

LAKE CITY/ VICKERS AREA

CRYSTAL LAKE

SPERLING GULCH

NEW CEMETERY

WATERDOG LAKE

SLAUGHTERHOUSE GULCH

OLD CEMETERY

NEOGA ▲ MOUNTAIN

UPPER   RANCH

CANNIBAL PLATEAU

LAKE CITY

STATION ELEVEN ▲

HORSE   PARK

UTE-ULAY MINE ●

● HIDDEN TREASURE MINE

HENSON

CROOKE HOME SITE ●

CROOKE FALLS

PARK CREEK

CORA MINE ●

GOLDEN PEARL MINE ●

VICKER'S RANCH ●

GOLDEN WONDER MINE ●

DEADMAN'S GULCH

NELLIE M. MINE ●
BUCKEYE MINE ●
TROUBLESOME MINING CLAIM ●
MONTE QUEEN MINE ●

GOLDEN HILL

BELLE OF THE EAST MINE ●

SUTTON'S PARK

CRYSTAL LODGE

ALPINE GULCH

ARMITAGE MINE ●

BELLE OF THE WEST MINE ●

DAWN OF HOPE BRIDGE

ROUND TOP MOUNTAIN ▲

SLUMGULLION SLIDE

▲ CROWN MOUNTAIN

BLACK CROOKE MINE ●

LAKE FALLS

GOLDEN FLEECE MINE ●

▲ RED MOUNTAIN

HOTCHKISS MOUNTAIN

LAKESHORE ●

LAKE SAN CRISTOBAL

SLUMGULLION PASS

TO CREEDE

RED MOUNTAIN GULCH & CREEK

N
W   E
S

road. Before this main road was built, that was the road down there."

He pointed out a faint track just above the waterline on the far side of the river.

"That road came up right where the Texan is now and turned off and had a bridge right above the falls. See that old road going up there across the river? That was it. Went over the bluff all the way to Slumgullion. That was the old highway. It branched off and went on the other side of the lake. J. J. Crooke had an old home right here on the right at the top of the hill. See where that old tree is? Now we're gonna leave the road here, Joe, and we're going up this little spur road to the Troublesome Mine."

He turned off the road to the right onto a narrow dirt track.

"Now this road here, if you go up there about a quarter of a mile and make a left hand turn, you come out to the house of Frank Poole. That's on the Troublesome patented mining claim. Vickers have had that for years. If you keep to the right, you go right around the road and you wind up about six switchbacks and come out right up on top of Round Top Mountain, where we got our TV station. It's a beautiful drive. You ought to do that sometime."

"I would never think of building a road up through there. It looks impossible."

"I donated a week's work with my brother, Jack. We built the road with county equipment. You see what happened, in 1958 my brother, Bob, was working with a concern out of Gunnison, trying to find out how we could get television. We'd heard about this TV stuff. So we went up by horseback, and we took these micro site deals up there, and they found that there was enough of a signal up on top of Round Top to get TV. So they took an electric power plant up there and experimented how we could get electricity by that wave. Then Bob and I said we were gonna have to get power up there to run that damn thing.

"So then, through the Chamber of Commerce and everybody, we raised enough money to buy a number ten Romex cable to go from my house 5,700 feet up to the top. Bob and I measured that by coming down that mountain with a fifty foot tape, in order to know how much cable we needed. Down over those cliffs. It wasn't easy. I could never do that again.

"We are on patent land now, the Troublesome Mining Claim. I sold it to Frank Poole. I divided that mining claim into two parcels. I sold Frank Poole the upper half, you can see his house up there on top. And I sold that other house there to J. C. Doss. He's dead. She re-married when he died, and the family has it now.

"Now this is BLM land right here. That is the land I'm trying to trade for and I think we are gonna get it done. Now we're going up here to the Monte Queen. Right up on the hill, this big tunnel is called the Buckeye.

"The Buckeye was started by a man by the name of Patterson around 1900. He run a tunnel right up on that hill, but I don't think they ever found the vein. They run that back in there 500 feet but I don't think they ever shipped any ore. It's possible that the vein didn't go down that deep. They could have missed it. Joe, over here is the Nellie M. They took some very fine ore from that Nellie M from on top."

"That mining report you gave me to read talked about veins in this country getting pinched off, or cut off. It was almost like they formed in a V shape."

"Called a fissure. This is the Monte Queen. That tunnel just above us, we put that in there in the '50s. The Monte Queen is an old mine. Up on top there they had what they called a surface operation. They cut that vein and they drifted in on it and they shipped a lot of ore. Then they moved down the hill vertically about another couple of hundred feet and ran another tunnel right in on that vein. And they shipped all that ore from that second level clear to the surface. That fissure was a high-grade silver ore, but not very much gold. Ruby silver, some of it."

"My father showed me some ruby silver when I was a kid. It was from a mine up Henson Creek, I think. It looked silverfish-black, but when he scraped it with his pocket knife, it turned red."

"That's right. They run that Monte Queen for several years and they shipped it by the railroad. What shut that mine down was they had nine carloads of ore shipped to the smelter at Leadville. Walter Mindenhall was in charge of the operation. The crew was there waiting for the return of the ore shipment so he could pay them, and they could afford to keep on working. As the story goes, and I suppose there's some facts to it, he went to Leadville to watch that ore being sold. When he got the money he went to the World's Fair in 1910, I believe in Chicago. And when he come back, he had already spent the money and these guys were mad. He had no money to pay them, and they shut her down. It's been shut down ever since, except for two or three little leases."

"Mindenhall owned it or he just ran it?"

"Another guy owned it. Mindenhall had an option to buy it. This isn't patented. So I keep up the assessments. We're still claiming it. The government during WWII passed a law called OME — Office of Mineral Exploration. They were loaning money to mining prospects 'cause they needed that silver for the space program. They were using it for bombers and stuff. So a guy by the name of Goodwin and another by the name of Reese from Houston, got an OME loan on this and leased it. So we run this tunnel in on the vein, 1,650 feet, and the streak of ore is about this wide all the way through. They stayed right with the vein, made a couple of stopes. About 150 feet in they ran an upraise to connect with the tunnel up above which was a couple of hundred feet vertical, and they took out some of that ore but they didn't make any money, Finally, the government ceased to finance those

OME loans, so they shut her down. Actually, they walked away from it.

"See, Joe, what all these fellas would do is, get a claim and go around and try to put together what they might today call a consortium, a group of men to put up the money. They would want a certain percent in return. And if it goes bust, they lose their money."

"That's what you are doing now. Promoting it."

"And if they walk away, and if you wanted to continue to hold it all you had to do is file the necessary papers with the government. That's what happened here on this one claim. I just kept this one — there's about six others tied to it — and I paid $100 a year to the government. It's what they call rent now. It used to be you had to do $100 of assessment work. But it made some sense when they passed that new rule. Now you can do it by just paying the government a rent, instead of going in there with a bulldozer and tearing it all up just to do the assessment work. I think it's a good idea. There's some good ore on this dump. That stuff would run forty or fifty ounces of silver. If it had run to gold, it would be very valuable."

"What would that vein look like in the tunnel?"

"Oh god, it was a beautiful, smooth vein. It had a beautiful foot wall and a beautiful hanging wall. See this tract of land we're hoping we're gonna get? It's probably gonna' take in this tract of land to the highway. Eleven acres of it.

"I hired a guy, a friend of mine, he's now in Montana, he's a well digger and I used him on some core drilling up in Cinnamon Basin and in American Basin. So I let him use this for him to put his equipment on. Well, he left here and went broke and now I got to get rid of that damn equipment he left there. It's a wonder the BLM hasn't got after me. I'm gonna bring up that dozer and dig a big hole right here and smash all that and bury it"

"That rail there was built just to run the ore out and dump it?"

"They had a big ore bin right there. See the cement foundation? They ran that track out, but the railroad is still there. There was a switch. If they had ore that they wanted to put in the bin, they threw the switch and came out here, and if they didn't want to put the ore in the bin, they would throw the switch and drop it out over the dump."

"So when do you figure these mines got started?

"This mine, the Nellie M and the Monte Queen started just before the turn of the century. They are old mines. During the boom. A man by the name of Jordon did the last work. I noticed one of the old newspaper articles that said 'Roy Madison and John Jordan are making great progress in the Buckeye Tunnel. They are making two or three feet a day'. And they was doing that by hand too, see."

"What is 'double-jackin'?"

"Double-jackin' is where you got a drill in your hand and another man hits the drill. It's a piece of steel with a bit on it. You turn the drill and he hits it with a hammer. And they'd trade. One guy swings the hammer a while and he'd hand the other guy the hammer and he'd get down and start turning. You got to keep putting water in the hole. Bang, bang, bang, bang, bang."

We turned out onto the highway and continued toward the ranch. East of the road, a scratch of a road crossed the face of a dark bluff that rose above the river.

"Now we're on the west side of the Highway 149, if you look across the road and across the river, the Lake Fork, you can see four patented mining claims right along there. Right along that old county road there. The first one you see is the Golden Pearl. Then you go just a little further and you come to the Lode Star. You can the see the vein structure there. They sunk a shaft on that Lode Star down about 350 feet and reportedly shipped some ore better than most of them.

"I could very easily believe that could have happened 'cause I took samples of that assay. Some of the stuff on that side of the river would run better in gold than the stuff on this side.

"Then next you come to the Rob Roy. They ran a tunnel in under that structure in an easterly direction, 500 feet, on the vein. And they did ship a sizable amount of ore out of there. But there's a situation, you had a contact of two structures. On this side you got the eureka rhyolite, and over there they got the granite. By god, they had the most beautiful silver there, but on this side, gold.

"Now if they could have found a place where those two veins intersected each other, you could have had a sizable deposit of gold, 'cause on the Golden Wonder, when they found that vein on top, it had set there for years and years. They had back and forth leases. When my dad run that #2 tunnel in there we found an east and west vein that was intersected by a north and south vein. That's what you call a junction.

"So we found the gold. That's why we sunk that shaft. After running the #2 drift, we sunk that shaft down 100 feet on the ore. Hand drilling it and sorting. So we sunk that shaft and then we came back down the mountain another 150 feet running the old #3 level, which had been started, but we finished it. We knew where we were because we followed that vein down.

"So then, Joe, I wanted to get that land there by the right side of the road. Ten acres. Now see when we got our deed, I gave my daughter that corner. She's got that tract of land, 750 front-feet of this highway. But it's not very deep. That's why, if we could get that 10 acres more, we could build her a house."

"Why do they call that mountain across the river, Station Eleven?"

"I don't know. The government set that up in the Indian days. It might have had something to do with the Hayden Survey in the 1870s."

"What are they doing down there at Crooke's Falls now?"

"Some guy is running hydro-electric power there. He's selling that power. According to the Federal Energy Regulatory Commission all the electricity he puts in that power line the Co-op has to pay him for."

"How can he just move in on that water?"

"Oh, they had a water right established there a long time. About 1890 they had an old power plant and a reservoir. They had hydro-electric power even that far back. They had an old dam there."

"And that water right was still there, and he just took it."

"He just bought it. The Texan Resort is on that placer over there. They bought it way back."

"What is a placer?"

"A placer is a patented mining claim. You know in the early days, if you could show that you had a good-size deposit of ore, you could call it a placer. See there were seven mines there at the falls. A lot of guys had those down through the years. J.J. Crooke got that land and he built that smelter up here at the falls. What they call Crooke's Falls. He had a smelter there. He is the fella that got the credit for inventing tin foil. If you notice there on the other side of the river where that smelter was, there's a great big pile of coal. There's also rock that was brought down by wagon from Red Mountain, down that difficult road. They used that for fluxing in that smelter. That's what they had to have to treat the ore. The road from Red Mountain comes down just this side of Lake San Cristobal. Very difficult road."

"So a placer is just a big claim?"

"You can get a hundred acres of placer. As a matter of fact, I bought a placer during WWII from some people in Grand Rapids, Michigan. It's called the Park Placer, and it's up near the upper ranch. It ties into the Golden Wonder Mine. I bought that after several years of negotiation, and I bought it on the condition that I had to straighten out the title."

"I still don't understand the difference between one standard-sized claim and a placer."

"A placer is a surface operation. They don't go down deep. In an ordinary mining claim, you got to do your fissures. Veins. A placer is a deposit of ore on the surface. When a fissure vein is formed, some of it comes up to the surface, but most is underground. See this road here, the old road went right out by the Texan, right up the hill. See this vein here?"

He pointed out a rusty streak running up the road cut we were driving through.

"Right around here they did a little tunnel work. Well, right down under this road, just across from the Texan office, there's a tunnel that goes under here where we're driving over. They run that tunnel in there about 800 feet. They cut that vein and they drifted on the vein and they found out that it had a tremendous deposit of what you call talc. Nothing but white talc."

"What ever happened to that guy Gibson that used to own the Texan?"

"He's the guy that built the Texan. He's dead. It's changed hands three times since he built it. Ol' J.J. Crooke's home was right up behind us. They had a dam there to store the water. Now they can't do it. We won't let them. We've got a little ski tow there. It's the only one here."

"You've gone from mining to skiing. How come there's no big skiing development around here?"

"We don't get enough snow to justify a winter resort. Isn't that strange? Over there at Telluride, they get all kinds of snow.

"We're coming up on these mining claims now. Look across the river, there up the hill on the east side. Just above the falls. The Golden Pearl, the Lode Star, the Dolphin and the Dolphin mill site. They're all patented claims. I bought them during WWII from a tax sale.

That's where our subdivision is. You've been down several of those tunnels as a kid."

I remembered wanting to, riding horses with my brother, two young prospectors, along the road to the mouth of the tunnels. But the dark tunnels looked pretty threatening. So we settled the issue by filing our own claim at the site of an old mine — one with no tunnel — across the river. We called it the Texan Lode. Perk had gone to the courthouse with us to help us file the claim.

"When you buy the mining claim, you can develop the surface too and put a building on it?"

"You own the surface rights, yeah. If it's patented. Right there where my house sits, it's on another patented claim called the Crown Mountain. That is part of that land we got from the Department of Interior."

"Why did you build those fish ponds on the ranch?"

"Well, I decided to store some of that water and save the fish, so I just built one or two ponds at a time. I designed them. We didn't have to do any engineering, we just designed those ponds so that you take the water out of the river. We had to have a permit, which we had. You can get those permits as long as you're what they call non-consumptive. We ran it right out of the river down through one pond and down to the river through another. All ponds go out through the fourth pond right back into the river."

"Then you can raise fish in there?"

"Oh yeah. We raise fish all the time. We don't get much natural reproduction of the fish. We buy the little fingerlings, then we buy some seven and eight inch fish and put 'em in there at different times during the summer so we have enough fish for the customers. We put some in the river too. You've got to have fish for the tourists. Otherwise you won't have any tourists. One pond is reserved for the women and children."

"I like that story you told about the guy who dressed up in the dress and was down there fishing in the pond for women and children."

"Yeah. He was a retired a military general. Can you believe that?"

PART TWO

SOUTH OF TOWN TO CINNAMON PASS

"There's No Hope Now For The Satisfied Man"

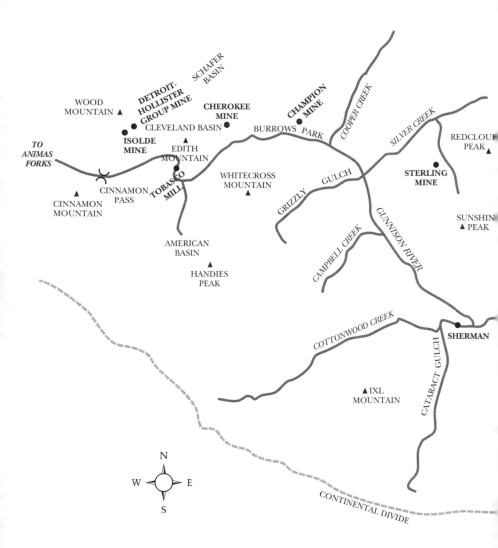

SCHAFER BASIN

WOOD MOUNTAIN ▲

DETROIT-HOLLISTER GROUP MINE

CHEROKEE MINE ●

CHAMPION MINE ●

COOPER CREEK

CLEVELAND BASIN ●

BURROWS PARK

SILVER CREEK

REDCLOUD PEAK ▲

ISOLDE MINE ●

EDITH MOUNTAIN ▲

TO ANIMAS FORKS

STERLING MINE ●

CINNAMON PASS

TOBASCO MILL ●

WHITECROSS MOUNTAIN ▲

GRIZZLY GULCH

▲ CINNAMON MOUNTAIN

SUNSHINE ▲ PEAK

GUNNISON RIVER

AMERICAN BASIN

CAMPBELL CREEK

HANDIES ▲ PEAK

COTTONWOOD CREEK

SHERMAN ●

▲ IXL MOUNTAIN

CATARACT GULCH

N
W ✦ E
S

CONTINENTAL DIVIDE

CINNAMON PASS ROAD

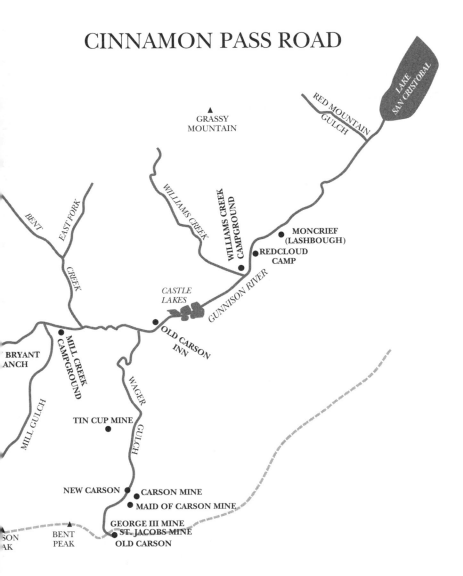

LAKE SAN CRISTOBAL

RED MOUNTAIN GULCH

GRASSY MOUNTAIN

WILLIAMS CREEK

WILLIAMS CREEK CAMPGROUND

MONCRIEF (LASHBOUGH)

REDCLOUD CAMP

GUNNISON RIVER

BENT

EAST FORK

CREEK

CASTLE LAKES

OLD CARSON INN

BRYANT RANCH

MILL CREEK CAMPGROUND

WAGER GULCH

MILL GULCH

TIN CUP MINE

NEW CARSON

CARSON MINE

MAID OF CARSON MINE

GEORGE III MINE
ST. JACOBS MINE

SON AK

BENT PEAK

OLD CARSON

*I*n the spring of 1874, Otto Mears, Russian immigrant-entre-
peneur, set out to build a toll road from Saguache into the
developing San Juan mining district, a 5,000 square mile
wilderness ceded by the Utes in the 1873 Brunot Treaty. Mears'
one hundred sixty-mile Saguache and San Juan Toll Road
would ascend the Saguache River to cross the Divide at
Cochetopa Pass, bear west to the Lake Fork of the Gunnison, follow the Lake Fork southwest to its headwaters, cross Cinnamon
Pass to Animas Forks and then to Silverton.

The engineer in charge was a young man named Enos T.
Hotchkiss, a road builder and some-time miner. Accompanying
the party was John A. Randolph, an artist for Harper's Weekly,
who wandered onto an abandoned campsite near the outlet of
Lake San Cristobal, where he found the mutilated and rotting
remains of five men. Within a month the search began for Alfred
Packer, a hapless drifter and the sole survivor of the ill-fated
prospecting expedition. He was suspected of murdering the five
men and living off their bodies during the severe winter that had
trapped them.

While prospecting in the area around the lake, Hotchkiss
found a promising mineral deposit, staked the Hotchkiss Claim
and did some initial assessment work. When he abandoned the
claim a year later, George Wilson and Chris Johnson relocated it
under the name of the Golden Fleece, the mine whose great wealth
and promise brought John Vickers to Lake City.

"That's the Golden Fleece up there," Perk said pointing to a series of ochre mine dumps that spilled down the
steep hillside from under a large rock outcropping at the
foot of the lake. "Enos Hotchkiss came in there and
found that deposit up there where they run the number
one level of the Golden Fleece and they started taking out

ore. They took a lot of gold out of that Golden Fleece, from #1 tunnel clear down to #3.

"That Golden Fleece was one of the biggest gold mines we had in the San Juans in the early years. Before they run the first lateral cut the Hiwasee and the Black Crook had started in production too. See, when they found that Golden Fleece, everybody got so excited. A man by the name of J.F. Steinbeck started the Black Crook a little bit north of the Golden Fleece. Some of his associates staked out the Hiwasee a little bit further north. There was so much excitement about gold up on the mountain at that time that everybody was staking every-thing else. They was shooting each other and everybody was high grading. In the end the Golden Fleece and the Black Crook came together.

"The biggest dump there, that is the Golden Fleece main level. Up on top, where they had all that gold, they had a surface operation. They had #1 and #2 levels. They went in and cut those veins and produced a lot of gold. They finally decided the thing to do was to run this tun-nel in there to see if the structures run deep. Well, they had a deal with the Black Crook Mine just to the north of them, so they combined them both into one group. They run that tunnel when they got in there about 800 or 900 feet, they turned and went to the right in to the Black Crook. They had some of the best mining engineers in the world, from Scotland and all over. They found that the Golden Fleece vein was a fissure vein, but it was a fault fissure. Fault means that there was a vein running easterly and westerly direction. Another vein from the north and south in the opposite direction cut through that and cut it off. It was a fault, and they spent lots of money trying to find where the other end of that vein was. They never did. But they produced a lot of ore.

"And then they decided to come down and run that big tunnel down by the shoreline of the lake. They run that tunnel in there about half a mile, and then the vein split. They hoped to cut that vein down at that depth, you know, about a thousand feet deeper. By gosh, they didn't find the gold. But then they come back and cut to the right, which was north, and cut the Black Crook vein.

"They shipped a lot of ore out of that Black Crook vein. They stoped it all the way from the lake level up to the Black Crook surface operation which was about 1400 feet."

"Where was the Black Crook?"

"It was just to the north of the Golden Fleece. They were both on the same hillside there."

"The first tunnel they put in there, was that up near the Pinnacles?"

"The first level of the Golden Fleece was just under the Pinnacles. Yes."

"And they went in high and kept going down lower and lower."

"Well, they found a lot of ore on the surface, so they kept sinking on it and drifting on it and when they got down there, I guess, about 300 feet in depth, the vein was faulted. They spent a lot of money trying to find, after it was cut off, where it went."

"I heard the ore in the Golden Fleece was 'pockety' ore. Have you ever heard that term?"

"The ore in the Golden Fleece was a little different than it was in most of the San Juan mines. They hit what they call 'glory holes' once in a while. There would be a big deposit of ore and then it would peter out 'til it wasn't so good."

"What was that? Gold and silver?"

"Gold and silver. Yes."

"That was the best gold mine in the area, wasn't it?"

"It was then. You know, right across the hill from the Golden Fleece is the Golden Wonder. The Golden Fleece never had as rich a gold as the Golden Wonder. That's a Vickers' mine. The Golden Wonder never has produced that much 'cause it never had that much development. As far as rich ore is concerned, the Golden Wonder has more free gold, yellow gold, than the Fleece had. The Fleece had what they call Hinsdaleite and Tellutrite. The Golden Wonder has some of that same thing, but the Golden Fleece never had any free gold like the Golden Wonder does."

"You think that's on the same vein, or is it a different vein?"

"I don't think it's the same vein. The Golden Fleece vein has always been considered to come across the hillside down by where the Crystal Lodge is and clear down by Crooke's Falls. But it never did go across on the other side of the river. But on the other side of the river, of course, they had the Belle of the West and the Belle of the East. They adjoin the Golden Wonder. That was a strange thing there, too. They had silver and lead and copper, but they didn't have the gold. To the north and east the Golden Wonder had the gold."

"Now when your father came to Lake City in 1888, he started to work at the Golden Fleece?"

"He did. He got a room at the boarding house and he stayed there a couple of years. He was what they called a fish eater. They had a boarding house, and they used to catch big fish out of the lake, and one guy that knew my dad was from Canada and liked fish. That guy came up to the boarding house with a five or six pound rainbow trout and he bet four or five of those other guys that he had a man working for him who could eat that in one meal. So they cooked up that big fish and my dad ate the fish and took the empty bone and held it up in the air and said, 'Well, there she is, boys.'"

"So he could eat fish? Trout?"

"Yeah. He said he left Canada because he got tired of living on codfish and mackerel. When he got down in this part of the country he wanted to eat some trout. Rainbows and brookies."

"How long did he work at the Golden Fleece?"

"He worked up there until he met Charley McKinley. He said, 'Mr. Vickers, you're a young man. I got a better deal for you up at the Ute-Ulay.' And that's how come he moved from there to the Ute-Ulay."

"What happened to the Golden Fleece? Did they finally give up on that vein?"

"They were in debt. They ran that big tunnel under-neath at the lake level. And they did a lot of development work in every direction trying to find out where that vein went after it apexed. A lot of times when they have what's called a false fissure, it gets cut off. It's what they call faulted. When that gets cut off, sometimes they find it and sometimes they never find it. They probably spent more money on the Golden Fleece trying to find the apex in under that long tunnel than they ever made money out of it. I doubt they ever made a net profit out of the Golden Fleece at all."

"What do you mean the apex vein?"

"Say you got a vein going north and south and you got another one going east and west and one vein intersects the other and cuts it off. That's what they call apex.

"Down through the years a lot of guys working on the mine would steal some of that gold. Carry it out in their lunch buckets. I knew of a case, not so many years after that, when I was young, a couple of fellows work-ing at another mine got a lease on the Golden Fleece, and they knew where there was about four or five tons of gold ore that had been stolen and sacked and put on the hillside there in some timber. After they got the property leased they went over there to get that gold in the timber and the sacks were rottener than the devil. They had to pick the gold up a piece at a time. They reported around here that they got $50,000 out of it. And it's possible they did."

"I heard that the Golden Fleece ore was running $400 a ton at one time."

"Well, see, that's low-grade ore. Some of that Golden Fleece ore would probably run $5000 a ton. Hand-picked."

"If they got into one of those pockets or 'glory holes'?"

"When they got in the pockets. They hand-sorted, see. That's why they had to search the men and everything else. They had one room, where when the men come off shift they had to change clothes. They'd even search their lunch buckets. They were afraid they'd take it home in their lunch buckets."

"Well, how did those men manage to get that ore out of there?"

"They had ways of stealing it. They put it in their jaw. They put it in their clothes. They would hide it out. One guy would watch while the other guy would go across the hillside and hide it out among the trees. It was a hard way to make money. But it was always going on in the mining business. Over to San Juan at Silverton they had those high-graders all the time."

"When did the Golden Fleece shut down?"

"It shut down around 1915, or thereabouts. After that, there were a lot of people that bought or leased and worked up there and tried to do something. There has been a lot of activity. They had a mill right down there below that first level, and they ran that mill a long time."

"Were they mining the dumps any?"

"In recent years. During the last forty years, there has been a few different outfits trying to mine that dump. But I don't think they made any money out of the dump. Those old miners, they were smart. They were crafty. They knew what ore looked like and they didn't throw any more on the dump than they had to. Although, in some areas in the Lake City vicinity, I've known cases where they went back in later years and mined the dumps and made quite a lot of money."

"Who owns the Golden Fleece now?"

"Well, most of it has been subdivided. There's a lot of homes up on that hill."

"So the Golden Fleece was made up of several patented claims and they have been sold off one at a time for home sites?"

"Yeah. There were more lawsuits filed on the Golden Fleece than all the rest of the mines in Hinsdale County put together. People would trespass. They would locate on another man's claim. They would go to court. Seemed like there was always some litigation. But, that's pretty well the history of all mines. There's always a lot of litigation goes on."

"I thought an English company owned the Golden Fleece at one time."

"Well, so many different people had it. I think one of the companies was from England. There's been so many different people that have had that property that I never did keep up. Once a guy by the name of Reeves from Dallas or Houston, and Al Goodwin, worked out some kind of a deal, lease-purchase, and they opened up that lower tunnel. They were all the way in there. Re-opened that tunnel and timbered it. But I guess after they got in there and re-evaluated the veins and the ore body, it wasn't going to be profitable, so they quit. It's just been sitting there. Al Goodwin is dead, and Mr. Reeves is in Houston. I think he's dead too."

"Do you personally think there is any ore left in there?"

"I doubt it. There could be a lot of ore, but it would take a person with a lot of luck and a lot of money to find it. I doubt if you'll ever see it. I know you won't now because it's all subdivided. Although, those people who've got those homes on there probably reserved the mineral rights."

"The story I heard was that Enos Hotchkiss was on the other side of the valley surveying Mears' road in 1874, he saw the Pinnacles outcrop and saw the color and — "

"That could have been. Because as you come down Slumgullion now and look across there at the Pinnacles, even today when the snow goes off, you can look over there and see the vein structure. The formation changes, but you can see it from miles away. Well, anyway the vein that Hotchkiss found was just under the Pinnacles. It was actually what you would call a mineralized outcrop. There was a slide there and according to the story he got to fooling around there with a hammer breaking up some of that slide rock and he kept breaking that slide rock, and he found a little seam that had fallen out of the main vein. He dug down on that seam and that's where he found the gold.

"You know, a lot of people have always said that Red Mountain, right behind the Golden Fleece, had what might be the mother lode of all of it. But nobody has ever penetrated that structure under Red Mountain at all. Except the government did allow a company in here about ten years ago, to core drill on the top of Red Mountain. They came up with a huge deposit of bauxite and alunite."

"But no gold."

"No gold."

"So nobody's gone from the Golden Fleece straight back west into the mountain."

"No, they have not."

"They went down?"

"Well, that tunnel down by the lake goes in there a mile you know. That tunnel from the lake level goes right slap dab west in for a mile. That's why they were disappointed when they ran that tunnel in under there and didn't find the vein. Even though it was cut off above, they thought sure they could find it, I guess. They spent a fortune looking for it."

"They went down 2,000 feet and then went east under the lake?"

"Well, no. They was on the level about fifty feet above the lake. They ran that tunnel right in the mountain, straight. Due west."

"So they never did tunnel under the lake?"

"No, they never went under the lake."

"So they went back toward Red Mountain."

"Right straight under the Pinnacles. Right straight west into Red Mountain."

"So they were hoping that the vein was vertical and that they would cut it."

"Oh yeah. That's what they were hoping. Even though they knew it had been cut off above, about halfway down the hill. By god, they thought sure they could find it. On that third level where the apex occurred, they went in there in numerous directions, and they never did find it."

"So they were drifting in all directions."

"Every direction, to see if they could find it."

"Well, it's like you said earlier. A mine is a hole in the ground owned by a fool."

Perk's eyes crinkled and he laughed remembering he had told me that. It was an observation he would make often.

"Tell me what a winze is."

"A winze is an underground shaft. It goes down from a tunnel. A digging that goes from a tunnel to the surface, that's a shaft. A winze is an underground shaft. Now you also have upraises. A stope goes up. A stope, you might say, is an overhead shaft."

"A stope doesn't necessarily connect two tunnels."

"Not necessarily. It could connect two tunnels or it could go clear to the surface. A shaft can connect two tunnels. Now, just for instance, suppose you had a tunnel right here going into the mountain. Down here a little farther you had a tunnel going in under that. They both run right in under each other. In a separate tunnel you're going to sink a shaft, or a winze, to keep going right down on the vein and you come to that tunnel below. If there is a tunnel below."

"Is it a stope only when you are trying to follow the vein?"

"Not necessarily. Sometimes you'll just stope up to get air."

"So if you've got a tunnel in and you dig up, that's a stope and if you dig down, that's a winze."

"Absolutely."

"So, you're not really mining out of a tunnel. You're just going to the vein."

"No. Sometimes you'll have an outcropping and your tunnel will go in right along the vein. And you'll be mining all the way through."

"And then when you get on the vein, if you stope it, it allows gravity to bring the ore down."

"Well, sure. See, you got a tunnel here, and here you got an upraise, a stope. In the tunnel you got tracks or a buggy. You can take an air compressor and drill a hole up and blast 'em and the ore falls right back down. It's called the gravity system of mining. Of course, if you go down in a shaft, or a winze, you have to hoist the ore up."

We stood by the jeep looking up at the dumps and rusting rails.

"So that gold is still in there somewhere."

"Maybe. All those years somebody was trying to promote a core drilling program. Now it may never happen because that's all in a subdivision. There's houses all over that place up there and half way up that mountain. You see the Black Crook dump shining through the trees there? There were a lot of problems then. The men couldn't get together and one guy would start mining ore off another man's property. Some of that they call apex. There's been many a lawsuit fought over what they call apex. It's generally understood, and it don't always hold up in court, that if you were to were to discover a vein in one spot and you locate it and you drift and start working on it, you could follow that vein even if it runs across another man's property. That always caused a lot of trouble. The rule of thumb is that you can do it as long as you're following that vein. The best policy is to get together with the other guy and work together or buy him out or some damn thing.

"Anyhow, the old road was on the other side of the lake before this main road was built. It came from Saguache over Slumgullion. Then they had another road right up on the mountain above this one about 100 feet. It was parallel to the one we're on. To service the mines. I'll bet you in that Golden Fleece, there's four miles of underground tunnel."

"But they never actually went under the lake?"

We drove on south around the edge of the lake and the valley opened up before us. Along the western, shore remnants of a few buildings were scattered over the treeless slope.

"This right here was the old town site of Lakeshore. They had a lot of houses up and down this valley by the lake. And they found out in recent years that all this land still belonged to the government. They made them move the houses. Some of 'em they burned. But there was a Roxie mining claim right here. It was about 300 feet wide and 1500 foot long. This is where the French family had their hotel. The Lakeshore Hotel was right here."

"What's that cement building there?" The crumbling walls *of a broken, gray box stood atop their own rubble.*

"Well, that hotel burned. The man that had it was a man by the name of French. He said he was gonna' build everything out of concrete so it couldn't burn, but it did. Come to find out his wife was a firebug. She burned that hotel. He and his wife didn't get along after that hotel burned. He had an option on the property and later bought it. Hugh McKee, Joe Axlebaum and Ole Olson all had cabins right along the shore here. They lived here all their lives and finally the government took 'em away from 'em. Didn't have title at all."

"So French built the hotel to cash in on the tourist trade. When was that?"

"That was in the '20s and '30s. It was a nice place. People didn't have automobiles then. They had the railroad. He'd meet 'em at the railroad station and bring 'em up here."

"You know, when we first started coming up to Lake City, you couldn't drive along the east side of the lake."

"That was the original road. The old toll road to Silverton. But after they opened this road here along the west side of the lake, they didn't use that road any more. We opened that road up through the Chamber of Commerce, several years ago."

"There used to be a mine tunnel that opened right out on the road here."

"That was closed. The government took that away from the people. You know, it's hard to believe. You'd think if you came up here in 1880 and took up a little tract of land and your family had been there all their life, you'd think they'd have some equity in that land. The government says no. We tried that on a lawsuit on our ranch on what they call a "Color of Title." Color of Title means that if you had quiet possession of a piece of land, thinking you owned it and paid taxes, you could get a title. But they kicked that out in a hurry because they said we knew we didn't own it because we made application under the Homestead Act. We found out under that application that the land had been withdrawn under an old government power of withdrawal."

"Fishing still good in that lake?"

"Oh, I think the fishing is pretty fair, although the Division of Wildlife has not been stocking it for the last four years because the trout got that whirling disease. But I think they got some fish this year on a limited basis. Some of the hatcheries are disease-free. We buy our fish for the ranch from a disease-free hatchery."

"There was no mining up at this end of the lake?"

"No. Not 'til you get clear up this side of Carson. Now we come around here to what they call Red Mountain Gulch. That goes up to the Red Mountain where there's that big deposit of bauxite. Largest deposit in the free world. So, the County, they got a grant to put in this Red Mountain Campground for day-use."

"You can't do anything with this land now without talking to the government?"

"Oh, man. That took a lot of doing just to get that campground."

"Weren't you on the County Commission for a while?"

"I wanted to be, but I got defeated. By five votes."

"But didn't you have something to do with the roads?"

"Yeah, I had something to do with all of them."

"But that was as a private contractor."

We rounded a corner and stopped for a group of workers patching the asphalt. Perk leaned out the window to talk.

"How's it going, Walter? Where in the hell did you get that machine? All the way from Colorado Springs? Is that the County's? That's a dandy, ain't it? Hell, I never saw one like that. That's a new one. See ya' later. Take it easy you guys.

"Now this land here, belongs to some people from Lake Charles, Louisiana. See the house over there on the mountain just above the lake? They got 110 acres here. Name is Frochet. I built that house for the Forchets. My brother and I built that house thirty years ago, the year that Kennedy got shot. That's a four-bedroom house. It's a pretty nice place. We didn't take a contract. He was a good friend of mine and he just had me to do it. I got help. I got three and a half dollars an hour for my work. It's on a patent mining claim. This little stream coming down here is called Red Mountain Creek."

"I used to jump the fence and fish in that stretch of river there."

"They don't keep the public off. They've got it posted but there's nobody here. Nobody's looking after the property at all. They got about a half a mile of damn good water. As a matter of fact, their land runs out into the lake a couple of hundred feet."

"From here it looks like there's two Red Mountains up there."

"It's all one mountain. Double peak. It's a huge mountain."

"So all that aluminum ore just bubbled up."

"It's what they call a secondary replacement. Someday you'll see this road paved all the way to Sherman."

"Why do they want to do that?"

"Well it's less grading. Better driving. More comfortable ride."

"You got to play to the people who want to come here, don't you. Tourism is the only source of income."

We turned at the end of the lake, bumped off the pavement onto the gravel surface of the river road and re-entered the canyon it had cut from the fluted cliffs. For two miles the road climbed slowly up out of the canyon and then, turning like the river itself, leveled off and wound across a broad alpine meadow toward the sloping, criss-crossed flanks of the mountains that filled the perfect sky.

"Now there is Carson Peak. See it right ahead. The town of Carson is just to the left of that. On the right side is what they call Tincup. That Carson had some big mines. There was George III, the Carson and Maid of Carson. The silver that came out of the Carson was so rich you could damn near cut it with an axe. In the Colorado Museum there's a big slab of Carson silver.

"The main mine of Carson was called the Saint Jacobs. A good friend of my dad's was the engineer. He was from Scotland, a graduate of the University of Scotland. His name was Gus Zacharias."

"Those mines were late getting started up there, weren't they?"

"Hell, I remember when they was packing ore out of Carson all the way down to the bottom of the hill there at Child's park. Then they would ship it by truck. A man by the name of George Corey Franklin was involved in that. Now this road on the right goes up to Red Mountain. The guy that built my house has got 100 acres of placer up there. Joel Swank. He built a home up there. About three miles of road to get to it. That is a county road. I don't think they're doing much with it."

"What does that mean if it's a county road?"

"They get highway user money, and the county maintains it."

"They plow it in the winter?"

"No, they don't keep it open in the wintertime. Up there on the left where that fence starts, that's the Moncrief Ranch. He just took it back. Some guy made him a deal for $5 million about three years ago, and he couldn't make any more payments so Moncrief took it away from him. That was the damndest thing you ever saw. This guy Kraft, you read about it in the paper I'm sure, bought this place for $5.5 million and he had a contract to pay 12% interest, but for the first two years they never did close the deal. He kept paying interest, but he never did close the deal. The reason I know so much about Moncrief, I was on their board of directors. They had camp there for children with terminal illness."

Here the river meandered through a lush meadow. A group of log buildings was tucked under the trees at the far end.

"Was this the old Red Cloud Ranch?"

"This is the Lashbaugh place. A man by the name of Lashbaugh got the patent on this."

"This is a nice log house here on the right. I looked at this house to buy it in 1990. Great view out across the meadow and the river to the mountains."

"A man by the name of Wade owns that. Has his own shop. Computers for doctors."

"They wanted $60,000 for that and I thought it was too much."

"That's a bargain. It would go right now for $260,000. Now, right next to the Lashbaugh place, we're getting on what you call the Red Cloud Ranch. Red Cloud bought this when it was the old Clawson ranch and now it's a religious camp. They got a lot of stuff over at that Red Cloud. They got two new trucks. They got them from the army. For religious purposes. To haul these kids and stuff."

"You know, I wouldn't think you could make a living ranching up here."

"Oh, there wasn't any of these ranches that made any money."

"Well, why did they bother with cattle anyway?"

"Well you take Clawson, he run this little ranch. He had a dairy ranch, and ran a few milk cows. He made a few bucks. As far as money was concerned, he didn't make any money."

"So there never was much money in ranching. It was just subsistence."

"That's right. They may have made $1000 a year."

"You think eventually you'll break your ranch up and sell those as individual cabins?"

"I don't know, but we are gonna start leasing some of 'em. We got some leased out for five years."

"That's what's happening all over town isn't it? 'Cause you could get more for one cabin than the whole place is worth."

He ignored me — or maybe didn't hear me — and changed the subject. Maybe I was getting too much into his business.

"On the right here, this is Williams Creek here. That goes up to Grassy Mountain. If you go up that creek and over the ridge you come right down Alpine Gulch. Now the Forest Service has got a campground right here. A real nice one. And you know, that's always been something that bothered me. The government won't give you any land, but they'll take a piece of choice land and make a campground and charge a dollar a day to use it in competition against the guys that pay big taxes on their private land. If they were charge for those campsites they ought to charge the same as if they were gonna rent a cabin. Or maybe a little less. Well it don't make any sense to me to see those people get taken for all that tax. In this county the government owns 95% of the land and only 5% in private ownership."

"Is the property tax in Lake City pretty high?"

"Pretty high. They have to have a lot of land to maintain the roads, schools and all that. The land's the only source of income."

"Do they keep the road to Sherman open all year?"

"All year. There's a guy up here at Sherman who just finished his house — a three-story red brick house. Three-story and it's got an elevator in it. Can you believe that? He's a good friend of mine. A man by the name of Tommy Thompson. His house is on a county road. They keep that open all winter for him. Oh there's a lot of people who bought that Sherman. It's all private ownership now. It's all been divided.

"Right here on the left is Old Dick Sherman's place. He is putting up that hay. Looks like pretty good hay."

"One crop a year?"

"One crop. They can't make any money raising hay. But they can do exactly what they want to do. That power line goes all the way to Sherman. They got the telephone in too."

"Sherman started out with mining?"

"Sherman was promoted as a mining camp. They had a strong vein called the Black Wonder vein. It's a true fissure vein. You can see it for miles. They did some development, but not much. They built a huge mill, then they ran that pipeline all the way up to pick up the Lake Fork water to run that mill and the power plant. I think they went broke in the late '20s. I remember when I was a kid; they had so many people in Sherman. They would come down to Lake City in trucks — I never saw a truck like that — to go to the baseball games.

"This place here on the right has changed hands — The Old Carson Inn. It's a bed and breakfast now. It's a nice place. It sold for $850,000 a while back."

"I wouldn't want to run a bed and breakfast, would you? Can you imagine those people in your house all the time?"

"And the next morning they got to get them the hell out of there and clean the beds and the bathrooms, do the linens. Bed and breakfast, that is, without a doubt, the poorest business you could even think of getting in."

"And everybody thinks it would be the greatest thing. 'We're gonna retire and buy a bed and breakfast.'"

"It's losing its popularity now though."

A rough dirt road turned off to the left and immediately began to climb steeply through the trees.

"That's the Carson road right up there. Wager Gulch. You've been up that, of course. You know a lot about Carson."

"Well the thing I remember about it is that it's the worst road I've ever been on in my life. It's just like driving up cement steps."

"It still is, too. They're trying to sell the townsite of Carson now. There's seven hundred acres in there. All those mining claims altogether is seven hundred acres."

"Who owns it?"

"Bell Helicopter out of Dallas."

"They haven't put those buildings in the National Historic District?"

"No, but they're talking about it. They fixed them up."

"They ought to be saved."

"Well, they are. They're trying to sell that whole town site. Somebody will buy that someday. It's got a lot of potential."

"They'll tear those buildings down."

"Well, I doubt that. You never know. I think that whoever buys that will recognize the historical value."

"Boy, I hope so."

"I do too."

"I don't think that's changed a lick since the first time I saw it."

Carson had always been one of my favorite secret places and my memory of it had been clearly etched since that August day when I first went there. For the first few miles, the road to Carson, if it could be called a road, followed a streambed up a narrow rocky canyon. The spring run-off had washed away all the loose dirt and rocks leaving only a series of stone ledges. At the head of the canyon, the road crossed the streambed and labored up a steep shelf road just wide enough for one jeep. The road wound up the side of the canyon in a series of tight turns, and as I approached each one, I strained up to see over the hood to pick a line through the turn that would avoid as many obstacles as possible. Along side one tight turn, a patch of lupine crowded the shaded hillside.

Rounding a last wooded turn, the road leveled off, passed through an aspen grove and came out into a small meadow. There ahead, in the lee of an overhanging circ, just at the tree line, was what was left of Carson, a group of old wooden buildings weathered the color of cinnamon. It seemed strange to see the buildings, so complete, sitting there at the edge of the empty meadow. No people. No streets. It was as if the buildings had been set down in this unlikely spot for storage, and then forgotten.

"I haven't been up there in four or five years," Perk said, "but I know he hired some carpenters to put some roofs on. Some new metal roofs."

"You know there's tongue-and-groove ceiling in that stable?"

"I know it. Can you imagine that? That was old man Child's private residence in the mining days. Boy, they did a lot of mining there. That George III and Jake Jacobs, they put a lot of mines in there. That was his horse barn.

"Look over there. Some guy come up here and bought that house and moved into it. What the hell you gonna do? Well, you walk around and walk around and pretty soon your wife says, 'Well, hell, lets get out of here.' Women don't want to stay here. It takes a special kind of woman to live here.

"Emma Jean and I have been married for fifty-seven years. I remember the first three or four years, I thought it wasn't going to work at all.

"Now this is Bent Creek. This is a subdivision here. He's got it all approved and ready to sell. The guy that owns it has got one home and is offering it for sale. I noticed in the paper that he wants a million and a quarter. He'll catch a sucker. There's more suckers born now than you think there is. Those are the most expensive houses you can build. Log. That's a nice place, though. We used to hunt up Bent Creek all the time. Lot a water in that creek. Some of it goes all the way down into the Colorado. Some of it ends up in Yuma, Arizona, and even Old Mexico."

"How come they diverted that spring box up on top of Spring Creek Pass? You know, there used to be a box and part of the water went out in both directions, on both sides of the Divide."

"Well, that was a lawsuit. That's what you call trans-mountain diversion. The San Luis water users had that water right and secured it. Then they wanted to divert it, drop it over the mountain into the Rio Grande River and pick it up down on their ranches in the district. Some comes this way. In the lawsuit they agreed to split it up."

"You know I have never seen the white cross on the mountain at White Cross."

"I'll show it to you. It's easy to see. Now right over there, there's another situation. The government took this tract of land — that's Mill Creek — and built that bridge and made a beautiful campground over there. They don't charge enough there. They are in fact competing against Dick Cooper who's got the camps on the lake down there. I don't think that's right.

"Now this ranch here, right beside the road. It's one of the old ranches. In the '20s a guy by the name of Dan Bryant bought this place. I think he got the patent too. He decided he wanted to go in the goat business. He bought him a herd of goats and he ran those goats for a year or more and then he decided he was gonna raise fish. So he put a fish hatchery up here and started raising those fish. And he wasn't hardly making a living at all. He had two boys and they worked on the roads. I worked on the road with both of those guys.

"Dan Bryant, he and his wife got a divorce. I was working with one of the boys on that shelf road up above Sherman. One day, damn if Ol' Bryant didn't go outside the kitchen door and killed himself. That was awful for them two boys. The mother, she just lost her mind and she disappeared. They had a hard time finding her. Somehow she got over the mountains on the Rio Grande side over to Hermit Lakes. Walked over the mountain. She had house shoes on. Lost her mind. There's a lot of history there. It ain't all pretty. This is all subdivided now. You see they got some land for sale now."

"That's all swampy."

"It's what you call wetlands, but the river's way over there. It's not that bad. You could build on that, if you built a foundation. This is a good place to be in the real estate business. You can buy that land and then sell it again. That's called IXL Mountain. Up on top of that mountain is a mine called the Sterling. Right here's where Dan Bryant's fish hatchery was. See that old house? That's all fallen in now. He had all the ponds in here. He raised a lot of fish. Didn't do any good with it. Then when he died, it sold to a family by the name of Bell from Midland, Texas. He had a big old barn. That's all fallen too. That's where he kept his goats. That's the old house right there. Mrs. Bell, when she bought it she built another one right up here. A newer one. I stayed in that old house two or three summers when we were working on the road. I don't know what's gonna happen to it now. It sold."

"Well, the next thing you know there'll be convenience stores up here."

"See, now that's Cataract Creek. There's Cottonwood Creek right there and the Lake Fork goes this way. There's a lake up in there. We used to go up there a lot of times. Boy, that's good fishing."

Ahead of us, a mobile home teetered on a small space cut into the side of the steep hill.

"Now, I'll show you what the guy did here. See that place up on top that he leveled off? He' gonna build himself a house up on there. Right now he's living out of a great big travel home, and he couldn't get it up there so he parked it right over here on that corner for the time being. Can you imagine a man crazy enough to build a house on that kind of a place? By god, a snowslide or a flood will get him surer than hell. That's a slide area he's in.

"Now you turn down here to the left and you cross the river and you go right into Sherman. That goes to the old town site."

"What happened to the old town of Sherman? Did they tear it down?"

"It all rotted away, and they tore it down. It's subdivided now. There's some beautiful homes. I was telling you about the guy who has the three-story red brick house. Well, there's a lot of people want to get down in these honest to god wilderness areas. Then they want to live like they're in the city. They can't ever have enough. But, I'll tell you right now. There's no hope now for the satisfied man. By god, that's a fact.

"I've taken my bulldozer up this pass so many times you won't believe it. They've always had a lot of mining going on and I was always working on the mines. I promoted a lot of work in American Basin. The Gnome Mine. We spent about a million and a half dollars in there. I had a company out of Houston called Houston Natural, spent a lot of money up there. We didn't find the gold. If we had found the gold, we would still be mining."

"So a group would put up the money to develop a claim for a share of the take?"

"Generally they would buy the land on a purchase contract. They would make payments intermittently. If they don't find what they want, all they have to do is walk away from it and give it back to you."

"So as long as they're paying on the development they're entitled to some of the take?"

"They just take it all. Just pay me a royalty. Or they could pay me the cash, and I'd just walk away from it, and they could have it all. And a lot of times I worked for them cause they knew I had the knowledge to do it. And I had the equipment to do it with.

"Now you see that big black dike going across that mountain up on the left? That's called the Black Wonder vein. See that big vein? It's a monster. It's a contact is what it is. A geological contact. That's where two formations come together. They had gold but, honest to god, they didn't do enough work to prove or disprove anything. There's a tunnel up here goes right in under it. They put all their effort into building that pipeline and building that mill.

"We used to run our cattle from the upper ranch, when we were young, all the way to Sherman. For the pasture.

"There was a man by the man of John Gavin who had a cabin there that he lived in. He was one of the last guys. One of the last of the Mohicans up there. He died in that cabin. He had a mine right up there at the top of what they call IXL Mountain. It was way up on top. What they called the Sterling Mine. And that old guy worked on the Sterling off and on 'til he died. We used to come up here and visit with him — Bob and Joe and I — when we had cattle up here at Sherman. We'd set there and he'd give us a biscuit or something. We didn't have anything to eat besides flour and bacon. He loved the Vickers boys 'cause he didn't see that much company anyway.

"He knew they were building a railroad from Silverton up to Eureka and he had so much confidence in it. He kept thinking that train was gonna come right over the hill from Silverton and come right down Cottonwood Creek. He was kinda watching. We'd be sitting there visiting with him and all of a sudden he would say, 'Hey. You guys. Listen. Listen. Listen. Listen. There's a train a coming down Cottonwood.' He was so sure that this was gonna boom any day."

"But that's so steep up there."

"Oh, they can build a railroad any place they want. Damndest thing you ever saw. That's Cataract Canyon right there. Beautiful falls up there. Sometime you ought to walk up Cataract. There's a 30-acre lake up there. Now I worked on this road. That's the first work I ever had in my life, working for the county. Fifty cents an hour. Now, look down there to the left and you can see part of Sherman. That's a big flat down there. There's a lot of room there."

Where Sherman once stood and thrived, a plaited stream wound along a sandy flat shaded by cottonwoods.

"Now that's the town that washed away when the dam broke?"

"That was it. It's in a flood plain. They got the stream pretty well stabilized now. It's not running where ever it wants to. Now see the road going up there into the canyon to the left? You can drive up Cottonwood Creek for about six miles. It's a county road."

"I bet it was a slow trip up here in a bulldozer."

"I've ridden this road so many times. The money I was making when I was working outside, I would take and put right back to the ranch. My brothers, they did the work on the ranch. I had the best brothers a man ever had. They was doing all the work and I was bringing in the money. Otherwise, that ranch, you couldn't have done what we had to do 'cause the revenue was not there. Then just when we got it up to where it looked like we could make a few bucks, get things on a paying basis, I lost three brothers in one year. Joe and Bob and Ivan. Three of them."

"What happened?"

"Joe had surgery on his leg and he got a blood clot. Bob had a cancer of the liver, and my older brother, Ivan, he died. He was retired after working for the U.S. Department of Interior."

The road climbed around the hill and curved onto a narrow shelf chiseled from the cliff face. Over the unguarded road edge, the river was just visible in the canyon a hundred feet below.

"There was a guy here a few years ago who started to back up and he backed up right over that bank. In a big pickup with a camper on top of it. Didn't kill no one but it smashed it all to hell. It just rolled over twice and hit the bottom. Lucky. Some of that stuff is still down there.

"When I was driving that bulldozer I stopped here many a time to get a drink of water at that spring. The old road, I'll show it to you, was on the other side of the river. Way down there. That was the old road a hundred years ago. The reason why we moved the road over here was that the old road across the river crossed a lot of snow slides and it was always muddy. It was all solid rock over here. You see those pins in the ground? Dig the hole with a jackhammer, drive the pin in it and strap the rocks against it. Made a cribbing. Made it all the way up. This was all blasting. I used to enjoy it. They would drill the holes and blast the holes and I would level it off with a bulldozer. Push those big rocks over the mountain. You'd see them go down there and hit that river and splash water half way back up here. The old road came right out of Sherman, right along that side down there, all the way clear up to Burrows Park."

"When was this road put in?"

"Well, we worked on this road from 1930 to about 1935 or '36. That's when I met Emma Jean. I was working on this road; her brother brought her up on vacation from Denton, Texas. To help take care of their baby. I went home one night, and Emma Jean was staying in one of those little apartments we had there. I came across to see my sisters, and she said, 'Well, what do you do here for entertainment?' She was only about sixteen. And my sister said, 'Ah, well, we got a brother, name of Perk Vickers. We go down to Mike Pavich's about once every night or two.' And that's where I met Emma Jean."

"So they had a trail on this side but there was no road?"

"No road. They had a trail. The reason they had a trail was a wooden stave pipeline came all the way from the river to carry that water down to Sherman. I don't think they ever got it finished. But they built the mill. In the mining business the promoters always screwed it up. They'd come in and promote the money and do a lot of roadwork and build a big mill and then a tramway. Then by the time they got that done, there wasn't any money left."

"But they got their money and they were gone."

"Some of 'em did. This road is a boulevard now compared to what it used to be."

We passed an oncoming car that slowed for us to get by on the narrow road. Perk leaned out the window to talk to the occupants — an elderly man and woman.

"Thank you very much for stopping! Beautiful country, isn't it? Where are you guys from? Illinois? That's good. My name is Vickers. We have a ranch down by Lake City. Vickers' Ranch. We're up here looking at the mines." They nodded, but we couldn't hear what they said. Satisfied, Perk waved and we drove away.

"There's a little vein coming right through here,"Perk said, pointing to the road cut. "See that little vein? Now if a guy was prospecting he would start digging on that. Says, maybe I'll find the mother lode."

"Now would all the ore in a mine be along the face of the vein?"

"On the same vein, either on the foot wall or the hanging wall. Generally on the hanging wall. There's another little fissure comes right through there. You've been up this road a lot of times, haven't you?"

"Yep. I like it."

"Can't beat it."

"Wasn't there a bridge over one of these canyons?"

"That's further down. That bridge was built solely for the purpose of supporting that water line. That was one heck of an undertaking there."

"Once I was driving up here and I passed a guy on a bicycle. Did you ever have a bicycle?"

"Never could afford one."

"Even as a kid, you never had a bicycle?"

"Never had a bicycle. The only bicycle I ever saw was when Larry had one when he was about ten or twelve. You don't have any idea how hard up we were. Ran the cattle and the horses trying to hold things together. Whenever it looked like one of my brothers wanted to get married, he had to leave. He either went to work for the county or worked for somebody else. He had to get away from the ranch 'cause there wasn't any money."

"He couldn't stay there even if he wanted to?"

"They would have all loved to stay there all their life. You take ol' Gary, Peggy's boy. Going to Colorado State University, he'd love to stay here all the rest of his life, but he can see we're getting too much family. He don't ever talk about it. It's just the normal kind of a situation. You know. Just not enough to go around. I've got some insurance policies that I'll give my daughters, if I keep paying 'em all the time. After Emma Jean and I die they will come out with some money. And if they're careful, that should keep 'em a going. They can always go to the ranch and fish and hunt and do whatever they want. It will still be home to 'em, you see?"

"No chance you'd move back up to the upper ranch?"

"No. No. But if a man ever wanted to make some money . . .. Did you ever hear of Ed Cox? He's the guy that bought the Valley View Ranch. It's the old Baker Ranch. Just this side of V C Bar. Those people are fabulously rich. I took him on a tour of the upper ranch. He's a good friend of mine. When we got up to that cookout place, up on Gold Hill where the Golden Wonder is — you and I'll go up there while you're here — Cox, he said, 'You know, I never realized what you had here. If you ever want to sell it, let me know'. He would connect it across the hill with his Valley View Ranch. It's just north of town. I bet we could put that on the market and sell the upper ranch for ten million.

"But then you are gone. If I was to leave Lake City, say I'd move, I'd last about a month. I'd be that bad. On that Alaska cruise two years ago, I couldn't wait to get off the goddamn ship. And it was a good cruise ship. Good people. But when I got up to Juno, Alaska, I got to looking around and I said, 'Well now Perk, what in the hell are you doing here? You just came from a more beautiful place, a private place. Open country.'"

"Some people say you didn't get that short leg because it was broken. They say you got it from walking around the side of these hills all your life."

"Just wore it off. That's exactly right. That's true. Makes it nice to have one short leg going around the hill one way. But going around the other way it ain't worth a damn."

"My father said you could always tell those hillbillies from Arkansas 'cause they all had one short leg from walking around those hills. Even the cows did. Speaking of hillbillies, what do you think of Clinton?"

"Well, I think he's a class A asshole. As a person. I think he's in all of this for him. He's the most selfish man that I've ever heard of."

"Where does he get the money though?"

"Well, he borrows it. Look, that guy bought the house in New York for him."

"A million dollars."

"'Cause he's trading favors. You know how that goes. Why a man, if he's true and honest-to-god involved in the government, got to be a crook like that? Why? Money don't mean a damn thing. It sure as hell wouldn't to me and you."

"You know what? He's just poor white trash. That's what my father would call him. He's over impressed by money."

"The crazy son-of-a-bitch and yet he's got some good government ideas."

"He does. But he won't do 'em. And she's worse."

"She's gonna be the senator of New York. Well, what do you suppose he'll do after his term is up?"

"I don't know. I've been wondering what he would do. Somebody showed me a picture of the Clinton Library, and it was an adult pornographic book store."

"I don't know who would have him around. Would you hire him?"

"Oh, god no," Perk said, almost shouting.

"You couldn't trust him out of your sight."

"No. I sure wouldn't trust the bastard. Hell, no. It's gonna be a long time to wipe out some of the damage. I hope this guy Bush gets the nomination. I hope that he'll do a good job, and I think he wants to. I liked his father. Now, you take Jimmy Carter. He's a Democrat, but I want to tell you, he's a good man. I see him every year. He's head of a group of foundations that raises money for unfortunate kids. He's got a great big meeting over at Crested Butte at the hotel. I go over there every year. He's just an ordinary guy."

"I think he was just in over his head when he was President."

"Oh, he couldn't begin to handle it. There's nobody that can handle this government either."

"You know who I miss? Harry Truman."

"Ol' Give-em-hell Harry. There was nobody like Harry Truman. He was one of the best presidents we ever had. And he made a quick decision in no uncertain terms.

"We're just about to Burrows Park. A guy by the name of Burrows came up here and he raised mules. He finally left here and left some of those burros. I guess no one ever knows what happened to him, but the old timers picked up some of the burros and I suppose some of them died of old age. Probably some of 'em died on account of the winter hazards."

"I've never seen a coyote up here."

"We got em on the upper ranch. Coyotes cause a lot of trouble with the sheep men. There's talk now of putting up some funds to hire the government to go back in and thin out some of the coyotes."

"I heard they're harder to trap than a fox."

"They're hard to catch. You have to poison 'em. We used to get pure cyanide and put into a piece of lard. Roll it into a ball. They'd eat that. There's a lot of people strongly opposed to trapping animals and stuff. Those coyotes are probably the smartest animal there is. But then, there's really no such thing as a dumb animal. The only dumb animal, in my opinion, is people.

Perk slowed to steer through several rock ledges exposed on the road. "They need to fix this road here. About a mile. Needs to be blasted and fixed up. This is called Campbell Gulch right here. Now we're coming into Burrows Park. A big slide came down there about four or five years ago and knocked all that timber down across the river there. It's hard to believe the strength of a snowslide. There's a lot of firewood up there but it would be a helluva job to get it over here, wouldn't it?

"Now see that mountain right straight ahead of us? That's Sunshine Peak. This one right up here above us is called Red Cloud. These are two of the biggest. 14,000 feet. The gulch between Red Cloud and Sunshine is called Silver Creek. I notice the flowers are getting pretty well gone."

"They're pretty up at American Basin, aren't they?"

"Oh, that's the prettiest place in the world, I think."

"What causes that cinnamon color to the dirt up there on Cinnamon Pass?"

"That's a heavy mineralized zone there. If you look way back, it goes clear through into Silver Creek. Goes all the way into Alpine Gulch. The geological report shows that.

"There's an old cabin there. Somebody put that there. That was his home palace, see. Lot of handwork with an ax. A chain saw is a little different. The government's got that road blocked off. Thank God."

"*There used to be an old building sitting by the road along here somewhere.*"

"They've restored that. That was Burrows Park. That belonged to a guy by the name of Clawson. He built that. Clawson had that mine, see right ahead of us? That's the Great Ohio. Old Clawson willed that to Cornell University. They own that and they are still paying taxes on it. They did a lot of development there and they shipped a lot of ore.

"Now that's Grizzly Gulch there on the left. You go up that gulch and come in behind Handie's Peak. We're coming up on the cabin you were talking about that belonged to the guy who owned the Great Ohio. Those are hand hewn logs there in that cabin. Look at that. You have to put a lot of hard work in there. With an axe. You see a lot of mineralized zones going up through that hill."

"*Are there mines up in there?*"

"There's prospect holes all the way up there 'til you come to the Champion Mine. This is the Great Ohio. They did a lot of work here. It had a deep shaft."

"*Now where is the vein they were going in on?*"

"I don't think it came to the surface. It was a shaft operation. Then they ran this tunnel in under it to put air in the shaft. I been all through that thing. The mine's been caved in for a long time."

"*They have any earthquakes here?*"

"No. Not yet."

"*And there's not much hot water coming out of the ground except down there below town?*"

"The only place. Well, just over the hill at Ouray they got a big one over there."

"*Now what's that road cutting across the face of that hill up ahead?*"

"That's a road that Joel Swank built over to some mines. You know, I told you going up Shafer Basin. That road goes up over the top of the hill to Shafer Basin. You go up that road and you can walk right down Shafer Basin to the road along Henson Creek. They couldn't build a road around the other side. It was too sheer. Too steep. Joel Swank did quite a bit of exploration work on some of these mines. Mostly built roads and stuff. All authorized. Most of em." He turned to me and winked.

"Well, that was a way of prospecting, wasn't it?"

"It's the only way you're gonna get it done. Looks like a storm coming in. Looks like it's gonna rain. You know there was a guy built a house right down here about ten years ago on patent land. He owned it. He tried to get a permit from the government to build a road from this road to his house. Didn't get it. They never would give it to him. So he did it anyway. I don't know who got that house anymore. All he did was cross his own land. You don't have to call it a road.

"See that mountain way back there to the right? That's called Wood Mountain. The one just this side, that's called Edith Mountain. It's not nearly as high as Wood Mountain. It's about a thousand foot difference in elevation. Now we're at Burrows Park. Coming into Cooper Creek next. All of this area is Burrows Park. At one time there was a lot of excitement up here in the mining business. People all thinking they were going to find the mother lode.

"But that didn't last. After the boom, everyone had moved away, taking the excitement with them and Burrows Park had been reduced to one log building surrounded by twenty acres of alders."

"So, most of the money that was made in mining wasn't from the ore they mined but when they sold their claims?"

"Oh, yeah. Just work it and sell it and find another one and work it and sell it."

"Just like real estate."

"That's exactly right. And so they would say, 'Oh there's a lot of ore in here. You ought to buy this.' They'd promote it and sell it. Show a few samples that looked good. They'd use their money to develop it and then sell it. They weren't exactly crooked about it. They were doing what you call marketing now days. Now this is Cooper Creek. C-o-o-p-e-r. Copper Creek is over on the other side where the Ocean Wave Mine is. There's a good fishpond up on top of there, up Cooper Creek. I've never been up there, but my brothers used to take horses up here and go up there fishing. Damn good fishing."

"You know where they hanged those guys from the bridge? That was called the Ocean Wave Bridge."

"Oh. yeah. Some called it that. I don't know why. It's right where the new bridge is below town. That goes over to the Ball Flats. There was a smelter there. They hauled the ore from the mine to the smelter there. That was an ambitious program. I would say somebody over promoted himself. Whoever did that."

"I always thought they ought to make more of hangings. If they're going to hang somebody, they ought to put it on TV."

"By god, cut their head off and throw it out in the street. Let the kids watch. This is what happens to you when you kill somebody."

"If they're gonna do it, they may as well get some mileage out of it."

He was quiet for a minute, then changed the subject "You know if a guy wants to go mountain climbing, there's no place in the world with as many places to go mountain climbing as right here in Lake City."

"Well, I'm like Mark Twain about that. They asked him if he ever exercised and he said every time the urge to exercise came over him, he sat down right quick 'til it passed. He said he could never see any advantage in being tired."

"What a guy! You know, you think about those old guys that wrote stuff like that. Well think about Shakespeare, for instance. I studied Shakespeare in school for about a year. Now that absolutely had to be a special kind of a man. There hasn't been anything since then that he didn't say first.

"See that property there on the right, that's part of the Champion mining property. They had a mine further up. I'll show you. That vein goes right across the mountain. They dug another gopher hole there. They have quite a few slides here. There's not any slides on this side of the pass that hit anything except up here at the foot of American Basin.

"A month ago there was sheep all over this area. They had a permit, but they had to have the sheep out by the 10th. If you look way up there in the gulch, on the right, you see that big pile of snow? We got a mine right there. That's called the Isolde, Hollister and Baltimore group. Here's Cinnamon Basin, and here's Cleveland right up here. On top of that ridge is where they had that Isolde Mine. They had a boarding house right there in that saddle. They stayed there year round. They used to cook there. My uncle worked on that Isolde, right on top of that ridge. He said he worked up there one winter for thirteen months."

Two bare, gray-green peaks pressed up for hundreds of feet above the timberline. There wasn't a sign of life, and it didn't look as if there ever had been.

"How in the world would you get up to that?"

"There's a road comes right around from the top of Cinnamon Pass. You can see the dumps. Now there is a place on top where they took out a pile of gold. Some people found the outcropping, extremely rich ore. So they started sinking on it. They called it the Isolde. Why they called it that, I don't know. And so they got down about a hundred feet in that shaft and there were two people by the name of Hollister and others. They found out about it, they said, 'Hey, you're on our property.'

"So it went to court. And the Hollister people and the Isolde people fought it out in court back and forth. First one decision and then another. The Isolde people claimed the vein apexed on the Hollister land but they had a right to follow through the Hollister. Well, some court ruled they did and another court ruled they didn't. So that shut the son-of-a-gun down for years and years.

"My dad, who had some property just over the hill in Cinnamon Basin, bought four or five of those mining claims there that were patented. We still got them. The Isolde, The Hollister, The Baltimore and the Philadelphia.

"Now I had a deal with Houston Natural Gas. A friend of mine from Breckenridge, Texas, helped me make the arrangements. We made them an offer for $750,000 and they gave me $25,000 cash. Hired a firm of engineers and geologists and I took my dozer up there. I got roads all over that area, so they could explore. We did a core drilling program on both sides of that mountain. We spent at least a million dollars of their money. That gold's right on top, we were sure. We set out to the side and run those shafts in there. All we got was sulfide. Some of that stuff was like solid lead and zinc, but it did not have the gold. Now there's a case where we missed it. How the hell we missed it, I don't know.

"Then they bought one of these electric power plants on wheels and they skidded it around with a tractor. It would identify the different kind of metal called the anomaly. They would identify the metals but they couldn't separate them. We found so many anomalies there you wouldn't believe it. Someday you'll see a pile of gold come out of that mountain.

"If you'll go just over that ridge, over the top of that Wood Mountain, right down to Hurricane Basin the Golconda Mine is right under you. Just right over the hill. You could throw a rock down into Henson Creek. But if you walk it you'd find out it's a long way.

"This here on the right is the Champion Mine. Now during our roadwork days, we stayed there about two or three months every year. In that little cabin. Pretty good accommodations. This house belonged to a guy by the name of Ed Kane. He died right there. They found him dead in that cabin. These people had the courage and the

faith and the confidence. They just stayed. They figured
that if they could not discover it, somebody else would
come along and help them. Optimistic people. Couldn't
beat em . . . . We stayed in that little cabin in the summers
for a month or two working on the road. Fifty cents an
hour. Big money. Old Ed Kane. Seems like he still ought
to be around there someplace.

"Over there on the right, that's the old Cherokee
Mine. There's a big dump there and a big metal head
frame over the shaft. That's a shaft house. I'll tell you
about that mine. The tunnel goes in right behind that
cabin. They sunk a shaft down in there 500 feet. Every
100 feet they drifted off. Boy, you talk about copper.
They had copper like you won't believe. Here about fifteen years ago a guy by the name of Reeves, and Al
Goodwin decided to open up that shaft. He put that new
headframe there. What shut that mine down was, they
were coming off shift, and one guy was up above the
other fellow on a ladder and he reached out with his
foot to act like he was gonna scare the guy and that fellow jumped off that ladder and fell down to the bottom
of the shaft and he killed himself. Well, they shut the
mine down for several years. And recently Gale Goodwin
made a deal and opened up that shaft. He died, but
before he did he opened up that shaft a long ways. No
caretaker now. She's abandoned."

"Who puts up all these bluebird houses?"

"Oh that's a guy from Denver. He does that all over
our country. He's researching the history of the bluebirds
to see why they're becoming extinct. He's retired. He
married a preacher's daughter and she has a little bit of
money and he retired. I don't know what he used for
money. That little program cost him a lot of work. I
haven't heard the final report. They've been doing that
for four or five years. He ought to be coming out with
some kind of a report before too long, hadn't he?

"Now we're coming into what they called White Cross. Right around the corner is a mine called the Illinois Boy. At that Illinois Boy they did quite a bit of development work there, and they were supposed to have hand sorted quite a bit of that ore, but it wasn't big enough to justify big development. So they quit. It's patented. Somebody owns it. That's Cleveland Basin up there on the right. That's a lot of basin. I've come down that basin a lot of time. You think that's a short ways, but it isn't. I've been down that two or three times with those engineers and stuff."

The dirt road climbed a low hill and, leaving the alders and the grass, entered a dark copse of spruce trees and bumped along over the rotten corduroy of old logs. In the spruce shade, there was no undergrowth, only cones and needles that covered the ground like a brown mat.

"I like these spruce trees, don't you?"

"Can't beat 'em."

"This is my favorite altitude right in here. Where the spruce start."

"The government blocked that road off. I don't know where that goes. That's the start of a trail. Goes right up through. It's a good trail. That's where the government is letting the people down. They ought to come in and do some work on all the trails so the people could use them.

"Right up there to the left, Joe, there's the white cross in the rocks. It's on it's side. That white rock formation. If you look up just to the top, to the left, there's a flat place. A guy come in here way back and he saw this cross, and he said 'God marked this spot for me to find a mine,' so he run this tunnel right there. It's called the LaBell Tunnel. And he did find a vein. You look up here and see the outcropping? He ran a tunnel over this way to get away from that snowslide probably. After he got underground he probably drifted over that direction. I don't know. I couldn't prove it. That cross is quartz, they say, but I've never been up there. I've often wondered what happened in that LaBell Tunnel. He must have gone in there and drifted over there because there's the vein over there. There was a little village there at that time. There were ten or fifteen cabins right along side of that place."

"You want something to eat, Perk?"

"I'm just fine. If I don't eat a bite I'm just as well off. I rest better. I overeat all the time. And I know it. Well, now days you got so many different kinds of food that we never had when we were kids. Then it was meat, potatoes, gravy, flour and sugar. That was about it."

The road ahead, just at timberline, crossed a long talus slope then wound over a series of grassy hummocks toward a sheer rock wall that curved across the end of the high valley a mile away. From the base of the wall, the road turned back on itself and angled upward across the face of a wooded ridge at a forty-five degree angle toward the saddle between two peaks that marked the summit of Cinnamon Pass. Perk stopped at the bottom of the turn. A dirt track led off to the left and down over the bank into American Basin, a broad U-shaped valley that sloped upward to a nearly perfect semicircle of rock cliff that formed the walls of a cirque. Behind it and rising for another thousand feet was a row of stark, chiseled peaks, bare and gray except for long fissures, still whitened by last year's snow.

"That American Basin is the prettiest spot around. The wildflowers are gone now but in July they are as thick as weeds. Cover this whole basin. You can stand in one spot and count twenty or thirty different kinds of flowers. People who haven't seen it wouldn't believe it.

"We have a mine up there. The Gnome Mine. Now, that's a story with a lot of interest. The Gnome is right there in American Basin. That mine was filed on by a guy by the name of Dacey, I'd say about 1900. He was so sure that there was a million dollars worth of gold and stuff there that he kept the public from going up there. He roped the land. He took one claim right in the middle. He kept that for years, and Dad finally bought that mine.

"Dad had a friend by the name of Brooks Collings of Rockville, Indiana, that went in with my dad and they bought that mine. My dad kept working on it and trying to promote it but they never did anything with it. Finally, about twenty years ago, I made a deal with some people from McAllen, Texas. We had to buy Collings' half-interest before I could sell it to those folks. We had to put up $10,000 to buy him out. That's a lot of money. We didn't have the money either, but we finally got it. They paid me off with that silver saddle I got down there in the office.

"We kept it for many years, then I sold it to another mining associate of ours for $45,000. He quit, and I got it back. During my promotion days on that Gnome, the company from McAllen put up the money to run that tunnel. We run that eight-foot square tunnel right in on that vein. Beautiful fissure vein. We went in with that tunnel 600 feet right on the vein structure.

"Finally I sold it to some people that the government was trying to run off the land that they had, and then they traded it to the government. It now belongs to the Untied States government.

"What kind of minerals were there?"

"We expected to find gold. But we didn't get the gold. Plenty of lead, zinc, copper and silver. But it did not have the gold."

"What's a fissure vein?"

"A vein is a fissure that was made when the earth was formed and the mineral comes up through the earth in a crack It's not really a crack. It's a wide piece of solid rock quartz or rhyolite. Some of 'em are straight or vertical. It's always been a mystery how that can be formed."

Perk carefully put the car in gear and coaxed it up the steep road, steering carefully around the mud holes and rocks.

"We relocated this road up to the top of Cinnamon Pass. That's the old Tobasco Mill site up there on the right. The tunnel was up on top. They did a lot of work in there. Had a tramway all the way down the hill from the mine to the mill down here.

"There's quite a story on that mine. It was owned by two brothers from Philadelphia. One stayed here and ran the mine, and the other stayed back east and raised the money. They spent a lot of money — too much — but like a lot of others, they didn't develop the mine before they spent the money. Built that mill. Beautiful mill. Strung all that tramway. Finally, they went broke and one day the brother who was here took a pistol and blew his brains out. When the brother in Philadelphia heard about it, he shot himself too."

The road was above timberline now, and the route to the top of the pass traversed a wall of scree for a quarter of a mile. In the lee, just below its crest, a leftover snow bank was dusted with wind-blown cinnamon-colored dirt. At the top of the pass we bumped to a stop on a small rectangle of almost flat ground that marked the summit. A Forest Service sign indicated that the altitude was 12,800 feet. The summit was on the crest of a central pointed dome. Below us, in front and behind, broken, stained peaks and deep valleys fell away steeply to the tender pastels of the distance.

"Well, we're on the top." Perk said, shifting in his seat to get a better view. "You can see that Detroit-Hollister group there on the ridge to the right. The Detroit's in San Juan County. The Hollister is in Hinsdale County. We could put those properties together. They settled the lawsuit so we could do something with it. So we still got that. We're gonna sell it though. The minute you go over the top of the pass here and start down toward Silverton turn to the right and you're on Vickers' land. We got 110 acres there.

"See that monument up there?" He pointed to a ridgetop a quarter of a mile away. "The government came out here in the early days, and they set up these mineral monuments in certain locations. Geographically located. They knew that the mining would possibly be developed, so they had that mineral monument set up right there and they put it in the record. In the register. And if you are over here and find a vein you have to survey it out by a licensed surveyor and tie it to that mineral monument. It's a reference point. Then you could identify it."

We turned around and headed back down the pass.

Perk frowned as he eased the jeep over the steep, rutted road. "This road needs some work. That's a dangerous curve right here. You try backing up to make this turn and kill the engine and you go right off the edge.

"That snow bank over there, that's the last one here. Now the new ones will be coming on. I want to make sure I get this in low range. If we go over one of those cliffs, it's goodbye Perk and Joe. Down the mountain we go. Look at that scenery. God, this must be a thrill to a person who comes up here from Houston, Texas. And women folk say, by god, if I get off here alive I'll be lucky. If you got a vehicle and you know how to drive a vehicle in the city or where ever you come from, all you got to know is you got to be careful. And you got to take it slow. That's all. But they get in a helluva hurry. We don't get very many people killed here though, to come right down to the bare facts."

"This is about as high as you get in a car."

"Well, my brakes are good. I've come down out of here, and you won't believe it. Three or four drinks of that brandy, I'd take a couple of shots and hell, I'd whistle all the way home.

"In my operations, I made money in the mining business mostly by promoting and working for the people. There wasn't nothing crooked about it. I promoted the mine and sometimes you'd get a payment and sometimes you wouldn't. But I made money by working for them on the job. I always recommended they hire good geologists. Those guys, like Winston Sheehan, one of the most noteworthy geologists in the world, and Russ Meadows who's got that report I gave you to look at, those guys were very famous engineers. Russ Meadows was from West Virginia. He's dead. You know, most of the people I've been associated with are dead. I tell everybody today that I have outlived all my enemies for sure.

"You know I was gonna tell you about Jack and Betty Moncrief that's got that ranch down there. I'd check up with him every once in a while, and he'd say he had a $5 million deal at 12% interest. He never closed the deal, but he kept getting that interest money. All the people told him, 'Aw that guy's no damn good. He's never gonna close the deal.' It wasn't worrying poor old Jack 'cause he was getting that interest. You put a pencil to a $5 million deal. And one time he said to me, 'Perk,' he said, 'I'll tell you, these deals, back and forth, it kinda reminds me of the whore. She's got it. She sells it. And she's still got it.' He said, 'That's my case. I sold it and I get the interest money and I still got the ranch.'"

Perk pointed to an abandoned mine tunnel in the rocky hillside. A thin trail led to the opening. "Look at that," he said. "Somebody just had to walk over to that opening, see. Now that tunnel just goes in about 100 feet. Just suppose it was 1000 feet, and the guy walked in there. There's no signs, no nothing. Something happens to him. Who's fault is it? The owner of the mine or the guy that walked in it. Now, over there, there's one of the strongest fissure veins you'll ever see. Comes from the top of that mountain down and crosses here. Now you might wonder, if it's a fissure vein, with a foot wall and a hanging wall, how come it got so crooked all of a sudden? Well, being formed, the pressure from below had something to do with which way it shifted."

"I don't understand the foot and the hanging wall."

"Generally a vein, it tips like this." He held out one palm, tilted at a forty-five degree angle. "Here's what you call a hanging wall. Over here is the foot wall. It's like a wall that is leaning.

"After Emma Jean and I had been married for a few years, some of the folks from Texas would come up and say, 'My god, how do you stand this high country? Don't you get tired of it? What do you do in the long winter months?' I can always say, 'Well, I can tell you what we do. How do you think I got those twins?' And that stops 'em. Some of those people, if you think about it, have a tendency to make things look so dark. They'll unintentionally try to discourage you. 'Well, maybe I got to get out of here.' You know how that goes. I'm telling you, you ought to remember, in my lifetime, thousands and hundreds of people, there's a lots of double-crossers. There's more good people than there is bad. Don't misunderstand me, but there's lots of double-crossing son-of-a-guns, too, if you add it up. Especially for personal financial gain. So many of them you would not believe."

"You know. it's amazing what you can get along with if you put your mind to it."

"I'm the same way. I got quite a bit of cash in the bank. I don't go no place. Where in the hell you gonna go? I've been every place. We went on a Caribbean cruise. We went down there with Peggy and a couple of other guys. And after about three days out on that stuff, I said, 'Now Perk, you made a mistake. This ain't nothing for you either.'"

"I don't think there's anyplace like this."

"That's so true."

"I'm worried that somebody's gonna come in here and mess it up."

"Well, that's one thing they're not gonna' do," he said, setting his jaw. "There's lots of people now in the government in high office that's gonna protect this country. This Alpine Loop that you're on now, the government's trying to save that by buying it up. That's why I'm saying the government should start pushing to get these private landowners that don't want to mine to buy those lands back. They got a lot of money to spare, then they got to own it. Then they can protect it. If they don't, you take that Henson Creek as a good example. You see the signs up and down the road at Capitol City? That's all gonna be a housing development. Then you've lost something."

"Have you been over to Crested Butte lately?"

"Once a year."

"Well you know what that's like. That whole valley is full of houses."

"Absolutely. The snow's what led them to develop that Crested Butte. I got a friend from Atlanta, Georgia, that owns the biggest part of that. They have now invested about $225 million. They're starting to build a third hotel. Now they're wanting to sell the third hotel. Now what's gonna happen there, one of these days, is that Crested Butte is gonna merge with Aspen. It's only a short distance. You'll see if you go over the hill. You'll see an aerial tramway one of these days go right over the top from Crested Butte to Aspen."

"The other night you mentioned that Wayne Aspinall, a congressman from Colorado, was a friend of yours."

"Yeah. He was a congressman from Grand Junction. He was one of the best congressmen we ever had. He was the one who set up the Colorado River Compact and the Upper Gunnison. All those projects should be credited to Congressman Wayne Aspinall 'cause he did it all.

"Well, most of the congressmen are there with good intentions. Then they get promoted, they get to trading back and forth, you help me and I'll help you. I don't like those riders on those bills. I don't think they ought to be able to amend those bills. Once they get a bill written up, and present it on the floor, that ought to be the final one. But here'll come a guy and say I want to amend it now, and I got a bill here and they're trading around. I'll tell you, that seniority system they got, that's a bad deal. In my opinion, one of these days, and it may happen soon, you're gonna see a well-organized group of young people with a new program on a third party. The younger generation, under forty, those guys are burned out on Republican and Democratic. They see all this stuff going on in the newspapers and they say we need something different. It will someday happen. And straighten things out a little bit. Because like you very well know, these guys get indicted and get jail terms and get fined, it's getting ridiculous.

We approached a steep descending turn, so tight that the road before and after the turn were nearly parallel to each other.

The inside of the turn was a deep mudhole, and the outside, tilted dizzingly out toward the unprotected drop off, a series of rock ledges.

"Now this turn right here is tight. I'm gonna back up a little and then turn. I like that better. At least you're gonna save enough room to jump out. I'm always careful with these machines 'cause I gotta work like a dog to pay for it. Down these hills, if you're careful, there's nothing to it. It's a matter of fact. It's a wonder on places like this that we haven't had some accidents. You can't be too careful on these roads. You can get killed. If you run out to that banking and try to back up like I did right there, if they don't catch up right quick, you'll lose a couple of feet and first thing you know you're so far out and then you have to jump it back or you don't go. Yes sir, once I come down there in a snow storm when the road was covered with snow, I'm telling you, you won't believe it. Now I don't take as many chances as I used to take."

"Well, I tell you, with these hills, you can get in a lot of trouble in a hurry. You get a lot of momentum in no time. You probably learned a lot about momentum by bulldozing those rocks off the cliff and watching them drop."

"I have done that."

"What's the most dangerous thing about running a bulldozer?"

"Well, on the ice. You'll slide sideways. You got to watch that. I've had some goddamn close shaves riding off on the hillside. Once it starts sliding, it's just like a sled on ice. Now that old road I showed you down by the bottom of the hill, came right up through these timbers. So we come up, followed that old road in that bulldozer. We did it with the road supervisor when we were working with him to make a new road. Came right up here and had a downhill push. Always bulldoze downhill. It's a lot easier. Blast and bulldoze. Easy to do. Can't see the old road now. It's overgrown that fast."

We passed the turnoff to American Basin again and could see all the way to the end of the cirque.

"That's the Gnome Mine over there. That dump in the middle of the basin. We put a lot of work in that tunnel. That tunnel goes in there about 700 feet. It's on the vein. A strong fissure. You'd be surprised the lead and zinc in that mine. The road just goes as far as the mine. It used to go further. The government shut it off. I had it clear up to the Sloan Mine and I decided that I didn't want to go no further, so the government shut me off on that. It stops right at the Vickers Mine. That's the end of the trail."

"Pretty country in here."

"No question about that. We talk to people all the time, go all over Switzerland, go all over the world, and say that you can't beat this right here."

"What I like about it is that it is still a little bit wild."

"This is the only place left that I know of like God made it. It's about as close to heaven as you'll ever get. No doubt about that."

"How's you hip doing?" I had seen him limping and thought he must be having some trouble.

"Still nagging a bit. As a matter of fact, that's why I use that cane. It gives me a sense of balance. It don't take much, but it saves me. I can see that all the time."

"A lot of people are too proud to use a cane."

"You're right there. They say nobody wants to see ol' Perk with a cane. But it's just like fishing. Take a stick with you. Keep from falling down in the river.

"See that slide area there?" He pointed out a broad chute which began in the gray rock of the peak and cut down through the timber. Only grass grew in the slide area. Twisted aspen lined the sides and spruce logs were scattered along the course and stacked at the bottom like jackstraws.

"Now those snow slides will do funny things. This has been a common area for the last hundred years for snowslides. If you notice, over on that corner it changes course. Coming down over on one side over in the timber. Man, it's hard to realize unless you've seen the power behind a snowslide. It'll snap those trees off, eighteen inches thick, just like they were toothpicks. I've seen 'em run over on Henson Creek a lot of times. Here in the '70s, I was working in the Golden Wonder sinking that shaft for a company, Southern Union Production out of Dallas that had an option to buy it. I had two Indians working for me, Wato and his friend. They were damn good mining hands. They didn't know much about machinery, but when they learned it, they would take damn good care of that machinery, believe me. I love the Indians. I always thought we robbed them of their country. It had to happen, I think. Unfortunately.

"There are a few bastards I'd like to get even with. Sometimes I think it works out where I do get even with some of them. I'm a strong believer in 'you reap what you sow.' That's the old saying. I believe in that. There's a beautiful lake up that Cooper Creek. Good fishing. The problem you got up there is that the fish multiply so fast, and nobody fishes it much. They don't get the growth you'd expect them to get. Not enough food and too many fish. Just brookies and natives. Rainbow don't reproduce up there. They get skinny. Just like overloading your horse pasture with horses. But you know, Joe, the German browns reproduce awful well in our country. There are a lot of browns on the Lake Fork now. Oh yeah. It's full of browns."

"You know they talk a lot now about guns and gun safety, but I'll bet you there were more guns in this country in 1900 than there are now."

"There's always gonna be guns. They're gonna have to get a little more strict with outlaws and crooks. Cut their heads off and throw them out in the damn street. That way they'll be more careful. They know damn well, nowadays they'll get by with it; hire a lawyer and all that. If you know they're gonna cut your head off, you'll look at it a little differently."

"Who was it, an Englishman I think, that said, 'There's nothing that focuses your mind like the thought of hanging.'"

"Hah! That's good. I like that. No one could speak like those Englishmen. Oh, they had guns in the old days, but they didn't just go down the highway shooting. That's the damndest thing I've ever seen on some occasions. I see in the paper every day or two, where somebody drives down the street and just shoots. They don't even know who they shoot. Those guys are crazy."

"You want a candy bar?"

"No. How many you got?"

"About ten."

"Oh, well. I was afraid you were going to offer me your last god danged candy bar. I was just trying to be a gentleman. Pretty hard to beat a Snickers bar."

"So the train came into Lake City before you were born? Wasn't it just a dead-end spur up from Sappinero?"

"When I was a kid, some days you'd see a passenger train and then a freight train on the same day. It was a boomer, but it didn't last too long. Narrow gauge. That was the thing. You'd ship your cattle by narrow gauge, to Gunnison over Marshall Pass to Salida. Then they had to take 'em off and put them on the standard gauge. We shipped some of the cattle to Kansas City or Denver — to wherever the market was the best."

"When did the hunting laws get started?"

"That's a good question. I don't know but I do know one thing. If they hadn't of started, there would never have been any wildlife. They had nearly killed them all. When I was a kid, I never saw a live deer nor an elk 'til I was fifteen years old. You could go to the grocery store and buy an elk steak or whatever. Or mountain sheep. There's a few of them left. Hunters see one every once in a while, but I've never seen one."

"Now the hunters come in and pay for a state license to hunt on federal land."

"Now, there's room for an argument. What we're doing, we're discriminating against a non-resident. The non-residents are paying our bills. They're supporting us. When they come to buy a license, we charge them nine times what we charge a resident to hunt deer and elk on their own land. That is what you call discriminating. There has been a lot of talk by these out-of-state people to bring suit. To see if that's legal. It's not right. It's an unfair situation all the way through."

"You know the miners and settlers came into this country from all over the place."

"Yeah. Scots. Italians. Cousin Jacks. That was an old expression for the English. You don't hear that terminology hardly ever anymore. Emma Jean and I were up there in Nova Scotia a few years ago. I had my shoulder broke just before I went and my arm was in a sling all the time, but I enjoyed those Englishmen. In Sydney Mines, there in Nova Scotia where my dad came from, the people there are still living in poverty. I got a cousin named Stanley Vickers that has come out to see us a time or two. He lived in the same home that my dad was born in. You know they had four fireplaces in that house. Those winters there are bitter."

"Did you feel any magnetism or any vibrations when you were there?" I was referring to emotional attachments, but I think Perk must have thought I was referring to earthquakes."

"No. I didn't notice it. I heard about it but I didn't notice it. That bay coming in there is beautiful, and there are a lot of good places to eat seafood. They have good seafood. We flew in and Stanley picked us up at Sydney. That country is about as different from this as you could possibly get. My god, it sure is.

"See that rubber tube there on the road? They must be counting the traffic. Years ago when they were putting them on Slumgullion and we were working on the road, we'd go up there and drive across them a hundred times a day, back and forth. Get more highway funds 'cause they thought there was a lot of traffic."

"They burn coal for heat in Nova Scotia?"

"They do. And we've burned coal all my life. We still do. That coal is the best heat. Up there in Nova Scotia, they burn coal all the time. They have to steal it, too. I tell you what happened. The English government had that land there at Sydney Mines so they wanted to develop those lands. My dad's two uncles, and my dad's father were engineers. They went there and they set up their homes and they started raising their families there. The English government for their good work gave them one hundred twenty acres of land. One brother decided he was going back to England, and he did. My dad's dad stayed so he ended up with one hundred twenty acres. He had thirteen kids, my dad being one of them. So they divided that land. So you drive in that one street and it says 'Vickers Lane.'

"My cousin lives there in the house my dad was born in. They all knew we were coming. He told them he was going after ol' Perk and Emma Jean, so when we drove into that street I could see doors opening and people come out. You'd think the President of the United States had arrived. By god, I couldn't believe it. They were so glad to see us.

"Right behind the house they had what looked like a hole in the bank. And I said, 'That must be your cellar.' And he said, 'No, that is a hole in the ground. Whenever we want coal, we just go in there and take it.' The Peabody Coal Company owned the whole thing, but they'd steal that coal. That was how they got their coal. They didn't have to mine any coal at all, but a lot of 'em still work in the coal mines there.

"I had a cousin by the name of Purvis. That's where my name comes from. He was killed in an underground mine. It's all under the ocean. It goes way under the ocean. You'd swear you'd be scared to death to go down under that ocean. So anyway, we visited around there for three days.

"One day I said, 'Let's all go down to the hotel for dinner.' And so we talked to the man at the hotel, and he said, 'We'll just give you our meeting room upstairs.' And I said, 'Well, we're gonna' have to have some whiskey bottles.' And he said, 'I tell you what we'll do. We'll put a few bottles of whiskey up there, and what you drink we'll charge you for it. Otherwise we have to bring it up from the bar a drink at a time and it will eat you up.' Come to find out, Canadian Club, in Canada costs sixty-two dollars a bottle. And cigarettes were four dollars a package at that time. I said, 'What the hell is going on?' 'Well I tell you what,' he said. 'Our government says if you want to smoke and drink you're gonna have to pay for it. That's where our money's coming from.'

"About twenty-five Vickers showed up there. 'Jesus Christ,' I said, 'when we pay for this we're not gonna have enough money to get back home.' They all thought that was great. They all thought ol' Perk Vickers had a lot of money. He's a miner and a rancher and all that, you know.

"See that house right over there? You can buy that house for about a million bucks. Some sucker will come along and buy that. The owner and his wife stayed there for a short time. Then they left and it was back for sale again. I asked old Bill Hall one day how many houses he sold. And he said he has got houses that he has sold five times in the last six years. Same house. Just like the mining claims. Selling the dirt. It's big business. I should have got in the real estate business a long time ago. I made a mistake. I should have. I've been asleep."

"Will alfalfa live up here?"

"Yeah, it will, but it dies out eventually. You can get two crops a year but you have to replant it every two or three years. That alfalfa seed, it goes straight down and when it gets to where the water is, it's gone.

"The county needs to start doing a little work on those roads up there. There's three or four places up there I would call extremely dangerous for a stranger. Those switchbacks above that Tobasco Mill especially. If you haven't got it in real low gear and it dies out and you start back, look out. Dangerous."

"You know Perk, I think you're gonna live to see a resurgence of the dude ranch business because everybody wants to recreate his past. And some people miss that and they want to come back and do that."

"If they ain't careful they're gonna be too damn late. So many of the dude ranches are going into subdivisions. See they got a law in Colorado now they call the '35 Acre Tract.' I can sell all the land I want over thirty-five acres to a John Doe, but if I want to go under thirty-five acres I have to subdivide it. They're trying to keep all the land from being divided into small parcels. They make it a little hard to do a subdivision. We've had some cases where a guy buys 35 acres and he wants to split it. Say he's got a couple of kids and he wants to give them one half each. We'll let them go in on a one-time split. You get a one time split once, but you can't do it again. It's a onetime deal."

We turned down the west side of Lake San Cristobal and headed back toward the ranch.

"That's a beautiful lake, ain't it? That's the prettiest lake there is. No doubt."

"How deep is that lake?"

"I don't know. About 200 feet, I think, but I don't know that for sure. The Slumgullion Slide is what made that lake. Come down there and choked the river right off."

"So that road over on the east side of the lake was old Otto Mears' Saguache to Baker's Park Road?"

"Yes. Many years ago, the road below here come right through from town on the east side of the river where our subdivision is now. Then they had a bridge up here where the highway bridge is now called the "Dawn of Hope Bridge." Now why they called it the Dawn of Hope, I don't know. Then it continued right up to the lake and continued on that east side clear to Sherman."

"You know Perk, I've always thought it was interesting that at one time it was so important to get to a place that they had a big road to it, and after a while the road just disappears and you can't even find it. The place that was once so important to get to, isn't important at all any more. Now, tell me about this rock dam at the end of the lake."

"Well, that's what we call an outlet weir there. It's a permit to store and stabilize a stream. We put that in there, a bunch of us. The outflow was wearing it down and lowering the lake. You take that dam out now, it will lower the lake about eight feet. It raises the water level and establishes it. We got help from the Colorado Division of Wildlife. It raised that lake about three or four feet. If that should wash out completely, that lake would lower eight feet. Down to bedrock. You can see, over there on the east corner of the lake, how that Slumgullion Slide is, in fact, starting to fill that lake in. I can remember that slide used to come way back here. You give it another hundred years you may not even have a lake."

"Now tell me about the Slumgullion Pass Road."

"Boy, that Slumgullion dirt is dangerous stuff when it's wet. Used to, when you got to the top, the road went on down Mill Creek, down by Deer Lake. Then it went up over what they called the Gardener Ridge till it hit the Savoy (Cebolla Creek) and come back up where Spring Creek is now.

"The road went right through where the Oleo Ranch is now. In 1958, through the county, we got the U.S. Bureau of Public Roads to survey the road from the top of Slumgullion where the road is now to Spring Creek Pass. There was several miles of road to build. They let a contract to take all the timber off that road right-of-way and clean up the timber and put a road through there. My brother and I bid on that contract and we got the job. Man that was a tough job.

"That's the Gladiator Mine in the canyon down there on the river. The guy that bought this, a guy by the name of Jack Eagan, is gonna build a house up on that dump. The Argenta Falls is right under us here. They shipped quite a lot from that Gladiator. There's a lot of tunnel work in there. Right now it's into a problem with that water quality. Right by the Argenta Falls is what they call the Lake Falls Mine and the Minerva — two patented mining claims. We had them for a great many years. During WWII we got short of money 'cause my dad and I were the only ones here. My brothers were in the service. The need for money caused us to do a lot of things we wouldn't have done. We sold those two patented mining claims for 1500 bucks. Now the guy has got two houses on that land. There's twenty acres there and he wants $250,000. And he'll get it, too.

"This is the old Contention Mine. This was a big mine right here. It's all tied in with the Golden Fleece. It would be safe to say this is part of the Golden Fleece Group. You look at that map. This on the left here is all what you call Hotchkiss Mountain. It's named after Hotchkiss. He's the one who found the old Golden Fleece Mine to start with. Right down there is the ponds where the tailings went.

"Now right around the corner on the left is Silver Coin Gulch. Right up Silver Coin Gulch about a half a mile, an attorney and his associate discovered a vein, and he run a tunnel called the Armatage. We own that water there. We changed the course of the diversion. We were piping it right around the other way, but it soaked up the ground. Then when they built that Crystal Lodge there they were complaining; so we decided to change the point of diversion and pick it up down in the field. Just to hold it.

"You go up this road, about eight or nine switchbacks and you come to a huge deposit of iron ore. There's where they got their fluxing for that Crooke's smelter. Brought her right down this road."

"Those old-timers must have walked all over this country to find all of this stuff. Climbing all over here."

"Oh, they did. They don't make men like those people any more. Sure don't."

"I mean, what would they have to pay you to walk to the top of Round Top and back?"

"Most of these guys today are not able. Just like you told me that you couldn't walk up on those peaks. That you didn't have enough wind."

"You guys raised up here don't need oxygen! I don't know what you live on."

"You waste too damn much of it in the first place. That Crystal Lodge is built on the Groves mining claim. Some guys by the name of Dilly and Foster did a lot of mining in that gulch there."

"It sounds like almost every inch of this ground was claimed."

"Most of it. Yeah. Now you can see, across there, the Golden Wonder up on top. Now that gulch where the Golden Wonder is, that's called Dead Man's Gulch. The Golden Wonder Mine is right at the top of that. Then you come right around the hill and you come to the Belle of the East and the Belle of the West, just down by the highway."

"Are they on the same vein?"

"It's always been a question. It's never been proved or disproved which. I don't think they are on the Golden Wonder vein 'cause they do not have the gold the Golden Wonder has."

"Now was there an outcropping up there? Is that what prompted them to dig there?"

"On the very top of the mountain they found an outcropping up there on the surface. Over here on this side, there's the Gold Quartz. They had another outcropping on it and it has copper. Where the water comes out of that tunnel, if you put a steel cup or something in that water and let it set two or three years and then come back, the copper would replace the metal. It would be a solid copper cup. It's hard to believe."

To the east, two grassy mountains rose against the skyline and rose to the summit of Cannibal Plateau.

"Now that's your place over there where those road cuts go across the mountain?"

"No, that goes to Sutton's Park up on the mountain. Up on Cannibal Plateau. That's part of our hunting territory. That's up near where our cookout place is. Up on Gold Hill."

"Why do they call it Dead Man's Gulch?"

"I think they named it after the Packer Massacre. The Packer Massacre site is right where that gulch comes down to the river."

"Last year I was over at Grand Junction and a guy came in from the museum there who said that he had been interested in the Alfred Packer story all his life and he was collecting Alfred Packer stuff there at the museum. He thought he had more stuff than any one else. He said a few years ago somebody brought a pistol to him that he said was found at the massacre site. Do you remember anything about that?"

"No, but I've heard of two or three guys who showed up with a pistol they said was Alfred Packer's pistol, but they never could prove nothing. There's one of them down there in the museum, I think. I'm not sure. They make a big story out of it."

"Were you up here when this guy dug up the bodies?"

"Yeah, I was there. I was the guy that promoted it. I made a trip back to Washington, D.C. to get Starrs. (James E. Starrs is Professor of Law and Forensic Science at George Washington University. He was Director for the Alfred Packer Victims Exhumation Project) He's the nicest guy you ever saw. He's at the University in Washington, D.C. I think I've got a copy of the final report someplace. He claimed that they were nothing but cold-blooded murders. Probably right. Caught them in their sleep I suppose."

"You know they are putting on a play now in New York about Alfred Packer. "Cannibal: The Musical," they call it. I saw a notice of it in The Wall Street Journal. *Playing to standing room only crowds."*

"Is that right? I didn't know that."

"I sent a clipping to Grant Houston and he called someone in New York to find out about it. Said he was going to do an article on it for the Silver World. *"*

"Oh, I did hear about that. Grant went to Grand Junction to meet with these people, the guy that's promoting it. He's gonna get some money out of it. He's claiming that the story was not accurate at all. He's claiming that it was all self-defense on Packer's part. Although, when they dug the graves here ten years ago I was part of that. I went to New York and Washington to get this thing started. When they dug up the graves, the best experts — archaeologists — they said it was cold-blooded murder. This guy, Bailey, from Grand Junction who claims he got the pistol is gonna make a story. The guy is going to London."

"Bailey told me that the pistol was a five-shot Colt revolver. There were two bullets still left in the chamber. They took a piece of lead from one of those bullets and compared it with a fragment of lead they found among the clothes fragments in the grave. They used an electron microscope. Said it was a perfect match. Apparently, in those days, and maybe even now, bullet manufacturers used different formulas for their lead bullets."

We pulled into the ranch and stopped in front of the house.

"Aside from those four dead guys that were frozen stiff by that snow slide up Henson Creek, what's the earliest thing you can remember about growing up in Lake City?"

"Well, that is a good question. There was a lot of things. There was a calamity, economically speaking, when that railroad went out. When the railroad went out, on the 23rd of July, in 1933."

"You remember the exact day?"

"Yeah. I remember everybody up and down the valley was there to kiss her good-bye. There was some of the people crying saying, 'Well, that's the end of us. That's the end of Lake City. The railroad's gone out. We got no highway. Got no roads. The mines are shutting down.' That's why right then people started moving out of Lake City. Man, the Depression was goin' full blast. We didn't have a damn thing. Our bank had already gone broke. There was a lot of banks in Montrose and Gunnison and other places in the Depression that just closed their doors. If you had any money in the bank you just lost it. There was no chance of getting it. So Roosevelt — I give him a lot of credit — he called that bank holiday, and that saved the people. Now Roosevelt, when you think of some of his programs, they were fantastic programs. Some got out of hand. The welfare program. They needed that. Now it's plumb out of reason."

"Well, you earned your keep today, Perk."

"I enjoyed this. I had a good day."

"It's good getting up in there. I like it up there in the high country."

"Yep. Never get tired of that. Where do you want to go tomorrow?"

"How about up Henson Creek. To Engineer Pass."

"By god, that's beautiful country. Lots of mines, lots of history up there."

That night when I got back to the cabin I re-read the Alfred Packer article Mr. Soderholm had given me fifty years ago.

THE TRIAL OF ALFRED PACKER
AND
THE SENTENCE

Packer was first tried in Lake City in April, 1883, before M.B. Gerry. His name was Alfred Packer, and his age 34 years. Judge Gerry was a man of the highest type, a southern gentleman of the old school, a jurist of deep learning and knowledge of the law. He was, as many readily understood, an ardent Democrat — and therein lies the refined, subtle humor of this story.

At the time of the trial there was living here one James (Larry) Dolan, a saloon keeper, an Irish wag of rare and sometimes profane or vulgar wit. Dolan had been one of the principal witnesses against Packer, having met and associated with him at Saguache when Packer was making his getaway out of the country early in the winter of 1874. It has been said that Dolan had a grudge against Packer and had threatened to kill him should he be acquitted of the charge of murder. At any rate, it can be easily understood that Larry Dolan maintained a keen interest in the trial from first to last.

The story goes that Larry was about the first man to come from the courthouse after the verdict was in and sentence passed. "Well, boys it's all over; Packer's t' hang." Pressed for particulars by the habitues of the saloon — bustling, active mining camp of the new west almost half a century ago — pressed for particulars, Larry took an appropriate attitude before this motley audience and delivered himself thus; "The Judge says, says he, 'Stand up, y' man-eating son iv a bitch, STAND UP;' Then p'intin' his tremblin' finger at Packer, so ragin' mad he was, 'They was siven Dimmycrats in Hinsdale county an' you eat five iv thim, G—d—ye: I sentins ye t' be hanged by the neck ontil ye're, dead, dead, DEAD, as a warnin' ag'in reducing the Dimmycratic popyalashun in the state.'"

The crime for which Alfred Packer was tried occurred in 1874 near Lake San Cristobal, above Lake City. Packer and his companions were caught in raging blizzards that winter. They ran out of supplies. Later, human remains were discovered in shallow graves, and Packer was arrested several years later on charges of having devoured his companions to keep from starving. He was supposed to have lured them away, one by one, and then killed and eaten them. It wasn't until 1884, in

Gunnison, that he was brought to trial and finally convicted at the second trial.

The sentence of forty years in the penitentiary, eight for each man eaten, would have been carried out, but at the turn of the century, the Denver Post, in one of its periodic stunts, actually got the man pardoned, and he died five years after that in eastern Colorado, about 1907. The evidence against him was circumstantial, but the first trial in Hinsdale County in 1883 — after Packer had been discovered hiding under the name of Swartz, in the mountains of Wyoming — resulted in a verdict of guilty and sentence of death.

Considerable fiction has grown up about the case. Those who love "western thrillers," are fond of alleging that District Judge Gerry, following conviction in Lake City in 1883, declared:

"Stand up. ye son-of-a-gun and receive your sentence. When there was only six dimocrats in Hinsdale county you et five of them."

As a matter of fact, Judge M.B. Gerry, of Macon, Georgia, who had been a federal jurist, used formal and elegant language in sentencing Packer to be hanged. The following are the words of the actual sentence.

"Alfred Packer,' said Judge Gerry, 'a jury finds you guilty of willful and premeditated murder — a murder revolting in its details. In 1874 you, in company with five companions, passed through this beautiful mountain valley where stands the town of Lake City. At that time the hand of man had not marred the beauties of nature. This picture was fresh from the hand of the Great Artist who created it. You and your companions camped at the base of a grand old mountain in sight of the place where you now stand, on the banks of a stream as pure and beautiful as ever traced by the finger of God upon the bosom of the earth. Your every surrounding was calculated to impress upon your heart and nature the omnipotence of the Deity and the helplessness of your *own feeble life. In this goodly favored spot you conceived your murderous design.*

"You and your victims had had a weary march, and when shadows of the mountain fell upon your little party and night drew her sable curtain around you, when your unsuspecting victims lay down on the ground and were soon lost in sleep, and when thus sweetly unconscious of danger from any source and particularly from you, their trusted companion, you cruelly and brutally slew them all. You then and there robbed the living of life and then robbed the dead of the reward of honest toil, which they had accumulated.

"To other sickening details of your crime I will not refer. Silence is kindness. I do not say these things to harrow your soul; you, Alfred Packer sowed the wind; now you must reap the whirlwind. Society cannot forgive you for the crime you have committed. With God, it is different. He will not forget, but he will forgive. He pardoned the dying thief on the cross. He is the same God today as then — a God of love and mercy, of longsuffering and kind forbearance — a God who tempers the wind to the shorn lamb, and promises to all the weary and heartbroken children of men; and it is to this God that I commend you."

THE SENTENCE

"It becomes my duty as the judge of this court to enforce the verdict of the jury rendered in your case, and impose on you the judgment which the law fixes as the punishment for the crime you have committed. It is a solemn, painful duty to perform. I would to God the cup would pass from me. You have had a fair and impartial trial. You have been faithfully and earnestly defended by able counsel. The presiding judge of this court, upon his oath and his conscience, had labored to be honest and impartial in the trial of your case and in all doubtful

questions presented you have had the benefit of the doubt. A jury of twelve honest citizens of the county have sat in judgment on your case and upon their oaths they find you guilty of the willful and premeditated murder — a murder revolting in all its details.

"Close your ears to the blandishments of hope. Listen not to its flattering promises of life; but prepare for the dread certainty of death. Prepare to meet thy God; prepare to meet the spirts of thy murdered victims; prepare to meet that aged father and mother of whom you have spoken and who still love you as their dear boy.

"For nine long years you have been a wanderer upon the face of the earth, bowed and broken in spirit; no home; no loves; no ties to bind you to the earth. You have been indeed a poor, pitiable waif of humanity. I hope and pray that in the spirit land to which you are so fast and surely drifting, you will find that peace and rest for your weary spirit which this world cannot give.

"Alfred Packer, the judgment of this court is that you be removed from hence to the jail of Hinsdale County and there confined until the 19th day of May, A.D. and that on said 19th day of May, 1883, you be taken from thence by the sheriff of Hinsdale County, to a place of execution prepared for the purpose at some point within the corporate limits of the town of Lake City, in the said County of Hinsdale, and there between the hours of 10:00 a.m. and 3:00 p.m. of said day, you, then and there, by said sheriff, be hanged by the neck until you are dead, dead, dead, and may God have mercy on your soul."

The arrastra at the Golden Wonder — before it was moved to the main ranch. (Vickers' Family Photo)

Lake City about the turn of the century. The view is to the north. (Colorado Historical Society, #4451)

Parts of Lake City look just like they did a century ago. (Muriel Wolle photo: Denver Public Library, Western History Department, #X-21)

Perk's Dad owned the Senate Saloon, the second building on the left. (Courtesy of Grant Houston)

An interior shot of the Vickers' saloon. Perk's dad is second from the right. (Courtesy Grant Houston)

Perk's parents' wedding photograph. His mother was married at the very early age of seventeen. (Vickers' Family Photo)

The Presbyterian Church — the first church building on the Western Slope of Colorado. (Denver Public Library, Western History Department, #X-68)

The Old Cemetery at Lake City. The Vickers' family is buried here. (Muriel Wolle photo: Denver Public Library, Western History Department, #X-57)

The Hinsdale County Courthouse, where Alfred Packer was tried. (Denver Public Library, Western History Department, #X-71)

The Old Occidental Hotel which burned in 1937. (Muriel Wolle photo: Denver Public Library, Western History Department, #X-32)

The Vickers' home (left) and the Catholic Church on the northwestern edge of Crookeville. (Denver Public Library, Western History Department, #X-11)

The 1881 Lake City school — now torn down. (Muriel Wolle photo: Denver Public Library, Western History Department, #X-44)

Perk's dad — second from left. He was active until he died at ninety.
(Courtesy Grant Houston)

Perk's brother packing horses to take Muriel Wolle (author of Stampede
to Timberline) *to Carson City — 1946. (Muriel Wolle photo: Denver
Public Library, Western History Department, #X-3003)*

The Vickers' Ranch — 1947. It looks much the same today. (Muriel Wolle photo: Denver Public Library, Western History Department, #X-3623)

Perk and Emma Jean — both are still very active. (Vickers' Family Photo)

The Empire Chief Mill located high up Henson Creek. (Photo by Bob Stigall)

The Ute-Ulay Mine near the high point of its production in 1885. (Frank Dean photo: Denver Public Library, Western History Department, #X-61914)

Golden Fleece miners pose for the camera about 1880. (Denver Public Library, Western History Department, #X-60892)

Perk and his son Larry, who helps run the ranch. (Vickers' family Photo)

Rose's Cabin on the way over Engineer Pass. (Courtesy of P. David Smith)

American Flats is a huge area way above treeline — beautiful but easy to get lost in. (Courtesy P. David Smith)

The Vickers' Ranch brochure, which helps market the Vickers' guest cabins.

WEST UP HENSON CREEK TO ENGINEER MOUNTAIN

*"Those Old Timers Was
Tough Hombres"*

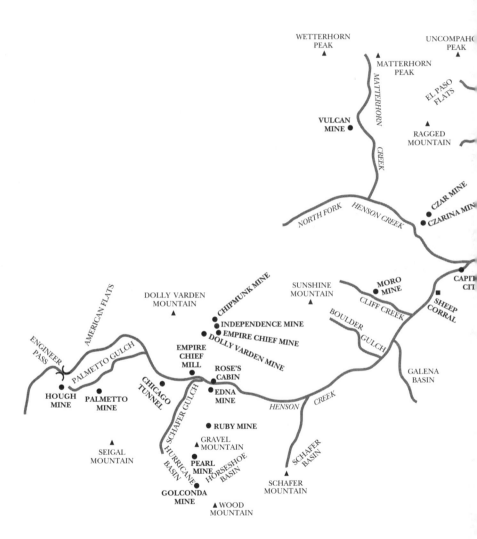

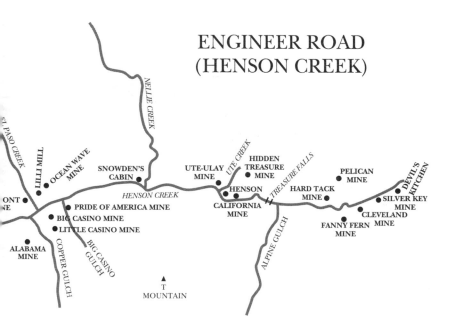

ENGINEER ROAD
(HENSON CREEK)

*T*he earliest recorded prospecting in Hinsdale County was in Henson Creek Canyon. In August of 1871, Joel K. Mullen, Charles Goodwin, Albert Mead and Henry Henson located a claim that would become the Ute-Ulay Mine, but since the land still belonged to the Utes, who were hostile to prospectors, the miners had to await the signing of the 1874 Brunot Treaty before returning to work their claim.

Other prospectors poured in seeking their "Golden Fleece" and, quickly, the narrow canyon was filled with the sounds of hope and industry. Aerial tramways criss-crossed the canyon, hauling ore from mines to mills. The road rumbled with stages and teamsters' wagons that crowded the Henson Creek and Uncompahgre that connected Lake City with Silverton and Ouray. And high in the crags that formed the canyon walls, the air rang with the measured, rhythmic song of the hammer and drill.

Henson Creek Canyon is quiet now except for the liquid machinery of the river. A few derelict buildings, timeworn and sun-dried the color of gingersnaps, tilt against the inclines that threaten them. The only vehicles on the road carry fishermen to Henson Creek's productive trout waters or sightseers seeking the scenic wonders of the Alpine Loop.

On a bright autumn day, with Perk at the wheel, we drove out through Lake City up this canyon, into the mountains and back into time.

"There's the old Vickers' house up on that hill to your left. Overlooks the whole town. I remember years ago when I was a kid I'd look out the window of that home by the church and you'd see pack horses, wagons, sleds and everything else going up the canyon to bring supplies to all the cabins from here clear to Rose's Cabin and on up to Engineer Mountain. The road went all the way over to Silverton. When the mines shut down they quit using the road 'cause it wasn't any use. Then later on, when the automobiles came in, in the '50s, they started fixing the roads up so you could use them."

Just as we left town, we passed Perk's granddaughter walking on the road. We stopped to talk and after a chat, drove on.

"She looks like a Vickers," I said.

Without looking away from the road he replied, smiling, "A bull always marks his calves."

Henson Creek has cut a deep narrow canyon in the brown volcanic breccias and for the first few miles above town, the road is at the base of the cliff along the side of the stream, matching it turn for turn. The roadbed is made from crushed rock cut from the cliff face, then spread with a grader, forcing the stream into a narrow pocket-water channel.

"They're going to develop all this unless the government buys it back. I hate to see it developed."

"Where would they get the water for the development?"

"You can drill a water well around here anywhere - two hundred feet over on our subdivision."

"Who owns a stream that runs between two pieces of property?"

"The property line is in the middle of the river bottom. You can float the river, but you can't put your foot on the bottom. You can own the land but not the water. Can't walk up the river. Not the bank or the high water mark. But where is the line? There have been lots of suits over that."

"I didn't expect the aspens to be turning."

"Yeah they're generally good by about the 10th of September. They're going pretty good now. Now that cave there to the left is what we used to call the Devil's Kitchen."

A broad, shallow cave had been cut by the stream, along the base of the roadside cliff. The ceiling was darkened by the smoke from old campfires.

"We used to come up here as kids for cookouts. I don't know where it ever got that name. Now, let's see if we can see that tunnel. Right here's where that vein comes through. This is the Silver Key. Right down there on the water across the stream. Up there is the other part of the Silver Key. Across the river. They didn't produce much. Oh, they shipped a little ore. In those days they worked like hell for nothing. They had a little bridge across the stream. It washed out every year. Some of those old guys were smart enough that they had the bridge on a cable, and when the high water came it would wash it right into shore, and they didn't have to build it over again. That's the vein there. It crossed the river and goes clear back down there to the TCM tunnel below town. That rusty colored rock."

"So these guys knew what they were doing. They weren't just out there digging holes."

"They had a pretty good indicator. Some kind of formation change. This land here up on the left belongs to a guy by the name of Brown. A contractor. The tunnel to the mine is right up on the hill there. See that house there. A couple of guys built that house and they sold it to this guy Brown. That vein there is called the Edna. Right up on that fence. There's a road that crossed the stream right here. Right up there about a thousand feet, across the stream, there's a mine called the Cleveland. The Cleveland had about five patented claims in it.

"My dad bought that Cleveland Mine. The Cleveland Mine had a big mill. A guy named Brown has a subdivision over there now. To get to that Cleveland Mine they had to cross that river and go up that hill about a thousand feet. The tunnel was up there. My dad was in that for a great many years and he finally ended up owning it. Then a man come in here from Kansas by the name of J.R. Greenleese and my dad sold him that mine for $45,000 cash. It had to be about 1915, along in there. At that time that was a lot of money. That really put Dad in business.

"Dad bought these draft horses. He had a pure breed Percheron stallion shipped in from France. To breed that mare. He raised those big horses. God, those draft horses was where the money was."

"Anyhow, Greenleese got promoted, or my dad promoted him, I don't know which. So my dad used that money to get those horses and the upper ranch and help keep the kids from starving to death. So Greenleese left for a while and we didn't hear anymore about it, not another word 'til 1934 right after I got out of high school. Mr. Greenleese came back and was visiting with my dad. They got to talking about the Cleveland Mine and Mr. Greenleese told my dad he wanted to reopen that mine and see if he could do something with it. My dad said, 'Well, yeah it would be a good idea', and he told me all about it. So Greenleese hired me to go up there and locate those levels. I took my two brothers and we worked all summer, Bob and Joe and I.

"Come fall, Mr. Greenleese come in and said, 'I got a man by the name of Frank, Mr. Ben Frank from Eldorado, Kansas, who is gonna help me get this moving financially.' He wanted to build a mill. Built it right there. A big mill. See that foundation up there on the left? All that's been cleaned up. So Ben Frank said we got to get another mine that's got a lot of ore that we might put into the mill. So we made a deal and bought the Fanny Fern. Up on top. I built a road to the Fanny Fern, so we could get up there.

"We bought a tramway, the one up there at the Ocean Wave. We had to go up there and tear that tramway down and bring the cable we were going to use for this tramway. A jig-back tramway. You know what a jig-back tramway does?"

"No idea."

"It has two standing cables with one bucket up there and one down here. The guy at the top fills that full bucket and opens up the brake and gravity pulls it down and pulls the empty one up. So there's no power needed."

"That's a pretty clever way of doing that."

"Yeah. It shows how god damn smart the people were. Oh, those old bastards forgot more than we'll ever know. That's my opinion anyway. I knew a lot of those prospectors. They were great folks. Oh, you had some bad ones. Once in a while some of them guys would get down there and get drunk and they would get kinda dangerous, but when they sobered up, they'd go back in the hills and then you wouldn't hear no more about them for a long time.

"So anyway, by god, we got that cable down and strung it up here to the mill. It had a pretty good-sized bucket on each side. Hell, those buckets would carry a thousand pounds. The first day of operation that cable broke and that big bucket went right down straight through the middle of that mill.

"So they brought in an expert from Denver by the name of Hill, A.G. Hill. He was known nationwide as a tram builder. So Mr. Hill came in and he measured the distance and I went with Mr. Greenleese to Denver and bought that new tramway. But the tramway had a traveling cable and we had to put a power plant here to get power up there to run the traveling cable. That worked fine for about a year or two, but it didn't make any money.

"Then a couple of guys set up the Pelican. See that road there to the right? That goes up to the Pelican. That mine produced a lot of ore for several years. They finally got the mill that belonged to Greenleese, but they couldn't make any money. They got in debt. They owed bills. And I lost my wages too, and it sat there 'til about 1950.

"The Vickers family had been working that mine on the ranch, the Golden Wonder, off and on. I had a friend in McAllen, Texas, and he wanted to put the Golden Wonder in operation. He had a friend in Oklahoma and they organized what they call Gnome Mines Company. And they owned that mine in American Basin called the Gnome. They took the Golden Wonder in on that deal. Two mines. So they made a deal with the man who had this mill to put the mill in operation with the ore from those two mines. Well, they put the mill in operation and we started hauling the ore from the Golden Wonder. About 3,000 tons. All of it was probably about two ounces to the ton. Well, things were going along pretty good, but they didn't have any scales or anything to weigh the ore with. So they finally decided to make a shipment of the concentrates. They assayed the concentrates and they had a lot of assays to show.

"They hired a trucker out of Telluride and he got that truckload of concentrates and hauled it to Utah where they had a smelter. They had a deal with the smelter, but they didn't have any way to weigh that ore. They had to load the truck by wheelbarrow. So they put a few buckets in each wheelbarrow so they would have an idea how many tons they had in that wheelbarrow. So they loaded that truck and the guy took off with a load of ore.

"So about two weeks later they hadn't heard anything about the ore so they contacted the smelter. One of the guys, Paul Jackson, went out there and they found out that the truck was ten days late getting there. They got to checking around and found out that the guy that hauled that ore from here went home, back to Telluride, before he went to Utah. When they weighed the ore and they got the settlement sheets and they found out that the gold was weighing out about a half ounce a ton. They claimed that the guy went to Telluride and took off the good ore and loaded some other ore. So they had the FBI check it out for them. At that time the FBI was checking gold-stealing shipments, but they lost out and they couldn't prove or disprove anything.

"So they shut her down and that mill set there again for several years until Jack Downey from San Antonio came up and got well acquainted with Roy Pray. Roy built the Crystal Lodge up by the lake. Roy was in the mining business and was always wanting to promote mines. So he called on Jack Downey to take on that mill and the

Pelican Mine. They took over that mine and started reha-
bilitating it and they worked that Pelican Mine. They got
the yard cleaned up and ready to go. I made that road so
they could drive up there and haul that ore down and
dump it in the bin. And they run that for two or three
months. But they weren't making any money.

"On the second level, one of the employees, Lester
McComb, one of the local boys working into that tunnel,
stepped over a ladder and fell down four hundred feet. It
killed him instantly. Broke his neck. So Downey shut the
mine down. It has never worked since. Downey got sued
and all that. It was in the '60s. They only took the real high-
grade ore out in the beginning because shipping costs were
so high. Those old time miners were smart men. They
selected what they wanted and what they didn't, they threw
on the dump. Nowadays these companies come in and
open up a tunnel and with modern equipment widen that
tunnel so they can work it. See that black headhouse way
up there on the south side? I built the road to that headhouse, too. That's the Fanny Fern. That tunnel goes in
there about two thousand feet."

*"Is that their bridge? Is someone going over there to work that
Fanny Fern Mine?"*

"No. Gene Brown built that. He's subdividing that
land over there. He's selling home sites."

"He's turned his mine into a housing addition?"

"He doesn't do any mining at all."

"So that's a switch, isn't it?"

"Hell, yes. It's gone from a profitable mine down to a
subdivision. Can you imagine going up this Henson
Creek with wagons? In the wintertime, sleds and pack-
horses and mules. All the way to Hurricane Basin. The
Golconda Mine is up there. Years ago when my dad had
the Independence Mine and the Empire Chief, he
brought ore down on that old jig-back tramway and piled
it up down at the bottom. When he wanted to make a
shipment, he had to come up in a wagon or a sled in the

wintertime, and sled that all the way down to the railroad, and shovel that ore into the boxcar. Coming down here in the wintertime you had a snowy road all the way. This canyon, when the sun hit it, had stretches of it, maybe five hundred feet, that would be bare ground. Some guy would go along with a shovel to shovel snow out onto the tracks. Man, you would not believe the hardships the old folks went through to try to make some money so they could support a family.

"The younger generation are not taught that. Well, you know most of the young generation are spoiled. In fact, since WWII, in my opinion, we have been living beyond our means. Now this whole government is going the same way. The government is spending far beyond their capability to repay their debt. Some day, I don't know what will happen.

"That claim way up on the hill is called Little Chief. It's just past the Fanny Fern on the opposite side of the stream. It's about a half mile above the Pelican on the right. Just another vein, just another outcropping some guy thought he could do something with. See that trail there on that slide across the stream? That trail's been there all my life. That's a wildlife trail, its cut that way by deer and elk. You'll see the deer and elk use it. They use that to come down and get water, but in the wintertime they use that to get over on this side 'cause this is the sunny side. It's bare all winter. Over there it snows in."

"Who did your dad get the Cleveland from? Did he do the prospecting?"

"He bought from a man named Johnny Atkins who was a miner and a bar fly. He was always hanging around Dad's bar. He was a good friend of my dad's. Somehow they got together on the Cleveland Mine. My dad had been making a little money in the saloon business, so he started grub-staking a couple of guys that worked over there. They worked there 'til he sold it. They didn't make any money but they thought they were going to make some.

"Here about twenty years ago I built a road for a company from Nevada. See, it takes off right here, down here across the river. See that tunnel over there? That's called the Hard Money. They ran that tunnel in there about five hundred feet on that vein. There are two tunnels. One up there and one right here on the water.

"They did a lot of work down below. Then they ran that tunnel up above to get away from all that water. They had a little aerial tramway across there. There's a cabin up there in that gulch. They had that tramway for their own personal usage.

"Up here on the right we're coming to the Hardtack. The Hardtack now is where the Hurt boys have this mining tour. This is the tunnel, right here by the road. This is right at the foot of Alpine Gulch that comes down from across the stream there. There's several mines up there. Several of them are right around the corner.

"Those oldtimers had some good names for these mines, didn't they?"

"You wonder where they got names like that. They had a big mill here. This is the Ocean Wave Mine. Alpine Creek comes out of Alpine Gulch over there across the stream. See the headhouse way up on the mountain? Over to the right. That's where that aerial tramway was that I told you we tore down."

"How in the world did you string that cable across this canyon?"

"Well they had an old wagon road. We took it up by pack mule. You'd be surprised how much cable you could haul. You take a mule and put about two hundred pounds on each side, all rolled up. He couldn't go any place but straight ahead. There's the Hardtack Mine there. They got it open now. There's a tour. You can go in there.

"See the headhouse way up there on the right? Just follow the ground level. It's just before it hits that big bunch of cliffs. That's Hidden Treasure. Let me tell you about that Hidden Treasure. Now that shaft goes down there about a thousand feet. And right around the corner, we come to the Ute-Ulay. The Hidden Treasure and the Ute-Ulay are all connected underground. If that tunnel was open there you could go in that Ute-Ulay #5 level, climb a ladder and come out on top. I've done that.

"Right now we're on the Ute-Ulay property. These old buildings and that track and trestle are all that's left. This Ute-Ulay has got a lot of history. I had that Ute-Ulay for ten years, you know. And then I sold it. Couldn't afford to keep it. It had that brand new mill there that was worth a half a million dollars. I had to pay all those taxes. I had to keep a caretaker.

"Right around the corner they had this reservoir. Out of the reservoir they took the water to run the mill. Run a hydroelectric generator. You knew about the dam washing out. It happened right here. See that old cement dam? That all washed out and killed all the fish between here and Blue Mesa Reservoir. Those guys that had their ranches down in the valley, it screwed up their irrigation systems. There was three or four lawsuits filed just because of that reservoir."

"Who did that dam belong to?"

"The dam belonged to a guy by the name of Ed Hughes. Not the mine. The Ute-Ulay is owned by a company in Seattle. They've got an option to sell to the people who have our Golden Wonder — the mill and all. They're not going to use the mill. It's a concentrate mill. I don't think you'll ever see this mill operating again.

"See, there were two mines together. The Ute and the Ulay. There was the Ute on the left side, the west side. Right next to that is another parallel vein called the Ulay. They went down in that Ulay a thousand feet. I got all the maps."

"Why were they putting down that deep shaft?"

"They were on the vein. Every hundred feet they went down they run a drift off. They finally got down to eleven hundred feet, clear in under Henson Creek. They went on into Red Mountain I guess two thousand feet. They had good ore all the way, but it was mostly zinc. Lots of zinc. But the Ute, just a little bit east of them, a parallel vein, had lead, zinc, copper and silver. That's why the Ute-Ulay was so profitable. Some of the bigger companies like ARCO had it. American Smelting had it for years. It transferred hands to a lot of people."

"And you owned it for a while?"

"That mine ended up owned by a poor old country boy by the name of Vickers. I had it for about five years. I was lucky."

"It wasn't producing then."

"Both the Ute and the Ulay were shut down. Idarado Mine had them. I knew the manager out of Telluride. He knew that I had some mines and that I was interested in expanding. His name was Johnny Wise. He said, 'Perk would you be interested in buying the Ute-Ulay Mine?' I said, 'I wouldn't have a chance to get the Ute-Ulay Mine.' He said, 'I'm coming through Montrose, meet me at the Belvedere Hotel.' He had been to New York to the head office. Numark was a big outfit. Still is.

"Well, we got into the Belvedere Hotel and had a couple of drinks — some kind of Scotch, or something — and he said, 'I'll sell you that Ute-Ulay for . . .' I forgot how much it was. It was a small amount of money. He said, 'I'll give you thirty days if you can produce the money.'

"Well, I produced that money. I got hold of a friend of mine in Ouray — the guy's still living — and he helped me promote the money and I bought that Ute-Ulay. But I had to get the money from other people 'cause I didn't have the money. So I finally got all that property in my name, but I had a hard time hanging onto it. The taxes were expensive. I had to have insurance. I said, 'I've got to get rid of that dang thing.' I should have kept it, too. Really. Now that land is worth a lot of money. There's seven hundred acres there."

"All home sites."

"Yeah. I sold it to a friend of mine by the name of Ed Hughes. He had made some money in the uranium boom. I come out of it with $10,000. That was the whole deal."

"We have talked about this before. They used to say 'the gold is in them thar hills'. Now the gold is the hills."

"That's exactly right. You get a mining claim then you put your houses on it and then make a housing development. The tourists say it all the time. 'Don't worry about the gold, Perk. You got the gold right here in your cabins.' And that's the truth."

"How do they separate that ore in those mills? Do they just use water?"

"No, they use chemicals too. They use lime and a lot of stuff depending on the kind of ore. They have what they call floatation. The ore goes across a table that shakes it. The heavy stuff goes one way and the other stuff goes in the other direction. It's a very interesting operation."

At the site of the Ute-Ulay, the canyon widens to two hundred yards, and the road and the stream separate, the road bearing to the right up the wooded hillside. From this higher ground, the peaks at the head of the valley are clearly visible, stacked so close together that there doesn't seem to be room for the turnings of the stream or the road. The peaks' rocky tops are bare and gray. Spruce and pine woods, dabbed this time of year with yellow blotches of turning aspen at the lower altitude, rise quickly up the steep slopes to push at the timberline like dark green fingers.

Above the peaks the morning sky shone like fresh enamel paint. There wouldn't be any clouds until afternoon when the mountains tossed up the warmer air. Here on summer days, when the air is warm, the cumulus puffs bloom and turn gray on the bottoms and dump quick midday showers with a regularity you can use to set your watch. Then, just as quickly, the sky clears and the road is dusty again. But now in the fall with the cooler air, there was less risk of midday thunderstorms, which at stream level were a nuisance, but in the high country could be deadly.

"We lost a horse right here one time. By God, we took a bunch of horseback riders up to Uncompahgre and after we got down to the foot of the trail, we turned the horses loose. We knew all our horses always come home. That one horse didn't show up. We come back up and found some god-damned guy ran into that horse with his car and broke her leg. We had to shoot her.

"That mountain up there on the left, that's called T Mountain. Just across from where Nellie Creek comes in on this side. You can get in there from the Sherman side if you come up Cooper Creek. That's the ridge that separates this from the other side. Now we're coming to a little mine called the California. See there's some of the old ore veins there. A lot of ore come out of that tunnel."

"Why would you pick that rock formation to go in on? Does that look good to you?"

"They had a vein. They went in and cut the vein. It runs across ahead of us. They cut the vein and then they stoped it. You see that cribwork up there? That's holding that dump."

"So stoping is a way you harvested the vein? You went in 'til you hit the vein and then you just went up along it?"

"That way you got your gravity. You drill holes and you blast it and it comes right down where you want it. In a shaft, you go down. In a shaft, and by God, you got to hoist every bit of it."

"So the horizontal tunnels weren't the producers. They were for getting to the ore."

"Right."

"Was this earlier than the Pelican?"

"I think so."

"Why would a guy like you buy the Ute-Ulay Mine? Just to hold it?"

"Well I thought I could promote it. I sold it, but I made just a very little. You see that vein there? That's the Ulay vein. Right down here they sunk a shaft. They went down eleven hundred feet, straight down on the vein. When they got down in there about a thousand feet they followed the vein clear across the hill there for maybe another thousand feet. That's the second mine my dad ever worked in when he came here after he worked on the Golden Fleece. Down in that shaft, he used to tell me, in that hot steam, it was so damn hot you nearly suffocated. He met a guy there by the name of Charley McKinley.

"Charley McKinley was the guy that talked my dad into coming from the Golden Fleece to the Ute-Ulay. See, they were sinking that deep shaft at the Ulay. They had all those Dagos and all those foreigners working at that mine. They had about four hundred guys working there. Those Dagos weren't too happy with the operation. McKinley said we got to organize these guys. So he organized what he tried to call a union. It was McKinley that started the first labor union that I know of in the United States. He called it I.W.W. He got involved in that damn thing and all those Dagos in the mine would pay him so much money to promote them. And some way or other he pocketed the money he got out of those guys. Somebody said he left there and went to the World's Fair. Well, he finally come back and they had him arrested and he went to the penitentiary. McKinley ended up in jail over that union. *(IWW, or Industrial Workers of the World, was a labor organization founded in 1905 by revolutionary socialists to radicalize the labor movement. It reached its greatest influence in 1912-17. Its strikes, viewed as an attempt to exploit WWI, were considered treasonable and its leaders were imprisoned).*

"Before that, they had that Indian uprising from the Dagos. The Dagos weren't satisfied with the food they were getting up at the boarding house so they blocked off a tunnel and the road. You couldn't come up this canyon no place without the army. They got the army to open up the road for them. They had a lot of people working between here and Engineer Mountain that couldn't even get through. The Dagos took it over."

The strike in 1899 prompted Governor Charles S. Thomas — the man who would later parole Alfred Packer — to send in four companies of infantry and two troops of cavalry. The troop train stopped in Sappinero to pick up Dr. Cuneo, the Italian consul bearing a note from King Humbert requesting the Italian miners to meet for a peaceful discussion. Dr. Cuneo, dressed in silk top hat and an overcoat with a fur collar, rode up the canyon ahead of the troops in a buggy with a white flag tied to the buggy whip.

As they approached the crowd of silent miners, Dr. Cuneo commanded the buggy to stop and walked toward the assembled men alone. He stopped and after a tense moment, took off his hat and threw open his coat and stood before the crowd in full evening dress, a red, green and white sash across his chest. The crowd cheered, and the strike was over.

"Now you have to have a surface claim that overlies where you're tunneling, don't you?"

"You do, oh yes."

"You can't just tunnel off anywhere you want."

"You discover an outcropping that looks good to you. You stake it. Your discovery should be on that vein. You go six hundred feet this way. It has to be pretty well in the center of it."

"But if it goes on up the hill, you better have claims staked over it?"

"You could do it as you go along. Did it all the time. This is the mill. The tunnel goes right under us. See the railroad? This tunnel goes in here a mile. It goes in there and cuts that Hidden Treasure vein. They just stoped that all out, all the way to the surface."

"Well, now how do they decide who owns it? The Hidden Treasure or the Ute-Ulay?"

"Oh hell, there was always a dispute there. There was always a fight, but they generally settled them."

"So it was the same vein really?"

"Same vein, yeah."

"Is there always a caretaker up here at the Ute-Ulay?"

"Yeah. This is the old boarding house here."

The old wooden boarding house looked abandoned, except for the modern day litter and trash scattered around it. The

*weathered two story building, its broken windows boarded, its
roof gapped and partially patched, listed slightly to the downhill
side like a tree in the wind. No smoke rose from the crooked and
rusted pipe chimney. I tried to imagine the caretaker who would
live there.*

"Now this is the dam that broke?"

"No this one they blasted out. See they had a flume
that carried water down there to run the generator for
that mill."

"Why did they blow it out?"

"They thought they were through with it. They wanted
to get rid of their liability. They didn't blast it out all at once
— just a little bit at a time and they drained it. See that
wood flume? When the Colorado Standard bought that
mill here in the '50s — that was the year I got my new dozer
— I built them some tailing ponds right up here across the
road. They pumped the tailings out of that mill and they
run them down that trough into those ponds."

"When did you get so interested in the bulldozer?"

"I got my first bulldozer in 1948. I found out if I had
it I could get a few jobs here and there and it would pay
for itself. We needed it at home too, but we couldn't
afford it. So that's why I did a lot of outside work. But I
could never have done the outside work if it hadn't been
for my brother staying at home building. I was bringing in
the money, and he was doing the work at the ranch.

"See those tailing ponds there? They filled four of
them. Lots of tailings and they were getting in a lot of
trouble. I don't think you'll ever see that mill run again
on account of the EPA."

*"At one time, they must have just dumped the tailings in the
stream."*

"Oh, hell yes. But you still had old folks who wanted
to protect the environment too. They used what they had
but didn't waste it. See this little place where people drive
to get off the road? The BLM's got it all fenced off now. I
think that's a mistake. Nobody's going to hurt any

government property by driving down a couple a hundred feet to fish.

"But you think about the courage and the inspiration and ambition that those guys had to come in here and do all the work they had to do to open up a mine and try to find the mother lode and make some money. They had to be God-chosen people to do it."

"Did they work up here year 'round?"

"Oh hell they worked all the way up to Hurricane Basin. Year 'round. We've got a mine up on top of Cinnamon Pass. I showed you yesterday where it is. My uncle cooked there. They had that boarding house sitting right on a saddle between those two peaks. The mine entrance was on Hurricane Basin. Right outside the kitchen they had a cable. The wind would be blowing so bad in the winter time you just take hold of that cable and come right around following that cable and when you got in the mine it was just like home. Long winters."

"He would be probably be snowed in from the first of November."

"Well, up there in that country you get snow all summer, but generally it opens up about the middle of May 'til the first of November. Sometimes a little longer. It varies from one year to the next, of course."

"I can't imagine doing that hard work all day."

"Well, you see, the younger generation of people, they don't want to do it either. They look like they would be physically able men, but when it comes right down to hard work they're not there.

"Now you go right up this damn creek you come right to Uncompahgre. I built that road up there way back. That's a county road now up to timberline. You can drive up there within three miles of Uncompahgre.

"For a while, had a contract with this hiking club. Once a year we'd bring the horses up here and camp overnight at Pike Snowden's. We'd ride out the next morning all the way up there to the peak and then we'd come meet 'em to take the horses back. That's how come that one horse got hit by a motorist."

"Was there ever any trapping up in here?"

"Not much. Now right here a guy, a miner, by the name of Pike Snowden, had a cabin, and he had another cabin right up here. The government has taken that over — it's government land — and restored that cabin. There's a pretty good campsite up there. It's a nice little ol' cabin. Beautiful little cabin."

"So all this was going on when your father got here."

"Yep. Well, some of it was starting, but there was still a lot of it going on. There was prospectors all over this country at that time."

"When did the mining business really get hurt?"

"When the silver crunch came on in the early '30s. Most of these guys left here. A lot of people left here. All but a few of the Vickers. If a guy had had any money and any sense he coulda bought it all. Those days are over. That stuff has gotten way out of reach. I think we have probably reached a maximum price on those lots, don't you?"

"You'd think so, wouldn't you?"

"Christ, you would. Although there's more people making money now than I have ever seen in my life."

"But there's no money to be made in mining anymore?"

"Pretty tough. The only mine working in this area is the Golden Wonder Mine up there where the boys are working now."

"You still own that?"

"Well, I sold it for $500,000. I get a royalty. They are shipping some of that gold ore."

"Who owns that?"

"It belonged to a company in Seattle called LKA International. They've sold it to these guys that have got it now. They are trying to pay for it. They're hand select mining that stuff. They're picking the best ore. They're doing just exactly what I would like to do if I was doing it myself."

"How do they get it shipped out of there? Do they just hire somebody?"

"They bring it out of the mine and then they put it in a big bag. Did you see some of those bags in my yard? Those bags will weigh three thousand pounds. They pick 'em up with a forklift and set them on the truck. They can only haul twenty tons at a time on account of the highway. They put twenty of those bags on a truck and ship it to Helena, Montana. It costs $1,500 for a truckload."

"That's the closest smelter?"

"It's the only one left in the West. There was one down in El Paso. The last shipment of that ore we sold averaged about twenty ounces to the ton. Those bags will run about $6,000 a ton. I would come out of there feeling pretty good about it."

"They used to say the ore from the Golden Fleece was the hot stuff because it was running $400 a ton."

"The Golden Fleece never had as high a grade of gold as we have in the Golden Wonder. And I don't know another mine in the San Juans that did either. I don't think it's a big mine. It's a small mine, but it's a good grade ore. They've got about $3-4 million worth of ore at $300 an ounce, according to their report, from the sixth level to the surface. But now gold dropped. We're only getting $260 an ounce. These god-damned Africans, they've got control of their government and those Africans are selling a helluva' lot of gold. Driving the price down."

"Do you hold up selling it 'til the price goes up?"

"No, you just take what you get. They got to get paid or they can't stay."

"Most of the mines around here are owned by who now? Big companies?"

"I got a list of all the patent mining claims. Do you know there's 550 patent mining claims in this area. In the county. I got a list here. Look this over. You'll be amazed."

The list was closely spaced on one page. Perk was wrong about one thing. The list showed 562 patented claims.

PATENTED MINING CLAIMS —
HINSDALE COUNTY, COLORADO
Accompanying DAVIE'S map traced by
Glenville A. Collins Mining Engineer of
Santa BarbaraCalifornia

G. & A. Placer	Church Placer	Golden Pearl
Lode Star	Rob Roy	Dauphin
Dauphin M.S. *	Sulphuret	Cora
Mountain View	Empire	Golden Wonder
Golden Carbonate	Belle of St. Louis	Red Cloud
Golden Mammoth	Belle of the East	Western Belle
Belle of the West	Delphos	Index
Trenton	Extension	Fleece Basin
Bank of Slumgullion	Golconda	Nellie Gray
Lake Shore	Nellie Gray M.S.	Golconda M.S.
Ida May	Fast Side M.S.	Lake Shore M.S.
Nellie M.	Crown Mountain	Garlock
Groves	Silver Coin	Beckel
Armitage	Armitage No. 2	Helen Hunt
Game Cock	Nellie G.	Greek
Necessity	Pallas	Lake Falls
Minerva	General Sherman	Gladiator
Vandalia	Hub	Arcus
May Flower	Newberg	Hinsdale
Express	Golden Chain	Kearsarge
Certified Check	Yellow Jacket	Roxy
Mountain Echo	Fannie	Earl
Lake View	Gold King	New Year
Altair	Doctor	Carmi
New York	Emerald Isle	Contention
Florence	Palmer	Irma
Hiwassee	Black Crook	Golden Fleece
Duke	Enterprise	Loohoon
Anna May	Hot Corn	Dock Ash
Dock Corn	Jim Crow No. 2	Morning Side
Omega	Alpha	Gold Pot
Golden Fleece Extn.	Governor Pitkin	Jim Dandy
Jo Dandy	Iron Clad	Concord
Colchis	Jason	Denver
Gold Ram	Factor	M. Ellen

Velveteen	Red Bird	Princeton
Silver Bell	Evangeline	Mount Marris
Cleveland	Fanny Fern	Mammoth
Pride of Colorado	Annie C.	Pelican
Pelican No. 3	Cannon	Benson
Atlanta	Little Chief	Blair
Hunt	Mountain Chief	Pueblo
Risorgimento	Alpine	Cherokee
Sequoah	U.P.	Michigan
Wye J.	Florida	Talahassee
St. Gothard	Spokane	Eureka
Telegram	Martha L.	Crystal
Hard Tack	Don Quixote	Winner
Hard To Beat	California M.S.	Ulay M.S.
Equator M.S.	Equator	Mab
Auria	Mayor of Leadville	Maid of Henson
Ulay Extn.	Yankee Doodle	Cuter
Free Lanse	Ulay	California
Lightning Striker	Ute	Regualtor
Leadville	Steele	Albany
Windsor	Otis	Protector
Invincible	Hidden Treasure	McCarthy
McCompe	McCarthy No. 3	McCarthy No. 2
Metropola	Treasure Hill	SpanTwin Sisters
Porcupine	Klondyke	Big Casino
Pride of America	Little Casino	Ottumwa
Burro Cabin M.S.	CastleBurro	Cabin
Red Rover M.S.	Whitney M.S.	Little Hattie
GimletMeat	Augor	Ocean Wave
Wave of the Ocean	Alabama	Colorado
Mars	Neptune	Venus
Lellie	Saturn	Jupiter
Louise	Syndicate	Finis
Baltimore	Ceres	Delphi M.S.
Vermont	Alhambra M.S.	El Sud
El Norte	Pearl	Scotia
Fairview	Empress	Ajax
Ajax M.S.	Sliver Chord Ex.	Czar
Czarina	Silver Chord	Broker
Excelsior	Ottawa	Lilly
Mountain Belle	Yellow Medicine	Capitol City
Capitol City No. 2	Keystone Stabe	Ballarat
Iron Placer	Veteran	Golden Eagle
Roscoe Conklin	Phil. Sheridan	Yorktown

Jamestown	Guyandotte	Roanoke
Norfolk	Portsmouth	Richmond
Petersburg	Newport News	Galic
Vulcan	Julia	Milford
Capitol Iron Placer	Paymaster	H.M. Woods
Mary J. Lee M.S.	Anchor	Silver Queen
Newburg	Haarlem	Montezuma
De Sota	Moro Limited	Ajax Limited
Blue Bell	Montreal	Moose
Little Barefoot	Incas	Independence
Highland Chief	High MuckaMuck	Empire
U.S.	Jessup	S.C.V.
Hondee	Magnolia	Mathison
Bonanza	Bonanza M.S.	Petopah
Silver Medal	Silver Medal No. 2	Mydedly
Amazon	Wall Street	Brick Pomeroy
Bloomington	St. Louis	John J. Crook
Russella	Big Horn	Horn Silver
Printer Boy	Accidental No. 2	Mountain Giant
Iron Mask	American Eagle	Duval
Frank s' ance	Chipmunk	Dolly Varden
Frank Adams	Iron Mask M.S.	Shafer Placer
Jennie	Fanny	Lake City M.S.
Equator M.S.	New Brighton M.S.	Thunderbolt M.S.
Ophir M.S.	Ophir	Anelia
Palmetto M.S.	First Nat'l Bank M.S.	Ruby Queen
Carbonate Queen	Palmetto	Chimney Corner
First Nat'l Bank	Copper King	Superior
Dictator	Lilly	Polar Queen
Frank Hough	Shiloe	Gladiator
Corinth	Sarah Wood	F.X. Aubrey
Miner's Bank	Geo. M. Tibbits	Flower of San Juan
Emperor Wilhelm	Wyoming	Philadelphia
Anna Crook	Hoffman	Engineer
Silver Plume	Boaster	Little Helen
Watson	Ruby Silver	Empress
O'Connor	Equator	New Brighton
Lake City	Newport	Fort Doaldson
Colorado Central	Bob Ingersol	Slide
Goodwin	Dewey No. 2	Pearl
Ruby	Dick Dawson	Malpe Grove M.S.
Maple Grove	Burbon Country	Junction
Mountain View	Sonoma	Silver Ledge
Highland Chief M.S.	Sunshine No. 1	Sunshine No. 2

Midnight Belle	Mary Jane	Snow Slide
Rose Lime M.S.	Mary Lime M.S.	Mary Lime
Rose Lime	Lone Tree	Postal
Ellwood	Sycamore	Little John
Clarence W.	Crown Point	Joaquin
Mountian King No. 2	Mountain King No. 1	Meteor
Printer Boy	North Side	Portland
Dupre	Belcher	Inez
Hollister	Isolde	Baker
Nucingen	Puzzle	F.B.H.
G.D.B.	C.F.M	World's Fair
Toledo Belle	Aroostook Extn.	Aroostook
Oneida	Flower of the West	Gnome
B.C. Steinbeck	Tobasco M.S.	Crown Point M.S.
Addie Lovell	Bon Homme	Fannie
Golden Magic	Golden Crest	Golden Age
Copper Rock	Golden Sceptre	Golden Treasure
Palmer	Galena	J.C. Lindsey
Golden Wand	Little Annie	Good Prospect
La Belle M.S.	Snow Storm	Gunnison M.S.
Gunnison	Shirley	Cashier
Red Gulch	Ada J.	Silver Star
Seward County	Hoosier	Champion
Napoleon	Miner's Delight	Grand Central
Japanese	Japanese M.S.	Tokio
Uncle Sam	Mansion	Alps
Sweet Home	Snow Drift	Eugene
Red Gulch M.S.	A. No. 1	A. No. 1 M.S.
Royal Gem	Smile of Fortune	Little Franklin
Adelaide	Sterling	Dolphin
Nellie G.	Conalan	Minnie Lee M.S.
Minnie Lee	Morning Star	I.X.L.
No.2 Ruby	George Washington	Tillman
Crescent	Wanimoo	Gracie
Naigra	Come Up	Mineral Flower
Black Wonder No. 2	Black Wonder	Black Wonder Ext'n
Eastern Rebel Boy	Katrina	Gold Foil
Nancy Jane	Pinnacle M.S.	Wager M.S.
Wegde M.S.	Bachelor M.S.	Maiden M.S.
Naomi M.S.	Aeolus	Swail No. 2
Swail No. 1	Boxer	Miner's Fate
Gold Bluff	Bull Cinch	Red Snapper
Ben Bolt	Bachelor	Maiden
Sea Board	Pinnacle No. 2	Pinnacle No. 1

Burrows	Naomi	Cawnoo
Newton	May Flower	Royal
St. Peter	Marian	Soap
Cresco	Annie	George III
Bonanza King	Hard Cash	Hattie
Ajax	Mott F.	J.I.C.
High Line	Red Deer	Sitting Bull
Queen Bee	Bay State	Continent
Contact	Stoneblack	Autumn
Hoosier Girl	Jumbo	Macot
J.J.C.	Smoker	L.R.
Dutch Girl	Igo	Little Clare
Hamiltin	St. Johns	St. Jacobs
Maid of Carson	Big Indian	Brick Pomeroy M.S.
Wm. T.	Four Aces	Pueblo Placer

* M.S. stands for mill site

I have always been fascinated by the names the miners chose for their mines. They reflect a wide divergence in origin and education. Home locales and home towns from all over the U.S. were popular, as were women's names. (Wives? Girlfriends? Daughters?) Terms of endearment or luck or benefactors are about as frequent as references to power, temptresses, masters. Names of animals and nautical terms are frequent. Some less imaginative seemed to have used their proper names, or enigmatic initials. And there is a surprising amount of reference to history, literature, mythology, astrology and opera. There is little misspelling, unless you count 'Free Lanse', 'Shiloe' and 'Tokio.'

"Now you see that road going up there?" Perk continued. "Right there on the cliffs? They had a big mill up there called the Lilli. See the cement foundations there?"

A series of gray, box-like foundations lay along the face of the steep slope like some giant's stairway.

"They had that mill there and they had an ore bin that came down from the top right down to the mill. Right up there on that Lilli, by god, there's a lot of dumps. We made a deal on this Lilli company. I had an army 6 x 6 truck so I built a road clear up over that cliff to the mill. I'll show you. We hauled about 5,000 tons of that stuff all

167

the way down to that mill. Then they said they didn't see any need of it. I got paid for hauling the ore, that's all I got. I had a trucker, a guy that worked for me by the name of Wayne Forebearer. One of my best friends. He's dead now, he could run that truck. A great guy."

"So there was a lot of spin-off for you from the mining, wasn't there? Road building and hauling and prospecting and dealing around."

"Oh, yeah. That gulch going off in that direction, over to the south, is called Copper Gulch. Right up here on the right is where the Ocean Wave is. Now this guy, Roy Pray, that moved to the Crystal Lodge, he was quite a developer himself. He came up here and bought a mine right around the hill called the Pride of America. So he goes to Gunnison and bought a railroad car and had me put it in there. That railroad car is all steel. See it right across that bridge. That's been here for 30 years or more. Those mines right up there are called the Big Casino and the Little Casino Mines. You can see the dumps further up the hill. They shipped a lot of ore out of the Big Casino but not much out of the Little Casino."

"Who owned those when they were producing? Would one guy own it?"

"Well, no. Most of those mines after they got them going good were organized in to some kind of company. This road, fifty years ago, used to go right around this way. Followed the river. One year they got a big snow slide that blocked the road. The Copper Mountain slide. Comes right out of Copper Mountain. My brother, Jack, was highway maintainer for the county, so he built this road up here on this side of the stream to get away from that snow slide. Right here on the right is the Ocean Wave. You see this guy has a cabin up on the hill there. You see that cabin up there? This is all subdivided.

"This is El Paso Creek coming in from the right. Right up there is a mine called the Alabama and also the Vermont. Now right ahead here, they had a tunnel that went in under there at least two thousand feet. Big tunnel. Cut that vein on the Vermont and they built a little mill out there over the dump. And the ore at that depth, it wasn't as good ore as they thought it should be and they shut her down."

"Give me an idea what it would cost nowadays to dig a two thousand foot tunnel."

"Right now it would cost you about $200 a foot. See the dump out here? They had a mill that set out here. You can see the Big Casino and the Little Casino now. See that road going around the mountain? Solid rock. I had to blast every inch of that. Drill it and blast it. Drill it and blast it."

"Just like digging a tunnel."

"At that time I got about ten dollars a foot."

"So is that cut and fill?"

"I just blast it off and push it off with a bulldozer. Now you can you see that road going clear around the hill there."

His eyes twinkled when he talked about the roads he built with his bulldozer.

"Now tell me," I asked, "before modern mining, would a miner just dig as far as he could go with a shovel and when he came to rock he'd start blasting?"

"No, they had to hand drill it and blast it out."

"What are they doing now?"

"Oh, Christ with compressed air now and air hammers. Two good guys and an air hammer could make ten foot a day. Just below that mill site, where the Pride of America Mine is now, that's the worst snowslide we have in the Henson Creek area. One year that came down with such force it shut off the river. And the people working up Henson Creek — there were a lot of people working up here — they had to take supplies by the boat across that thing and meet up here. It was about a half a mile of reservoir in there. That's the most dangerous snowslide we've got on the Henson road right there. We haven't had many slides in the last ten years."

"You get slides on this side of the river?"

"That's the only one up to Capitol City. Above Capitol City you get them on both sides. Here the sun keeps the south side melted off. That south side of the canyon is always bare.

"A couple of gals from Iowa, at this little bridge here, bought five acres over there on the other side. Now right ahead of us is where Lee's Smelter used to be. You've heard of Lee's Smelter? He's the guy who started this Capitol City. Named it Capitol City. Now that gulch going up right there, that's called Lee's Smelter Gulch. Good hunting up there too.

"Now we're at Capitol City. At one time we thought we were going to get this land and build a reservoir. It would be a beautiful reservoir here."

Capitol City wasn't a city any more, and it never had been the capital. George S. Lee had wanted it to be. Capitol City — first named Galena City when it was founded in 1877 — had grown up around Lee's Mining and Smelting Company, and with its growth, grew Lee's fanciful ambition that Galena City, rather than Denver, would become Colorado's capital. Good thing it wasn't, lying as it did fifteen miles above Lake City on a rough, winding canyon road that is closed most of the winter except for snowmobiles.

The old townsite was in a small meadow. After driving up the narrow canyon, it is always a surprise to enter it so suddenly. Here the canyon is gone, spreading back quickly to make room for the grassy park, a mile long and maybe a quarter mile wide. Willows and alders grow along the stream that, quiet now, turns and returns through the meadow. Close on all sides, mountains rise above the horizon halfway to the vertical.

"So Lee is the guy who built that brick house that used to be here?"

"Yeah. It's all gone now. You remember that?"

"When I was a kid the walls were still standing. But that must have been forty or fifty years ago."

"That two-story house had walls three bricks thick, and they said he had those bricks hauled up here from Pueblo at a cost of a dollar a brick. They called it the 'Governor's Mansion.' Now where Lee's mansion was, right there, a guy from New Mexico built a bed and breakfast. When were you up here last?"

"June."

"You come up this far."

"I come up here every time. It's worth coming up here just to see it"

"You ever go up North Henson? God that's beautiful isn't it? I did a lot of work up there for Exxon. I had that D6 Cat up here off and on for five years."

"What was Exxon doing?"

"By God they were exploring for rare metals, uranium and some of those rare metals. We did a lot of core drilling."

"When was that?"

"Oh, that's been within the last twenty years. Man, I had a good job. They'd pay me by the hour. My job was to build a road. They had a permit from the Forest Service to build a road wherever we wanted to go. When they got through with their development program, my job was to re-vegetate the whole thing. Put it back like God made it. I felt bad when they shut down. I was making enough money to keep my brothers working on the ranch making those necessary repairs."

"You can get to Uncompahgre up that North Henson Canyon."

"It's a good way. You go up North Henson and turn up Wetterhorn Creek. You come to Matterhorn and Wetterhorn and Uncompahgre, and you can go right across El Paso Flats and right down Nellie Creek. That's a beautiful view."

"I'd think working up there that high on a metal bulldozer in thunderstorms would be dangerous. I can't imagine that."

"Nothing to it."

"Storms didn't run you off?"

"By God, there was one time when I was building that road, a guy brought me up and he was going to pick me up in El Paso Flats. He was financing us. He said he'd be back at 4:00. I worked 'til about noon and a goddamned storm come up. Lightning and thunder. Well I'm telling you, that lightning up there in the high country comes in just a great big blue flame right at you. Well, I got off that Cat and got under it and I thought, I've made a mistake. So I got up in the seat. That Cat's got some kind of sponge rubber cushion up under that seat and it saved my life. It got dark and that guy never did show up and I said, 'Hell, something must have happened to him.' So I started walking. I walked clear back down to that Ute-Ulay Mine. When I got back, Bob was there at the mine and ol' Bob took me home.

"Next morning, when that guy came by, I said, 'What the hell happened to you, you crazy son-of-a-bitch?' He said, 'Well I thought another guy was going to pick you up.' I said, 'Bull shit!'"

Perk pulled off the road. "Right here is where the town of Capitol City was."

The stream, crowded with alders and gathered here and there in beaver ponds, meandered through a narrow grassy valley. Mountains, their high tops bare, rose on all sides half way to the vertical. One original log building remained. Boxy do-it-yourself houses, tar-papered and tacky, were scattered helter-skelter over Capitol City's once-thriving town site.

"We just now approved a subdivision on this to a guy. He's got about seventy lots here. We approved it and the County commissioner has final approval. It's a big expense to get a subdivision approved."

"How many people lived up here?"

"Oh man, when I was a kid there was probably a hundred and fifty people lived here year round. We used to come up in a wagon. Mother would bring up all the kids so we'd have some kids to play with. Whatever game they had, baseball, whatever it was. They used to have a big schoolhouse and they had schooling just like they have today, but the schoolhouse burned.

"This is the Czarina Mine, right there where the road to North Henson branches off. That tunnel goes in there a long way. See the big structure where they started? Now they followed that vein in there a long ways. Then they got an upraise to connect with the Capitol City up on top. They shipped a lot of ore but it came out of the upper works. It didn't come out down here. They brought it out of the upper tunnel and hauled it down. That road goes back up North Henson Creek eight miles. It's a county road now. It was before I got my dozer — I'd say in the '40s — a guy come in and took over that Vulcan Mine. It set up there, up North Henson Creek about a mile, and they shipped a lot of ore from that Vulcan. He built a great, big modern mill, like you wouldn't believe. Beautiful mill. And after he got that mill built, they went broke. Shut her down and they dismantled the mill a year later. They didn't even run the mill. That's what called promoting something you haven't got.

"See, in the mining business, that's been the biggest handicap we've ever had. Building mills and aerial tramways without putting the necessary money into the development. Development is the key to the whole thing. They should have found out what they had first. Open the ore up and then say, 'I've got so many tons of ore to justify the mill.'

"Right down here they had a pipeline that run up North Henson for about a mile. Eighteen inch pipeline. And right down here they had a power plant. Hydroelectric power plant. The purpose of that power plant was not for Capitol City at all. It was to build a line for the Empire Chief where the mill is up there. The one they are starting to restore now. I'll show you. They planned to build that power line up there and it run for several years. And I finally got a hold of all that stuff. That's the stuff I sold Ed Cox and he's going to trade it to the government. But we've run into some problems right now. There's a watercourse coming out of those tunnels and the government is afraid to take the credit back for fear it will have to go to the expense of making the water better quality water. That's craziness."

Perk pointed out over the now-vacant Capitol City town site.

"When I was a kid there was houses all in here. Right here, next that side of the road there was a big building that had a big sign that said 'SALOON'.

"Ol' Buskirk had that cabin over there where that new one is. I told you about him. He's the one that talked that woman into quitting her husband and moving in with him down in the valley.

"Bill Gray bought the old schoolhouse. Tore it down and used that lumber to build some of those houses on Lake City heights.

"See that foundation? That's where the old school-house set. Right there.

"Now that basin right straight ahead there, that's called Galena Basin. There was some prospects up there, but I don't know of any of them that were very extensive. Look at that beautiful cloud coming up there over that mountain. Isn't that beautiful? See there's a couple of them power line poles. That power plant I showed you down below had a power line. That's all that's left of them."

"The government built these corrals here for the sheep men. They hold their sheep in here, then haul them in and haul them out. That way they don't have to trail them so damn far."

"Are the Basque guys still coming in here?"

"Yeah, they're the best sheepmen of all. They come from Spain. The Bascos are always running those big bands of sheep, you know. There's still a lot of them around. By god, I'll tell you a funny thing about those Bascos.

"See, the government hired these trappers. They controlled the coyotes and all the animals so they wouldn't eat the guys' sheep. They were trapping the coyotes and the beavers and all the stuff they wanted to get rid of. Bobcats. Whatever. And they were poisoning 'em too. So these environmentalists put enough pressure on Nixon, and he decided he was going to put a stop to it. So he sent that order up to stop all poisoning and trapping on Federal lands. And he run off all the trappers. Then the coyotes got so bad that the Bascos started complaining about it. They couldn't raise any sheep. They kept putting so much pressure on Wayne Aspinall and some of our Colorado representatives that they persuaded Congress to form a committee to study the situation over, to come in here and check it out, see if they could find out what would be the answer.

"Well, they held those meetings all over the West. Some in Colorado. They had this one meeting over at Creede and all those Bascos were all there putting in all the information they could. They had a lot of stockmen at that meeting too. At that time, we had a lady representative by the name of Pat Schroeder. You know who she was. She's a very fine lady. A strong person. Well, Pat Schroeder couldn't be at the meeting but she sent one of her lady friends down there to conduct that meeting. So these Bascos, they were madder'n hell to start with, and this lady was telling all about these problems they were having and that they needed to stop the poisoning to protect the wildlife and endangered species and all that. And these Bascos kept getting' madder all the time. And this lady finally winded up saying, 'Well, I'll tell you. We've got a solution to the coyote problem. We're going to round up all these coyotes and we're gonna castrate 'em.' And this old Basco he kept getting mad and finally he got up and said, 'Lady, goddamn it. You don't understand the problem at all. These goddamn coyotes aren't screwing the sheep, goddamn it, they're eatin' 'em.'"

Perk laughed again at the telling of it.

"You look along the road here and you'll see part of that cable in just a minute. It came down from up there. Came down from the Moro Mine. The old mill set right here. See some of the steel here? They rolled that cable up in loops and took it up on a mule train."

"Once you get one end of it up there, how do you get the thing pulled snug?"

"Every five hundred feet they had these couplings called connector pipes. They pulled it tight with turn-buckles. They strung it on towers. Every once in a while they had these towers like a telephone pole to hold the cable up.

"Now this is called Cliff Creek. This is the one we're in a dispute with the government. We got those four patented mines up there. We want to trade 'em, so they sent one of their so-called 'experts' up there to check the water. He said that three of them was alright but there was one of them that had a little bit of water oozing out of it. Therefore, they were afraid it might pollute this river all the way down to Lake City. My argument is, if you come up and take a sample of the water in that stream right there — sample it before it goes into Henson Creek — and if there is anything going in there that's detrimental, that would surprise me. But they say that we got to check the quality of the water. They may turn down the whole deal. The BLM says that if we take these claims back and then later on, the EPA finds out that the tunnel needs to be sealed, that the water needs to be shut off, they don't want to take that responsibility."

"So they could come down on you and do the same thing? If they thought it was leaking something, could they make you go up there and plug them up?"

"Well, they're threatening to, but they never have done it, yet. We'd file a lawsuit over it. You see that water going all the way down Henson Creek to Lake City from all these mines? Lake City checks their water four or five times a year."

"But these miners didn't put anything toxic in the mines. That's the same water that's been running out of there since the beginning."

"Of course! Before anybody ever heard of mining. But that's the government for you. Right now, what's holding that deal up for the Vickers is the solicitor in Denver who is waiting for a report back from the water quality people. You know, Joe. I could sit there in the office with those mining reports and give you the same stories."

"It isn't as good though."

"Well, I know it. But it's a goddamned site easier."

"But if you were home, Emma Jean would make you hang out sheets or something."

"Hah! Now that's Galena Basin up there. I've never been up in that Galena Basin. God, it's beautiful. Now boy, I'll tell you, I bet that's a good place to hunt elk."

"That looks like all gravel."

"If you go up there hunting a bull elk, you're damn sure gonna hurt him getting him out of there. See that Galena Basin? You know very well that valley had never been explored much. Someday somebody is gonna find a lot of minerals that have never been found before."

"Look how much trouble it would be to get up there."

"With modern equipment you could do a lot of things you couldn't do in 1900. For sure."

"Well, there's mineral nearly everywhere up here."

"There ought to be."

"But in all your prowling around up there, elk hunting and road building, you never saw something you wanted to file on and prospect yourself?"

"No, only on top of Cinnamon Pass on that mine we already got. I exposed that vein there. That's good ore. We still got that. We got a hundred and ten acres there.

This is a beautiful site here, this Whitmore Falls. You can walk down there. They got a trail right down there."

"I could walk down there, but I'd never get out of there."

"Oh, if you walked down there, you'd goddamn sure come out. Whether you think you can or not. You can do a lot of things you think you won't do. See there how they picked this water up here out of this creek and ran it around the hill and had a hydro plant down below there? To the old Moro Mine. Some of that pipe is still there, I believe. There is an eighteen inch pipe. You can imagine, you pick that water up the river here and let it drop vertical three hundred feet, man you got one heck of a pressure. That's what hydro-electric power is all about. Just like Blue Mesa. If it wasn't for the hydro-electric power they generate and sell, the reservoir would have never been feasible in the first place.

"What did you think about them building Blue Mesa Reservoir. Did you think that was a good idea?"

"Oh, I think that was a great thing. See, what you did was take out about twenty-seven miles of choice river for sure, but when you did it was private river too. Very few people got to use it. Now they have a reservoir there that's twenty-five miles long. And according to the record every year there's about five million people use it. You know, I've always wanted to walk up to that Galena Basin. I never did, and I never will now for sure."

"You could get a helicopter."

"Oh I had a helicopter up on top of Gravel Mountain. We hired a helicopter to check that Ruby Mine out on top. You understand, I never paid no bills. I promoted someone into doing it. By god, we landed right on top of that mountain. It looks like it's sharp but right on top it flattens off to about 100 foot square. I was sitting in the back seat on the right side, another guy sitting in the front seat. They shut the engine off and the guy stepped out of the front seat. He walked out there and he started waving his arms and he hollered, 'Jesus H. Christ, get me back on this plane and get me the hell out of here. That wouldn't be my mine there.' Hell, he got back in and we drove right up. He didn't like that altitude."

"That's where the mine was, up on Gravel Mountain?"

"Yeah, we got a mine there yet, too. That's the purpose of that Chicago Tunnel. I'll show you some history on that. That's Horseshoe Basin. Now you go up to Cinnamon Pass, where our mine is, and walk around that trail by Wood Mountain and come right on down this way. That's a goddamn good hike."

"I can't hike up there. I can't breathe."

"You'll breathe. It's ironic. You think you can't breathe. See the road up behind that mine there? Over on the other side of the valley? That's the old road. That road was there a hundred years ago. The county took this road up here to get away from that bottom and that mud and stuff. Now right around here is what we call the Rosaline mill site. Just past Boulder Gulch. There where that big brick chimney is. That was put up by a German. He was gonna build a smelter there. He claimed he had a new process that could save ninety-five percent of all the gold. But he never got it completed."

Across the stream, the lone, red brick chimney stood amid alders and brush and the rubble of the ruined mill. Like the weathered shaft houses and the crumbled mill sites, the chimney, too, marked the site of another unfinished or unrealized dream that remain in this quiet place like the grave markers of stillborn children.

"By God, that chimney's put together good too. It's set there all this time. A friend of mine from Houston bought that. And he wanted to put it into the state historical society. He petitioned the Colorado State Historical Society, but the BLM wouldn't let them move that old road. No sir. The government would not let him open up the road. He took it to court, but, by God, he lost. So that chimney's still sitting there. Up there, that's

Shafer Mountain right there. And Shafer Basin there just below it."

"You been up in there?"

"No, but on top of it, we got a road on top of Cinnamon Basin. You can come right around it in a car. I don't know if the road is open now or not, but you can do it."

"Was there mining all up in here, too?"

"Oh, all the way up to the top of Engineer Mountain. That's where the Frank Hough Mine is, up on top of Engineer Mountain. The ore that come of that Frank Hough Mine was hauled all the way down Henson Creek to the railroad. You'da thought they would have gone around by Silverton. They didn't have much of a road but they probably had as good a road as this way. That's Horseshoe Basin up there on the left. That mountain right on that side, that's called Gravel Mountain. That is where the Golconda and the Pearl and Ruby Mine is. We still got that.

"I'll tell you what happened. Charlie Slocum was mining on the west slope of Horseshoe Basin, on Gravel Mountain. He started that Golconda Mine in 1908. They had a boarding house there and it was fully equipped. They stayed in there all summer and all winter. Then a snowslide came down there one winter and smashed into the boarding house and killed everybody in there, four or five different people. That shut the mine down. They shut her down for the winter, and when the summer came, the company from New York and the East decided they wasn't going to rebuild up there in Horseshoe Basin. They was going to go around in Hurricane Basin and build it and put in a tunnel. So they did.

"They go to work and they made Rose's Cabin their headquarters. They didn't have a road, but they built that trail up there to where the mine is. I built a road up there since then, but they got up there back then by horses. That tunnel goes way in about a mile to connect with this hill, damn near through that mountain. Anyway, they went through 700 foot of ice before they hit solid rock. Roy Pray opened that tunnel. He built another tunnel to the side of it and come in beyond that ice. The tunnel is full of ice now."

"You mean they were going to put a tunnel from Horseshoe Basin to Hurricane Basin?"

"From Hurricane to Horseshoe."

"Just to travel?"

"They had the ore, and they wanted to bring it out in Hurricane. They didn't want to mess with this anymore on account of the snowslide hazard."

"Boy, that's a lot of trouble."

"They went to a lot of expense. Those are beautiful aspen right there."

"That looks like a lot of water in that falls. Is that more water than you usually see for this time of year?"

"Well, this year they got more water."

"Is there a lake up in there?"

"No. There's a little pond up at the top, but no lake. You see that cable there on the right? That cable goes clear up to those cliffs. We got a mine up there called the Independence and it's connected with the Highland Chief. My dad would bring the ore out of the Independence around behind the Chief to an ore pit. They built this tramway. He'd make a deal to ship his ore down to here and put it in this ore bin. You see some of the ore here. And they'd bring that ore down in that jig-back tramway, just a heavy bucket. Like the one back there at the Pelican. When they got a shipment, then he would come up here with a wagon and load it by hand. I don't know if he did it himself or if he hired it done. If it was in the wintertime, he'd haul it by sled all the way to Lake City and shovel it in those boxcars, and ship it to Leadville, Colorado."

"What assurance would you have that your ore got off at the other end?"

"Well, you didn't. You just had to trust it. A lot of times they was getting screwed and they knew it, but they kept shipping the ore anyway. Those are big cables. Can you imagine getting those cables up on top of that? They had a horse trail right up to the top. I don't know when it was, I had a deal with El Paso Natural to take over this whole operation. The mill had been dismantled — all the machinery — but the frame was there. So they hired me to build a road up on top of the cliffs to the Empire Chief, #3 level. At that #3 level, you climb up the hill about a hundred feet and go in the tunnel and come out on the other side of the mountain on the Independence. I went through that tunnel lots of times."

"A lot of these mines are connected?"

"Connected. There's still a bunch of mine cars in there. They'll probably always be there. Up on that cliff by the Highland Chief, they had a boarding house there. It was three compartments. There was a kitchen and two bunkhouses so the night shift had a different place to sleep. And right over the cliff they had an outhouse, about six or eight foot square. Up on a sign inside that toilet, when you take a leak, it said, 'a little bit goes a long ways'. Right over the goddamned cliffs.

"When we were blasting that road over the cliff above us, we would do it in the fall and the early spring before there was any traffic. Right here we put a cable across the road here to block the road off. Nobody could go by. We'd be bulldozing up on those cliffs and here'd come the rock bouncing like you wouldn't believe. Look over there at that waterfall. You know, you've seen the Coors Beer advertisement? That's the Horseshoe Basin picture they took. That waterfall. They didn't say so, but that's what it is. I know Joe Coors. He's an old friend of mine. In fact, Joe's wife, Holly Coors, is now retired. She was our national committee woman on the Republican side. They're a great family. Look at that Horseshoe Basin. Can you imagine anything any more spectacular than that?

"*That's the only reason I'm against people building houses up in here. Everybody's got to make a living, but I don't like seeing them next to things like that waterfall.*"

"That's why the BLM is trying to get all this land. They're saying like they did to Ed Cox, 'You want some land down there by your ranch, we'll trade you.' And it's delayed the whole process, dealing with those solicitors. Now, I'll just pull in here and show you this mill. That's the Empire Chief Mill."

The square, one-windowed tower stood three stories high, its wooden siding browned the color of Lincoln Logs by time and the drying sun. The only structure of the once-busy mill that remained, it stood on a slight rise near the road like a sinister watchtower, at once a guardian to the past and, a survivor of it.

"Back then they were trying to go up there and join with that other jigback tram I just showed you. They had this one run by power, that power line down by Capitol City come all the way up here to run this mill. I've been twenty years trying to get this restored."

"See the reason we want to restore that mill is you don't see anything like that. There's some good that comes out of the government madness too, see. They got the right idea. Now we're getting it restored. I got the BLM stuck on that son-of-a-bitch. They've already put some money in it. We got 'em by the ass."

"*At one time this valley must have been crisscrossed with tramways.*"

"Well, there wasn't any tramways on that south face. They was all on this side. See how they started reinforcing that mill shaft house? They're working on this son-of-a-bitch. This is one of my main projects, to get this son-of-a-bitch restored. The reasoning behind that was it's gonna fall down some day. It's a monument. It's the only historical monument I know of between here and Silverton. There's nothing like that.

"Let's go up to the tunnel and have a look. Be sure you get all of this stuff down cause, by God, we're not coming back up here again. By the way, you know how to change tires? If we have to change a tire, you're the guy. I can't bend over."

"You know, it's been twenty years since I changed a tire and just as soon as I said that . . . ."

"Oh, shit. Shut up! By god, we'd have to look at the book. I wouldn't know how to change a tire. I don't even know where the jack is."

"What was that tower for?"

"That's part of the mill. They had four levels on that mill."

"When you're traveling down there along the stream, you don't know any of this is up here."

"Nope. And if you didn't have someone to tell you, you wouldn't understand why it was there either. That's the reason you're here. If it isn't, you're wasting your time and mine both. See what they're going to be doing now . . .the roof on the other side of that building is good. It's steel. This side they got to put a new roof on it. See they got all the materials right here. We got 'em by the ass this time. They got to finish it."

"How come they agreed to do that?"

"Historical purposes. See the BLM and the Forest Service are supposed to do everything they can to protect this Alpine Loop Trail. This Alpine Loop Trail has got national recognition. You've heard about that, of course. And the only way they're gonna get to protect it is to buy back all the land along the god damn Alpine Loop and put it back in the hands of the government."

"So they could control access?"

"So there wouldn't be any development there. They don't want any development and I can understand that. You just got through saying the same god damn thing."

"You know, sometimes I get the feeling I want this country to be my private garden. I want to be able to come up here and look at it, but I don't want anybody else around."

"If they want to straighten it out, that's what I'd like to see done. But first they got to get rid of the private landowner . . . like Vickers.

"Now that mill had an aerial tramway that headed right back up the mountain and connected with that same tunnel at that other mill where the other air tramway is.

"This is the mill site. The Empire Chief mill site, right here. If you look straight ahead, you see that mountain way over there back down the valley? See that tunnel and that dump? You see those cliffs looking right at you, in the middle here? See that little house sitting there near that dump? Way up near the top right at the base of the cliff?"

I looked where he was pointing. High on the cliff face, a small cabin teetered on a narrow rock shelf between two slide areas. A trail, looking more like a scratch at this distance, angled up out of the tree line and across the cliff to the cabin.

"Johnny and Billy Rawson had that mine. They were brothers." They built that cabin right there so the weather couldn't get him. So a snow slide couldn't wipe 'em out. They stayed there even in the wintertime. They shipped some of that ore out of there. High-grade silver ore. I don't think he made any money but in those days if you had $100 you were a rich man."

"Is that a road cut there?"

"That's no road. Just a trail. They had a burro trail up there. Those old timers was tough hombres."

"How did they get the ore down out of there?"

"Well, they went up there and worked and when they found something good they fixed up a good trail and got a burro or a mule and carried their supplies and kept right on working."

"But they went up there looking at those outcroppings?"

"They saw the outcroppings, sure. That's how they found it. They used those jackasses. You take a jackass, they could carry 200 pounds of ore down at a trip."

"It must have taken them two days to get to Lake City."

"They didn't go to Lake City. They come down with the ore and then went back up. They may have gone down to Rose's Cabin. They had supplies and restaurants there. Come up here and let's look at the tunnel."

We walked around the side of the yellow dump and climbed to its flat top. Two rusted tracks ran from the edge of the dump into the blackness of the small tunnel. Timbers boxed the tunnel entrance and a crudely lettered KEEP OUT sign was nailed to one of the posts. When I looked into the dark tunnel, cool air met my face. Water dripped into a shallow pool just inside the darkness.

"That tunnel goes in there 2,750 feet," Perk said. 'They stoped that ore out of the tunnel. They was on the vein, all the way to the surface, 3,000 feet up."

"My father used to tell me never to go in a timbered mine 'cause if it needed timbers 100 years ago, it damn sure needs them now and they're all rotten."

"That's a good philosophy."

"There's a lot of water in there."

"That's what I say. Now if there is any of the Vickers mines that have got a bad water system, I'll tell you why. That tunnel goes in there on the vein. They stoped it all the way. That would make the water have more mineral in it than the water coming out of the other side of the mountain. But the government didn't turn this one down. Why didn't they turn her down? 'Cause they want that god damn mill there."

"Now is this yours?"

"Yeah."

"Oh, I get it now. You're getting them to restore this mill then they're gonna want the property."

"That's why Cox is buying it. He's gonna trade it to the government. He don't want this damn mine. He's gonna trade it to them so he can get what he wants. Some land down in the valley."

"Why don't you just trade it to the government?"

"'Cause I didn't want to. I had nothing to trade for. He wanted that land down there and they said they wanted him to have it. They said, they'd identify some claims up Henson Creek — which are Vickers claims — if you can buy those and get 'em titled, we'll trade you for the land you want down in the valley."

As he talked, I scanned the bare mountainside. Two thousand feet above the mill site, near the timberline, traces of abandoned foot-trails zigzagged up across the talus slopes to a score of ochre mine dumps just visible at the edge of the trees. For me, those trails worn into the side of the mountain were a link with the past, as durable as an old melody, and I found myself wondering again about those men who spent their lives struggling against inclines and gravity.

When I come up into the mountains, I don't want to see people. I am much too possessive a lover to share. But I like seeing the faded traces of man on the wild land. It is important to me that people had once been there, like benevolent ghosts warming the rooms of an old house. The majesty of the mountains requires the work of men for scale. But for me, people in the mountains were a problem I have never completely resolved. Somehow it was all right for the prospectors and the miners to have been there. It was as if they were a part of the country, like the rocks themselves. It was as if history had begun with them. But the others, the ones who came later with their helicopters and their pipes and their lights, they were the interlopers, intruders, defilers in a holy place.

It is a romantic notion, and I know it. I know that the miners abused the country. I have seen the pictures, the photographs of the shaft houses, the trams, and the mills. But the wounds they left had healed. The timbered slopes they had stripped stump-bare had regrown, the smoke from their mill fires had cleared away, and their trash had decomposed. The reality of their offenses was gone. Their careless muddy tracks in the garden were overgrown.

"There are roads all over up there," I said.

"There's trails all up in there, but no roads. No roads on that side of the mountain between here and the Pride of America."

"All these places in here were developed in the 1870s and 1880s, when the first mining boom started?"

"That's right."

"And they have just been swapping hands since then?"

"They were working around here 'til about 1929 when the crash came and that did it. Shut 'er down. Every one left the country."

"They were producing mostly what?"

"Silver and copper. A lot of copper. In those days copper wasn't worth a damn."

We walked back down the dump toward the car.

"Boy that's a god damned bad rock in the road there. If you was to hit that you'd be there for the rest of the day. Probably have to buy a new car."

"I always thought that a mill went with a specific mine, but from what you say, sometimes a group would get together and build the mill and do the milling for lots of mines."

"That's what they call custom milling. We never had much custom milling in this country. Most of the mills that was here was built for a very specific mine. This was built for the Empire Chief."

"That must have cost a lot of money."

"Oh, hell. Money didn't mean anything to some of them guys in those days. Now, it's a different story. In Silverton they had custom mills. They'd build a custom mill to handle all kind of complex ore. And they would buy the ore from you, see. That's a custom mill.

"A lot of those mills had what they call an automatic sampler. You'd run your ore through there, and they'd run it through the automatic sampler, and then they'd show you how much they thought it would run. And if you were satisfied they'd give you a check right there. If you weren't satisfied, you'd have to have another sample run and get some guy to umpire. An independent man to umpire and maybe get it settled."

"Pretty rough estimate."

Perk steered carefully around the rock he had pointed out and continued up the road.

"This is where Rose's Cabin was. Right here in this clearing. They had a headquarters. Rose had a hotel right here."

"So what you see there, what's left of that log building, that was just the barn?"

"That's right. They'd bring the stuff all the way up here from Lake City by pack horse and pack mules. They stored it here. When they needed some of that stuff up at the mine, they would carry it up by mule."

"Was Rose's Cabin a private enterprise?"

"This guy, Rose, had a hotel here, a halfway station. I suppose he had some kind of a deal. Whether he ever owned the land or not, I don't know. See those logs? That was a horse barn. Look at those logs how they sawed them and squared 'em off. Each of them god damned logs is worth a lot of money. That was the stable. A big cabin was right there. I got a picture of that house. It had twenty-two rooms in it."

"Who salvaged the lumber out of Rose's Cabin?"

"A guy by the name of Townsend. He built that house up there by the Baptist church. Tore all the lumber out. Well, we used to come up here years ago, when I was fifteen years old. My dad would make a deal with somebody that wanted to make a horseback trip. They'd drive out to the ranch and we'd ride the horses up the road, all the way up here. Spend the night right here. And we'd bring enough groceries to spend the night. Then we'd meet the guys the next morning and we'd saddle up the horses and we'd ride up that trail through Horseshoe Basin to Horse Thief Trail to Ouray and spend the night in Ouray at the hotel.

"That was a beautiful hotel. The Beaumont Hotel. Johnny Donalds had a livery stable in Ouray. He was a very prominent transfer man there. I was over there a couple or four or five years ago and you wouldn't even know that livery stable was there. It was right there on the river. I suppose all that manure went right in the creek. It's a different story nowadays. We'd go down to the livery stable in the morning and get the horses and bring them up to the hotel and ride 'em back over the hill."

"How far is that, about twenty miles?"

"It's about fifteen miles. And they're all there too. Now here next to Rose's Cabin, they had a boarding house right here. That was the Empire Chief boarding house. See that snowslide path up there across the stream? One time snowslide come down there, and knocked into that boarding house and killed four guys. It come across the road. The people got to the boarding house and started digging. They found the four bodies, one at a time, and they brought them out. Finally, about three or four days later they found two guys alive. One was a guy by the name of Strayer. He was in the boarding house sleeping when that slide hit. I worked with him on the road for four or five years after that. He had one eye. The other was a glass eye. First one I ever saw. He said he could hear them digging, but he couldn't talk to them. He was in there under the bedsprings. That's the only thing that saved him. It created a little air pocket. The air will go through the snow.

"I remember when they brought those dead guys downtown. I was going to high school. They was frozen stiff. They brought them down by sled and took them to where the Lake City restaurant is now, Ol' Tom Beam, "Elk" Beam they called him, had what he called an undertaker's shop there. They brought 'em down and put 'em there on the table at Elk Beam's place. I remember those guys laying there. They looked like dead people. That's the first time I remember seeing any dead guys. I remember there was four guys by the name of Wickersham, Kohler, Cutting and Johnson. Four guys. Isn't it funny how I remember those names? Can you imagine a man remembering that back from the time I was sixteen or seventeen? Well, it impressed me. It's too bad I can't figure out some way to replace some memories with ones that are more worthwhile. But it ain't that way."

"It's stuck in there."

"Yeah, but how do you get it out?"

"You can't get it out if you want to. You can only get it out if you don't want to. Now what's that road scratched up on the side of that place up there?"

"Joel Swank did some of that. He did some of that for uranium. Just this side of that road, up that gulch, there's another mine called the Chipmunk. And the Dolly Varden. That's Dolly Varden Mountain right there at the head of that creek. I built a lot of roads up there for Roy Pray. Built five miles of road up there. It's still there, but it's not usable any more. That Gravel Mountain up there, that's a big mountain. Up on top we got the Pearl and Ruby and that's the purpose of that Chicago tunnel."

"Horse Thief Trail, where does that take off?"

"Horse Thief Trail takes off just before you get to the top of Engineer Mountain. It's a good horse trail. It's narrow, but it's a beautiful horse trail. You get down that trail and you hit Highway 550 about a mile from Ouray."

"What about the road that comes from Ouray back over this way?"

"That comes up just to the other side of Engineer Mountain. That's called Poughkeepsie Gulch. That's the road they use all the time. It goes down about half way to Animas Forks. If you turn right you go to Ouray. If you turn left you go down to Animas Forks and Silverton."

"But Horse Thief Trail cuts off this side of the summit."

"Just over the ridge, you see it go right down. That's American Flats all the way across here clear past Uncompahgre. That's where they graze the sheep."

"Is that where the Horse Thief Trail goes down?"

"That's part of it. See, right up here is the Palmetto Mine. And just above that is the Frank Hough mine. They're all right up here just this side of Engineer Mountain. You go right up here about a mile and cross the river, that's Hurricane Basin. Just inside the timber, a road goes back here to the Chicago Tunnel. That goes back in

2,500 feet. That was started in 1890 to penetrate veins to the Ruby Pearl. It goes right in the mountain to try to penetrate those veins up on top. If they had continued, they would have come out in Cleveland Basin. According to the map, if that tunnel were to go in there another 800 or 900 feet, and those veins came down that deep, and continued to have the ore that they have on top, you'd have a multimillion dollar gold and silver mine."

"And you'd just stope the whole thing?"

"I've been trying to do that for years but I never got the money."

"Why do they call it the Chicago Tunnel?"

"I think there was a group of people from Chicago started that tunnel. They had a boarding house up in there. A good boardinghouse. They discontinued working that tunnel in 1932, in May, and the reason I can remember that is it was the year I graduated from high school.

"One of the guys working up there at the Chicago Tunnel was a guy by the name of Roy Pray. Roy Pray had some associates — they were all from Canyon City. That one guy by the name of Campbell, Joe Campbell, he liked my older sister. Well, she didn't like him, but anyway, he come by our house up by the church there. He'd bring up cokes and cheeses we never heard of in our life. He tried to promote us, see. Anyway, my sister moved to California, and the mine shut down. Campbell married a local girl in Denver. His son's got an RV court up by the lake."

"People always come back here, don't they?"

"They come back, very seriously, even if they can't afford to. They always come back."

"Now the trail to Hurricane Basin goes up through the timber there."

"You go up here about a half a mile and the road forks, and you go right down and cross the river an go right up into the heavy timber."

"That cabin on the left side of the road in Palmetto Gulch, what is that?"

"Old cabin? That's sheepherders headquarters. Now Cary Finn, just this side of Dolly Varden Mountain, he's trying to sell that house I know. He wants $450,000 for it. It's a beautiful house though. It's a lot of money, but it's not too much to people that's got money. You get a guy to try to promote that, get the right guy up there, give him a couple of drinks and T-bone steak dinner, he'd give you a check right off the bat. Anyway, that house has got propane tanks underground. He uses sunrays to heat the batteries. He's got toilets. He's got a cable bridge to get across to it. You got to walk across the bridge to get to it. I've got a key to it. I've come up and spent the night with him two or three times. He's a good friend of ours. He's down there in Dallas where he's opened up a new business and got tied up on that."

"Well, maybe he'd need us to go up there and watch after it?"

"Hell, about three days and you'd get homesick. Some people still own that Golconda. I tried to make a deal, but they're hard-nosed to do business with."

"That looks like smoke up there. Someone's camping."

Next to the stream in a copse of trees a makeshift tent had been set up next to an aging pickup. We drove up to campsite and a man came over to greet us.

"How ya' doing?" he asked.

"Well, at least I'm not lost," Perk replied, "and that's more than you can say. My name is Vickers. We got a ranch down in town."

"Yeah, I know you, Perk."

"Well, who the hell are you?"

"Jim Sayerds. I used to drive. I was hauling ore off your property from that mine there."

"The Golden Wonder?"

"Yeah."

"How about that? This is Joe Wise. What the hell are you doing up here?"

"I was just doing a little brookie fishing. Hiding out from the old lady mostly."

"Where are you from?"

"I live in Lake City."

"Well, where's your place in Lake City?"

"I'm renting ol' Van Warner's house there. The one with the hot tub in front of it."

"I know where it is. Well, I didn't recognize you at all. We just come up here. Mr. Wise is putting together a memorandum on the history of these mines as I know them. I know the history of all these mines and when I die, there's no history left. I'm the only one left."

"Well, did Swank die?"

"No, he didn't move over here 'til all the mines shut down. He's still here yet, and he's a good man."

"I've done a little work up there for him. I understand your wife hurt herself."

"She fell out of bed and broke her neck. She's doing alright, but it's a slow process."

"Are they gonna have to operate on her?"

"We don't know yet. We're waiting for an appointment with a specialist down in Grand Junction to see what he says. They got it in a brace now. If that's a healin', she's alright, but if it ain't healing, she might have to have surgery."

"In '91 I done that," the camper said. "I wrecked a truck out in Barstow, California, on a pipeline job. A gas pipeline job. The road gave out and the truck fell off and I flew out of the seat and hit my head on the bottom of the cab. Cabover International."

"Well, I'd better get back down the road."

"Well, I'd offer you some coffee."

"No thanks. You want some dynamite for those fish?" Perk asked with a mischievous grin.

"You got any?"

"I bet you there's some fish in that pond there."

"Oh, I've caught a slew of fish out of there in the past. I just haven't got down there to do it yet. I come up here last night. 'Bout froze to death last night. I'm gonna see if it's any better tonight."

"It won't be much warmer here. But those fish ought to be brookies. They ought to be pretty fat. Just the right size for a good frying pan."

"They fight like a booger, too. I snagged one and it took me ten minutes to land it. Caught him by the tail."

"Well, it's good to see you. Thanks for remembering me."

"Yeah. Well, I'm the one you got on to for coming across your bridge too heavy. You remember me, now?"

"With that goddamned old overloaded truck and screwing up my bridge. I didn't remember you, but I know you musta done it."

"Well, I couldn't tell how much they was puttin' in that truck. Gold ore."

"Well, they're still mining but they're not shipping by the truck load. They're sacking it."

"You know, the last time I drove by the mill that ore was still sitting there where I dumped it."

"I should have a royalty coming out of that. But that mill's over with. They'll never run that mill again. Every time we started that mill we lost money. That Ute-Ulay Mill. Small world isn't it? Glad I saw you, anyhow. I didn't know anybody could ever recognize me except by my nose, and my hat's down over my nose so I didn't think you'd recognize me."

"I like your hat."

"Thank you." Perk waved and we drove away. "Now, ain't that something?"

"Guys still have to get away, don't they?"

"Oh yeah. You know this is one of the finest campsites you'll ever find. It's a nice spot here. Look at that weather up on the pass. That looks like snow."

"I'm not interested in driving on Engineer Pass in a snow storm."

"I'd say that's good judgment. Let's go on back to town. We can come back up there some other time."

"Fine with me."

"You know, I told you a while ago I went up here and built a road to that Chipmunk Mine. You look out there on top of that mountain. You see a road going right around the ridge? That goes over to the mine that they did a lot of core drilling on. Silver ore. It didn't pay off."

"Looks like they could mine that by helicopter."

"They probably could, but those choppers are expensive."

We crossed a boggy spot where a beaver dam had backed the water onto the road.

"How do you tell a beaver house from a muskrat house?"

"That's a big house there. A muskrat couldn't begin to build a house like that. It's beautiful isn't it?

"That's Golconda Mine, it's right up at the head of this basin."

"Can you get across that bridge there?"

"You can't cross that. That's on Gammage's property. But you can go right up here to where the road forks, and cross the river and come right to the Chicago Tunnel. That's where that guy died the other day."

"Was there gas in the tunnel?"

"Wasn't any gas at all. He just run out of oxygen. You walk into a tunnel so far and if the air ain't there you're dead. We always recommend carrying a candle. As long as that burns, you're safe."

"Either that or a parakeet."

"That's right. But we never had many parakeets," he said, with a wink. "Any way, the purpose of that Chicago Tunnel was to from Horseshoe Basin cause Horseshoe Basin got the snow."

"When did the road open up over Engineer Pass?"

"Aw, generally about the first part of June."

"No, I mean what year?"

"Oh god, I don't remember. They took stages over it in the 1880s. Said the crossing on top was just about wide enough for one stage. They re-opened it, I'd say in the '50s."

"And that was mainly for jeep trips?"

"Yeah."

"Boy, the back side of that pass is slick, isn't it? I don't like going down that back side."

"Well, the other side is the most dangerous side of the whole trip."

"I go up Cinnamon and come up the other side."

"You're better off. There's Dolly Varden Mountain now. You see that color. You know, I never get tired of coming up to this damn place."

"I got to come here every time. Yeah, I'm just like a salmon going upstream. I've just got to come up here and take a look."

"Nothing like the mountains."

A group of motorbikes angrily roared past us in a cloud of dust.

"Perk, I wish you'd get rid of those motor bikes."

"Well, there's gonna be a meeting tomorrow night, and I may have to attend that meeting. I know it's the next day or two."

"I don't think they're up here for the right reason. They're just up here to ride a rough road. They could ride a rough road anywhere they don't have to come up here and make noise."

"The ATVs are not as bad. It's those mountain motorbikes; it's those son-of-a-bitches that tear up the country."

"And you can hear them for twenty miles."

"Yep. That's right. They're hazardous to the wildlife and everything else."

"My father used to like coming up Henson to fish. That was his favorite place."

"Oh, yes. It was always good fishing. It's still pretty good fishing, I guess."

"But you can't get in the water anywhere now. It's all private."

"Oh, you can get in most of it. Some parts of it by the mine you can't. Supposedly, most of it you can get to."

"I remember they used to have cutthroat trout."

"Oh yeah. Cutthroats are not as plentiful anymore because Colorado hasn't had much luck reproducing them. But I'll agree. They're one of the most beautiful fish we have ever had."

"Now, how about that whirling disease?"

"No whirling disease up here. The falls stops the fish from coming up from the reservoir. We didn't stock any. Lucky. They have discovered something in the water that causes it. They claim that it's a certain type of parasite that comes in with a certain kind of water. Now, instead of getting water out of the river, they're getting it out of wells. Now, they use well water in the hatcheries. They say they're gonna have that licked in about another year and a half. We'll soon find out. I just fish once a year, now. In a pond on the upper ranch in June. We stock those ponds. We pay $3.00 a half pound for fingerlings. You know, you can buy the same trout in the store for $1.50 a pound all ready for the frying pan."

"Did you ever get bad fish from the hatcheries?"

"No. We never did. We've been lucky."

"So all this whole area never did get any fish with whirling disease?"

"No, but the Lake Fork has them all down through but not up past Lake City on account of the falls."

"So they never got in the lake?"

"Nope. Not that I know of. See I built a road over there. That mine across the bridge, that's called the Edna. That's all government land. I had that, but I let that go back. I didn't want to pay the assessment fees. It went back to the government."

"So when your dad was working up in here, there were five or six hundred people working between here and Engineer Mountain?"

"Oh, yes. Between Engineer Mountain down into Lake City there was probably a thousand miners working in there.

"Ever seen that house down there in the woods? That's a shingle roof. That's the reason it's kept so good all these years. Have to cross the river to get there. There never was a bridge."

Coming back down the canyon it was easier to see the little cabin halfway up the cliff face between the slides that Perk had pointed out when we were at the millsite.

"I just can't believe anybody is living up there."

"By god, they did just the same. He's right at the bottom of that formation. His intentions were to run that tunnel clear under the workings above to see if that ore came down. Same as the Golconda. Like the Chicago tunnel."

"That's a helluva long walk to Lake City just for a newspaper."

"God damn if it isn't. Aw, it would surprise you, people in those days, what they had to do."

"When did he get out of there?"

"I imagine about 1920 or '30. He was up there a long time. For years."

"You hear a lot about claim jumping in the old West."

"Oh, there was always people getting in trouble jumping claims."

"Was that going on around here?"

"Oh, it was going on. People were getting killed over claim jumping."

"You got a line in your book that says, 'It wasn't all pretty.'"

"That's true. In those days you had to live with what you had. You didn't think much. We didn't have a helluva lot, and we didn't expect much. Nowadays it's different. I say right now, there's no hope for the satisfied man. If this country ever gets into a depression like we had in the '30s, there'd be an Indian uprising here that would kill half the people. Hope it never happens.

"Well, you see a lot of these prospectors, they'd get in here and find something good and spend a lifetime trying to open it up."

"So is all the ore here is in quartz?"

"A lot of it is what you call rhyolite."

"So they could recognize it easily when they got to it."

"Oh, yeah."

"Probably looks different when it's under the ground."

"Oh, yeah. But you can see it, the minute you walk in."

"Now how did they work those mines if there wasn't any oxygen down there?"

"Most of the time they'd run a tunnel in. They'd go a hundred feet and if they still had the vein, they generally follow it up right to the surface. There's two reasons for that. One reason would be for ventilation. The other reason, they might find good ore in the process of doing it."

"How come there is gas in some of these mines now when there wasn't when they were working it?"

"They had an air line that went in there. They had a compressor pumping the air in to run their rock drills. They had plenty of air going in. If you go in that Chicago tunnel — I've been in there two or three times, — you got to take an air compressor so you can explore. Some of those rails are still in there. For the first four hundred feet there are no rails. Somebody stole all the rails up to four hundred feet. That's as far as they could have air when they stole the rails. The rest of the way, the rails are all there. If you're walking in there, when the rails start, for Christ's sake don't go no further.

"See those mines over there? That is what they call Ragged Mountain. That's up above Henson. You see a lot mines up on that hill. That's the Capital City and the Czar and the Czarina. There are roads all up in there."

"Are you still having cookouts up at the Upper Ranch?"

"Every Wednesday."

"Are you going up tonight?"

"Yeah. Sure am. If the weather holds. Are you gonna be here?"

"Yes. That's a pretty view up there at that site."

"Oh Christ, that's outstanding. You'll get some good pictures up there, and I'll give you some good information while you're up there."

"Is Emma Jean coming?"

"Oh, I don't know, that cold air would make her neck so stiff. She has a hard time sleeping at night. I feel sorry for her. Just gets three hours of slecp a night. I get up every hour and go in there and check on her three or four times during the night to see how she's doing. If I catch her asleep, I'll go back to bed, otherwise I'll set around there. You know, a guy hates to go to bed and wake up and find his wife's dead."

"It's gonna take more than a broken neck to kill her."

"Oh, she's tough as hell. Tough ol' girl. It's six weeks now. We got two more weeks before we go to that specialist. What do you suppose he'll do? The x-ray we got we're gonna' take with us."

"He'll just x-ray it and make sure it's healing right."

But the weather didn't hold, so the cookout was held in the Rec Hall next to the ranch office — the building built from logs taken from the original Vickers' house at the Upper Ranch. About fifty people showed up, and brought a covered dish and their own steaks to be cooked outside on the grill.

After dinner, Emma Jean, in her neck brace, played "Amazing Grace" and "How Great Thou Art" on the piano. Everybody sang and afterwards Perk said, "Emma Jean knows two songs and I like both of them."

As I left, Perk handed me some papers.

"Here. Take these back to your place and read them. It's all about the ranch here. And the Upper Ranch. And the Golden Wonder. We'll go up there tomorrow."

PART FOUR

THE UPPER RANCH AND THE GOLDEN WONDER MINE

*"It's About As Close To Heaven
As A Man Can Get"*

Denver Post Empire Magazine 11/21/76
Land for Sale: Bodies Included

"The oldest abstract titles show that much of the land along the Lake Fork in the Lake City area was part of a placer mining claim with considerable turnover. In 1887, a 22-year-old Canadian named John Vickers joined the mining scene. After working the mines in Butte, Montana, Vickers visited an uncle in the Crested Butte area of Colorado who touted him on Lake City because "that's a good place to fish." Vickers expanded into another business — a saloon, a restaurant and bowling alley. In 1899 he married the 17 year old daughter of a railroad man who helped bring the tracks to Lake City. Health problems turned him to an outdoor life and John and Vera Vickers began horse ranching at Horse Park at the foot of nearby Cannibal Plateau in 1914. The growing family — there would be 6 boys and 2 girls — lived in town during the harsh winters. In 1920 Dan McLeod sold Vickers about 110 acres along the Lake Fork. The stream meanders through the property for more than a mile beginning just south of the Packer massacre site. McLeod had been on the land for many years and he conveyed it to Vickers by a simple quit claim deed. A common and usually effective means of transferring property, a quit claim deed conveys all "the owner's legal interest" whatever it is. It is not a deed guaranteeing a clear title. In 1922 Vickers bought a mining claim which had been located on the property in 1917. In the 1930s additional mining claims were filed by Vickers and his sons.

The county assessor suggested at one point that Vickers check out the title because the property wasn't being assessed. The records suggested it might be federal land. Tax sales certificates showed that improvements were sold and not the land and those improvements were listed under a column titled "Value of Improvements on Public Land."

No one challenged the Vickers title, and in 1929 the first of 19 cabins was built on the Lake Fork frontage to begin a dude ranch operation that would become the primary source of income. Cattle and hay raising continued, the latter being stopped only this year.

John Vickers died at the age of 90 in 1955 and his widow, Vera, conveyed the property to three sons, Perk, Joseph and Robert who continued the business as "Vickers Brothers." The mother's transfer was by warranty deed. It fell on the family's Denver attorney, Robert Knous, (then soon to become Colorado Lt. Governor) to break the news to them. They didn't have a clear title.

Despite a clear line of ownership for more than half a century, and despite the large amount of improvements on which taxes were paid, the land still belonged to the U.S. Even the U.S. could not have sold it to them because it was included in a 1927 withdrawal for federal water project No. 857.

The lawyers decided to first approach the Federal Power Commission to withdraw its old withdrawal and restore the land for public disposition. They ruled favorably on this on Feb. 25, 1958.

They then applied for the property under a 1928 law called "the Color of Title Act" claiming that they had held the property in good faith and in "peaceful adverse possession" for more that 20 years.

This was denied by the BLM citing that Vickers must have known that the land was owned by the U.S., citing the Hinsdale County assessor's records. This

*suggested that the Vickers knew that they did not have
title to the land and the application was rejected.*

*Appeals were rejected, and Vickers went to
Washington to contact Colorado Congressman Wayne
Aspinall and Senator Gordon Allott, and to Interior
Secretary Seaton.*

*Seaton said that the family should be given ample
time to get off the land and remove all the improvements
— to which Vickers responded that they had better come
with help because his brother was an experienced army
veteran.*

*In 1961 Aspinall and Allott each submitted a spe-
cial bill to their respective chambers requiring the
Secretary to sell the property to Vickers. It was sold as
157 acres. Congress approved the measure on Sept. 5,
1961. It was signed by Kennedy. It provided a U.S.
patent for the Vickers Brothers after they paid the
appraised value of the property and penalties for pro-
longed trespass. The total was $18,331. Vickers bor-
rowed the money and paid for it."*

I met Perk the next morning at his office. He opened his
door just as I was about to knock. "Morning, Joe. Did
you read that article I gave you?"

"That's quite a story."

"It is for a fact. By god, I thought we'd never get that
straightened out. Joe, I got to thinking. You know what
we need to do now. I want to tell you about some of
these nearby mines on the property. Like the Rob Roy.
They shipped some gold from it, but I don't know to
what extent. We'll drive over there. The Monte Queen
has a lot of history on it. They shipped a lot of ore from
that damn thing."

*"We got out of that high country yesterday just in time,
didn't we?"*

"Yeah, I talked to some guys who said it snowed about
four inches on top. We got out of there just right."

The office that serves as both Perk's office and the office for the tourist business is on the first floor of the house that Perk's father bought from McLeod. The walls of the office are covered with large aerial maps and photographs of the ranch, of elk hunts and high country jeep trips. A deer head hangs from the wall above a counter that divides the room. Behind the counter, Perk's desk is crowded into a corner under four mounted trophy trout and beside a bookshelf cluttered with rocks, ore samples and other memorabilia. Perk settled at the desk, leaned back in the spring back chair and put one boot on the corner of the desk.

"Those fish come from here?" I asked, indicating the fish mounted over his desk.

"This one came from just below the bridge. Emma Jean's brother caught that one. Bob and I caught that one in Waterdog Lake through a hole in the ice. That one came from over there above the bridge a long time ago."

"I'd like to make another pass through town, and sometime I'd like to get up to the Golden Wonder."

"We'll go up there this morning after this weather clears off. Well, let's see. Want to go down by Lake City first? I called Grant Houston's office. They are finding us a copy of that article in the *Silver World* about the Golden Wonder. That's important. You ought to read that into the record 'cause there's a lot of history in that Golden Wonder mine. Lawsuit after lawsuit."

"I read about the Chicago Tunnel. That's fascinating."

"That Chicago Tunnel, it's too bad they never got the finances to penetrate that tunnel. 700 feet more. Now, you're gonna put some of that in your report just the same as if I told you.

"You know about the history of this house. It was built in the '80s. Dan McLeod built this two-story ranch house."

"I always thought this house came down from the Upper Ranch."

"No. The rec hall did. That's where we have the cookouts if the weather is bad. We tried to have a restaurant there, but it didn't work out. Dan McLeod was the guy that built the highway bridge down there. He was a great carpenter. This house is built out of logs."

"Those are great aerial photographs. I'm always surprised that country up on top of those mountains is so bare. If you showed somebody that, they would say you're in the desert. I guess that's the thing that surprised me most about the mountains. They look so sharp from a distance, but they're so flat on top when you get up there."

"You're exactly right. Here's a picture of Deer Lakes."

"What did they do that for? To hold up the water?"

"For recreation. We did that for fishing. Here's a picture of Cinnamon Basin. My dad had a house right there. That old building was still there at this time. See that old house? That's the boarding house I was telling you about. That's right where we were yesterday. This one is the Upper Ranch. We got nine ponds up there. This is that balanced rock, in Sparling Gulch. Just above the VC Bar. Old Jackson had that VC Bar. Those god dammed kids of his shot that rock, kept shooting at it and it fell off. Here's Quiet Valley."

"Where's that?"

"Just over the hill just this side of Spring Creek in what we call now the Oleo Ranch."

As if a thought had just occurred to him, Perk eased his foot from the corner of the desk and stood up. "Let's go into town a get a cup of coffee."

We walked out to get in the car and drove to town. Everyone in the cafe knew Perk and spoke to him. He asked about their families. They asked about Emma Jean.

"Now that Carson we were talking about," he said, stirring his coffee, "that's one of the older mining camps in the country. They had that way back there. They started shipping that ore off the surface just over the top. More or less over on the south side. That's right on the Continental Divide. That was the St. Jacobs Mine. That's where the high-grade silver comes from. They sorted that

ore and carried it over the ridge just to where Carson is.
Then they brought it down that old wagon roads on
mules and horses down to Child's Park. Colonel Meeks is
supposed to have started that Carson. He built that big
building there. That was an eight or ten-room house."

"I always thought that was a hotel."

"I don't know if it was a hotel or not, but he probably
used it for some of his mining associates. You've heard of
George Corey Franklin, I'm sure. He's written a lot of
books about Colorado. I don't know if he owned the mine
or not, but he had a guy by the name of Wes Lee who was
carrying that ore from Carson down to Child's Park.
When they got down that shaft, I don't know, maybe 400
feet, the ore was good, but the water was pouring in. They
retimbered that time and again, but pressure on the side
walls of the vein was so strong, it kept breaking the timbers. So they come back on this side of the mountain —
that was old Carson on that side — so they come on this
side and started Carson, George III and some of the other
mines in that group. They run a tunnel right in the
mountain. That was George III."

*"What was the shaft on the other side of the mountain
called?"*

"The St. Jacobs. So they got down and set up Carson.
Man they did a pile of underground work there. The evidence shows it. They had a steam boiler. Those steam
boilers didn't come up from Lake City. They came up
from Creede and, man, how they got 'em over that
Continental Divide to Carson. They come up west Lost
Trail, all that way. They had to be tugged on skids by
mules and horses. Probably two or three feet at a time.
You know, when you think of people like that, they did
that by hard physical work. Now, you'd just take a bulldozer and drag it right up."

"When did that mining district get started?"

"That had to be going strong by 1910. They were mining silver. Just silver. Then it shut down. Although, Joel

Swank tells me, he spent a lot of money up there reopening that mine — he's part owner of Carson now. Joel did a lot of backhoe work on the outside where he found a couple of veins. He opened up the George III. I think he told me some of that would run in gold. And right down below that big building, they had a post office. Imagine. A post office. They had regular daily mail, believe it or not. They have restored that post office to some extent. Just south of the post office, they had a big mule barn. It's still got the tongue and groove ceilings in there. Man, you think about the excitement there. That was before my time, but I'm just telling you what I remember hearing.

"My dad had a partner by the name of Gus Zacharias. Zacharias was associated with Carson, and he was associated with my dad in four or five different mining ventures — the Cleveland and the Armitage there just this side of the Golden Fleece Mine. All those guys, my dad and others, they generally took advantage of those great engineers like Zacharias and Mr. J. D. Fisher. J.D. Fisher was brought here right out of Scotland University for that mine up Henson Creek, the Frank Hough. He was their engineer."

"Did the engineers tell the mining companies how to find the ore?"

"No, they didn't find it. Most of those veins were found by some prospector. And he'd promote it, so to speak. And when he promoted it, he got a hold of a company or somebody that had the money and they'd get a hold of some engineer like Zacharias. There was a lot of them around here. Those engineers told you how to operate."

"So, they told you how to do the tunneling."

"Well, they didn't tell you how to do the tunneling, but they told you how to run the tunnel on the vein. They told you about the fault fissures and the cross veins. A lot of times, when you start working on those fissures, when you go in on 'em, you might find where one vein intersected another vein. A lot of times that's where you find the best ore. You take the Golden Wonder where that east and west vein intersected that north and south vein, that's what made that extremely rich ore.

"That's what we worked on. We concentrated most of our work between the surface and that #3 level on that intersection. That's where the gold was. You get away from that intersection, fifty or sixty feet and all you had was a little vein with nothing in it."

"When you talk about the vein, you don't mean the ore but where the ore would be if there was any."

"A vein is just a mineralized streak. There are more veins that don't have anything than there are that have something in them. Up and down the Lake Fork, all over the San Juans, you got all kinds of veins."

"So, these mining engineers were really geologists, too."

"Oh, that's what they were. They were miners and geologists. That was part of their education. Like the Colorado School of Mines. We've got a lot of people graduated from there. By the way, that Colorado School of Mines is rated as one of the best geological schools in the world."

"Who discovered that Carson area?"

"I don't know for sure. Corey Franklin had a lot to do with that. He may have made one of the original discoveries, although I don't know. That's a way back."

(I later learned that Christopher J. Carson staked claim to the Bonanza King and the district, named for him, was established in 1881. A single year's record for the St. Jacob's, the best gold property, was $190,000. By 1902, the district was abandoned.)

"One time I think you said that a man by himself could get down about forty feet, and that was the end of it. After that it took equipment."

"We run a shaft on the Golden Wonder down about twenty-five feet with a bucket and windlass, but when you get down past thirty or forty feet, then you have to put a headframe and you got to have power to run the hoist."

"Well, what's gonna happen now? Is somebody gonna come in here and open all these mines up?"

"Right now, there's not much mining going on in the San Juans. As a matter of fact, the mines are pretty well all shut down. Even that Sunnyside Mine over in Silverton. Sunnyside Mine now is ancient history. Now, they're making it into a museum. Even those tailing ponds are being re-vegetated."

"So they've given up."

"Given up," he nodded. "There may be a few prospectors in Silverton, but I don't know of any."

"And all that Red Mountain district?"

"There's talk in the BLM to get all that into wilderness. There's gonna be a big fight about that. They're gonna take it away from the mining companies. There's some areas, right here in the Lake City area, where BLM is making arrangements to trade the land somebody else wants, like that Ed Cox wants, for some of the owners to get away from the Alpine Loop. BLM will go to John Doe and say we'll identify some of the land that we want along that Alpine Loop, and if you arrange to buy it, we'll trade you some land you might want. It makes some sense, because here's a landowner down in the valley who wants to expand his holdings and they get some of the government land to do it. You can't buy it. They can't sell it but they can trade."

"You think they will ever pave the Alpine Loop?"

"Oh, I doubt it. Some of those landowners with fancy homes say that we're getting the road between here and Silverton in too good shape. Too much traffic. I halfway agree with some of that. But I think we need to fix it, some of the chuckholes. I'm not talking about paving it, but make it a little safer. That road we went up yesterday, to the top of Tobasco mill, on top of Cinnamon Pass, is extremely dangerous. Somebody's gonna get killed. If they stall it going up a steep grade, kill the engine and have to start that engine, they're in trouble. If you take your foot off the brake and the clutch at the same time you got no way of getting at the gas. An automatic transmission is safer, but if you got an ordinary pickup without a hand throttle, you're blowed up. Every pickup I've had for many years I've ordered with a hand throttle. You sit there, start it and pull out the hand throttle and get the engine wound up enough and then put it in gear and go. The hand throttle will get you around the corner. Otherwise you're liable to get killed.

"I went to that BLM meting last night. They had about a hundred people there. They were there primarily to get some insight in regard to the Alpine Loop and the ATVs and the motorbikes. Oh, there were so many different ideas. I didn't say a damn thing. Wasn't any use for me to say anything. A lot of people wouldn't agree with me. Let me tell you why. A lot of these people come in here to Lake City and buy them a home, or buy them a piece of land. They got the home they have invested in. They come in and buy a snowmobile and motorcycles and all this stuff. They expect they got the right to use their land. That's what they expect. They say, 'It's our land. We ought to be able to use it.' And those guys are only here a very brief time and little they know about what we have to be confronted with, the rest of us, over the next hundred years. You got to protect that land. You can use that land in an orderly way, but you can't cross it with a motorcycle and ride up Cinnamon Pass. I know a lot of these guys. I didn't say nothing. I know how they feel. They come out here and they want to use it. It's their land."

"Coming down from Henson yesterday after I left you I passed about thirty, maybe forty, of those dirtbikes."

"Now the government, they're gonna control whether the people like it or not."

"Do you think they will distinguish between the bikes and the four-wheelers?"

"Oh, I don't know, but they should. The four-wheel drive OHV, they're not gonna do much damage. They got big wide tires and have very little air in them. You know. They can float across the top of the ground and not do much damage. But the motorbikes, they will cut a trench right up the mountain, spinning and throwing rocks back 100 feet behind them. They can outlaw those things altogether. I don't know what they're gonna' do. It's a ticklish situation. Now you've got our senator, Wayne Allard. I just visited with him. It's his first term in the U.S. Senate. He makes a trip to the area about once or twice a year. I have been encouraging him to put the pressure on the Forest Service and the BLM in regard to this wilderness study. In Hinsdale County we've got 300,000 acres they put into wilderness study. The whole area. And that's been sitting there under that study, I'll say, for twenty years."

"What are they studying?"

"They're studying to see if it's suitable for wilderness. It's a WSA — a Wilderness Study Area. If it meets the criteria that they think they want, they'll put it into wilderness. Now there's some good about some of that. They'll take a couple of hundred thousand acres and make it into wilderness. My point is this, that our senator should say to the Forest Service, 'Now look, you guys have been studying that for twenty years. If it doesn't meet your particular criteria, put it back into multiple use concepts.'

"And a lot of people don't want that to happen because they know as long as it's under study, nobody can touch it. No roads. No trails. No nothing. One guy last night that got up and talked about the roads. 'We need more roads,' he said. One of the guys, my best friends in our subdivision, he says, 'This is our land. We got to build more roads so old folks and people with crutches can get to it.'

"Now you go up Henson Creek and I'll show you. You leave Lake City and go right up the road, you go up to Yellow Creek, you can drive clear to the trailhead. A good road. County road. You go up to Capitol City, you drive up North Henson Creek clear to the top. Good road. Well maintained. County road. You go further up past Rose's cabin to Hurricane Basin. That is a county road now. You can continue right on over Engineer

Mountain. Now how many more god damned roads do you want up there?"

"There's no place to build 'em."

"Well, they could find a place to put 'em. But you get up on top of the mountain at American Flats, you got nothing. You go up the Lake Fork you got the same god damned thing. My point is, we do not need any more roads. We do need a program where they could rebuild a lot of these horse trails and foot paths for people who come to these mountains. All these people who went up Henson Creek — the old timers — they all had trails up those mountains. And they been neglecting the trails. They need to rebuild the trail system. Then people could walk and you don't tear up the land.

"That one guy there, he's a good friend of mine. He said it's a shame they can't go where they please on their own land. What do you tell a guy like that? You could make an enemy, so I didn't say a god damned thing. I made up my mind. I'm gonna call the BLM this morning, in Montrose or Gunnison, as soon as I get back, and tell them that I was at the meeting. After the meeting, when I was at the door, Art Anderson, one of the officials at the BLM said to me, he says, 'Goddamn it Perk. I'm surprised you didn't say something'. I said, 'Art, I'm getting a little older all the time and I'm getting smarter. I know when to keep my mouth shut.' You could never convince them. Now, you see that guy sitting over there at that table right there across the room? That's my son-in-law. He's one of those guys that think they ought to go wherever they please."

Perk turned in his chair and hollered across the room. "Hey, Clay. I want you to meet Joe Wise. I was just telling him that you were a very strong conservationist. That you believe in all the laws of the land. That you believe all these EP reports." He turned and winked at me. "Joe is putting together a memorandum on these mines that I have been telling you about for years. Hopefully, when we are done I will be able to hand you a little memorandum saying that this is the way this mine was. And up at the top, I'm gonna say, 'No bullshit. Just the facts.'"

Perk turned back to me. "Clay, he's a misplaced Texan. He's married to my daughter. He's from Austin originally. He's a native right now. He got himself in Lake City and he's got himself invested to the point where he can't get out."

Perk called across to Clay again. "When do you think we ought to pull the starter off that D6 Cat? I can start it with a rope. In a couple of more days I'll be through for a few days. We might ought to send it into Montrose and have it redone."

Clay nodded.

"He's a mechanic. That's his business."

"You start that Cat with a rope?"

"You can. See that pony motor has got an automatic starter, but they got a little deal about that big around and you can put a rope around it and give it a spin."

"That's the gasoline engine."

"That Cat's got what they call a pony motor. You start it with gas, and it engages the big engine. You get it warmed up enough and throw it on compression and if it's warm enough it will kick off."

Perk finished his coffee and leaned back in his chair. "Well, lets see now, we might go by the bank, go inside the bank and tell Peggy hello."

"And I need to go pick up that paper with the article about the Golden Wonder."

"Yeah, I put in a lot of work on that."

"In a way, that Golden Wonder Mine represents this whole story because it was discovered about the time your father got here. And it's gone through your father's lifetime, and you held it until almost the end of the century. So that mine spans your family and the whole century."

"We were involved in a lot of litigation over that. See that case over that land we had went to the Colorado

Supreme Court. That was a tough one. We won that. I told you about that. My dad had $45,000 in escrow in his hand, so when we won the lawsuit in the Supreme Court, we had to be able to show up with that 45,000 bucks. That was part of the deal. When the lawsuit was over, if we didn't have the money, we lost the deal. When the decision came out, the Supreme Court said well what we need now is the check. We did not have the money. We knew the money was coming but it wasn't there, yet. Monahans, my dad's attorney, wadded up some paper like that, put it in an envelope, wrote '$45,000 to the court of the United States,' handed it to the clerk who received it."

"He just wadded up paper."

"Yeah. And put it in an envelope. And the guy took it, wrote him a receipt and never looked at it. That guy never opened that envelope. And he put it in the safe. About two or three days later, when that $45,000 came in, Monahans went all the way back to Denver and said to that clerk, 'Now I want to exchange this letter for that $45,000 you're supposed to have in that envelope.' Well this guy said, 'Well, I'll be a son-of-a-bitch. If I'd known that I would have never taken it.' So that was how close it was to losing.

"You got to have a judicial system, but in some ways it's a corrupt situation too. Sometimes there's no justice in the court system. If you got the money you can get what you want. Take that killing in the church. Did you see that on TV. Two guns, opened up in a church and killed six people and wounded eight or nine more. Then he turned the gun and killed himself. So it shows you, you're dealing with crazy people."

"What's happening? That never happened in the past."

"TV. TV has caused the problem. Someway, sooner or later, they got to put a curb on that stuff that goes on TV. Especially . . . . One night I accidentally turned over to, it was one of those sex programs. If you ever watch some of that stuff, you won't believe what you see. Any young couple, young people, watch that stuff, they're liable to perform an act that they wouldn't even think of. It stimulates sex. Now, how you gonna stop that? The freedom of speech, they say.

"And gun control. I don't know how you can do it. The American people say they got a right to carry a gun. Maybe strong capital punishment is the answer. If you can't keep someone from going crazy and shooting someone, then take him right out and cut his head off like you would a chicken. And throw his body in the goddamn river. I'm a strong supporter of capital punishment. Got to do it. That's all there is to it.

"You know, TV has got a lot of good qualities and a lot of bad qualities. Every day you can see on TV some guy walk up and shoot somebody, for no reason at all. You bombard people with that violence every day and pretty soon they're not shocked by it anymore.

"Just like that crazy son-of-a-bitch that pulled a gun on me that night in the alley. You've always had a lot of crazy people, but now you've stimulated them to the point that there are more crazy people. That guy that pulled the gun on me, my brothers beat the shit out of him. That same guy, sometime later he got in a fight and some guy took a knife and stuck it in him and killed him. So you reap what you sow. A lot of times you do. I've done misdeeds myself and it always caught up with old Perk.

"See those men over there in the corner booth? Those guys, I don't know who they are, but I'll bet they are out here looking for the big elk. Black powder season's on now. I think it's bow season, too.

"You know, this world's changing so fast it's a hard time to keep up with it. I'll tell you one thing, if they don't slow down, if they don't wake up, they're definitely going in the wrong direction. Spiritually. I really don't know where they're headed myself."

"You know Perk, I think that's why places like Lake City are gonna catch on again. See, things go in cycles. You and I want

*to go back and live like it was in the old days. We'd like to have
more money, but we'd like things to be more like they were. Well,
so do a lot of other people. They're hankering for the old times."*

"They are. That's why I say this third political party may
amount to something. These young guys, they're getting
burned out on the Republicans. I'll tell you, I've been a
Republican all my life but I might vote for a third party.

"Anyway, if guy can make a living right here in Lake
City, it's a pretty nice place. You're right close to heaven.
You're right close to God. You're right close to nature.
You're close to everything. And I don't think it will
change much because the government's got 95% of the
land. A lot of guys sitting here would disagree, 'cause they
want to get rid of the government. That ain't a gonna
happen.

"As a matter of fact, they are buying back more land.
You know, it's crazy about money. You take this guy Bill
Gates. The money that guy's made. He invented his own
home. Sometimes I think God must put certain people on
this earth for some certain purpose. Those people that
invented the telephone. They're not ordinary people.
Anyway Joe. I've had a good time visiting with you this
morning. Here, I'll get the coffee."

*The newspaper office was closed, but a note on the door for
Perk said to come back in the afternoon to pick up the newspaper
article. We headed back through town toward the ranch. As we
drove, Perk pointed out the mining claims along the way.*

"The Golden Pearl, The Lode Star, The Dolphin and
the Dolphin Mill site and the Rob Roy are right up by that
subdivision on the east side of the river. Right next to the
Sulphurette. We had to buy those claims. That cost us a
little bit of money to buy 'em. We had to buy 'em 'cause
we found out one thing. Some of our cabins was on the
Sulphurette. My brother's house was on it. See that mineralized area, where that road goes right across the face of
the cliffs?"

On a cliff face, just above the river, a rust-colored streak of rock angled up across a road cut, where a dark tunnel had been blasted.

"It's right there. Without that work we wouldn't have got those mining claims. And we wouldn't have had no subdivision. All those homes are on mining claims."

"Now once you own a patent mining claim, you can develop the surface?"

"You can do anything as long as you pay the taxes. You can't do that on an unpatented mining claim. We got some of them. And all you can do is use it for mining purposes."

"So, once you have a mining claim that is patented, it's just like owning land anywhere else?"

"That's right. And you get the mineral rights with it. A lot of homesteads and Colorado ranch homes, they did not get the mineral rights. The government reserved it. That Cora Mine is right above the ranch by the Sulphurette. Just beyond the Sulphurette is the Dolphin and the Dolphin mill site. And, up in the gulch was the Silver Fleece, and that's where the boarding house that they used for the pest house where they buried the black men during the scarlet fever epidemic.

"But up on top, you see, about half way up that mountain, there's two claims there — The Belle of St. Louis and the Empire. They're up there by the Golden Wonder. I was on the Board of County Commissioners, and nobody had paid taxes on them for years. The county took a lot of those claims. Just took title to a lot of stuff. So I guess it would be safe to say I convinced the other two commissioners we ought to sell them. So, we advertised them for sale. Now I couldn't buy them myself, so what I did, I bought them in my brother, Joe's, name. He was in the service. The reason I bought 'em under Joe's name was that I knew if he got in trouble, I could say, for self protection, he was in the service and all that stuff. But we didn't have to do that. We got 'em for Joe — four or five claims — and after the war was over, we quieted the title. We had no intention at that time of going into a subdivision, I just wanted to get 'em so someone else wouldn't get 'em."

We turned in at the ranch, crossed the river bridge and headed up a dirt road past the tourist cabins. The dirt road became more and more narrow and wound up into the trees away from the river.

"So," I said, "the original ranch was way back up here on the hill. When you bought the McLeod house, did you get the land all the way down to the road?"

"No. Hell, no. Up there, where those mining claims ended, you run right on BLM land."

"Oh, so your place and the Horse Park place were separated."

"When my dad bought this place, the Upper Ranch had nothing whatsoever to do with it."

"So you had to fill in by buying more land?"

"That's why we kept buying all that stuff. We knew we had to have access. There was an old timber road that went from Lake City on the other side of the river, right up past the falls clear up to where our road is now. They hauled those timbers clear down to the sawmill. As a matter of fact, they had a couple of saw mills up there in Horse Park."

"When we got that land there was still about a quarter of a mile in between the two pieces of land. Then, we had to get a right of way permit from the BLM. Well that one didn't come easy either. We finally got them to give us a permanent easement on that road, so it's all connected now.

"You know this is the best time of year for a tourist to come up here."

"I think the fishing is better this time of year, too."

"The fishing is good in these streams right now. The water's low and clear. See, since we put this part of the stream from here down to the falls into a catch and release, it's good fishing. See those rocks I've put in the river? That creates a lot of good habitat for these fish. I'm gonna do more of it. This is Park Creek right here. We're gonna' subdivide all this land. We already got the electric power for these lots. Now see that tunnel I was telling you about where the mineral is. That goes in about eight hundred feet, but it's caved in now.

"I built this road. I had to blast this goddamn thing. I got a wagon drill and I blasted it. A wagon drill is a great big air compressor with a big drill that sits off to the side. You can drill a twenty-foot hole with that. Now, that tunnel where the water is running out, I went in and put a pipeline in there and piped it out for livestock purposes. They shipped a lot of ore out of this tunnel right here. It went in there about eight hundred feet, and then they stoped it out. I think, if you go through this tunnel, it might be connected with that Silver Fleece tunnel. Then, you come right out on top of the mountain. They stoped these tunnels out clear to the surface. Now this has all been subdivided. These lots here have all been sold. You can walk right out around the corner and you look at the most beautiful scene you ever looked at."

"Isn't it funny, those open parks up there where no trees grow?"

"You know what caused that? From what I understand, certain places aspen do thrive, but when they use up all the nutrient in that soil, they die.

"See that big rock over there, Joe? Across the river. There's a gulch that comes down just to the left of that rock. There's a spring there, right where the aspen are. You got a lot of water there. That's why there are aspen there. A guy by the name of Ramsey got an idea that he was gonna uncover that vein so he run a ditch from that spring right around the mountain and made him a little pond. When that pond got full — about 5000 gallons of water — he'd lift the head gate and down the hill she'd go, washing out all that dirt for him. So now you go up there and see a ditch fifteen or twenty feet deep and you wonder how in the hell that happened. It happened because Ramsey was storing the water and then releasing it and down the hill she'd go. Do his mining for him. But, it never uncovered a vein like he thought it would. My grandson, Paul, bought this lot and sold it to a guy from Bryan, Texas and he sold it to another guy who sold it back to Paul. Paul wants to build a house there."

"Perk, you ought to get in the construction business. You could build the houses on all these lots you sell."

"Well, we've done that. I put in all the septic tanks and blasted all the roads for all the houses on the ranch. Larry has built six houses on our subdivision for several people on a cost plus basis. But, he's quit that. He couldn't make any money.

"We own that horse pasture. Part of that was on that mining claim. But when we surveyed the land, after we got the bill through the U.S. Congress that President Kennedy signed into law, we had to survey the land and we had to hire a government surveyor to do it. That Park Creek comes out of Waterdog Lake, and we got permits on four or five other springs. You can't just use the water. You got to get it all legal. You take this Colorado River, for example. It's one of the most controversial and over-appropriated rivers in the entire U.S."

We passed an old truck motor that was connected to a circular saw blade by a broad black band.

"What's this rig here?"

"That's where we saw our firewood. Man, we've sawed millions of blocks of wood on that damn thing. We had a John Deere tractor and we had a belt that run off the flywheel on the tractor.

"Now this is the Sulphurette tunnel right above us. They shipped a lot of silver ore from that. This is all our land. When we got that bill, we showed the government where we wanted the line to go. That's why I'm sure I made a mistake in some respects. We went with the surveyors and showed 'em what we wanted and that's what we got. In some places I could say I wish I'd got a little further one way or the other direction. You know what I'm saying?

"There are three lots up here that belong to a guy by the name of Peter Jenkins. He's the guy that walked across America and wrote that book about it. He stayed here with us. He figured Lake City was halfway across. I gave him a good deal cause I thought he was gonna give us a lot of publicity. And he did. He published a story about Vickers Ranch in National Geographic. Put it in his book too."

We stopped on a wooded bluff above the river.

"That's Jenkins' place. Walk out there and look at that son-of-a-bitch. If that ain't one of the most spectacular views you have ever seen. I don't think there's any place in the United States any prettier than this. You can't put together a subdivision that is as attractive and add to the privacy and the exclusiveness on this ranch. There's no other place on the Western Slope of Colorado like this. One time I was sitting right here with Governor Vandergriff — he's retired now — he come up here and he said, 'Perk, you guys must have had good luck to put this together like it is.' Everybody has got their own little privacy. Hell, I wouldn't sell all those lots. Most of those lots right now are worth $90,000. I think that younger generation of Vickers will protect it and keep it just like we have it. All they have to do is handle and maintain it properly and they have always got it. Especially that Upper Ranch. That Upper Ranch is the biggest asset we've got because you go up that road and come into that three thousand acres, that beautiful hay meadow land and we got nine fish ponds up there — all good fish ponds. So you can stay at Vickers, rent a jeep, stay in a cabin, you can go up there and fish all day. Where else can you find something like that? There's not any left!

"This place is protected. I'm sure. Larry has got a great head for business and it looks like the younger Vickers has got a great head too. Yet they will have to work. And Peggy and Patsy, for their part of the family, they can always use it for anything they want to. I didn't want to divide the land up into four or five parts. There was a family of eight of us, and some of the members of the family are dead now. My brothers and I always got along fine with all of them.

"My sisters, they all felt like they got the worst of the deal. But they had nothing in it! They left here when they was fifteen years old. Still, when they got old, they thought they ought to have part of it. Well, if you start to divide up stuff like that — that's what got me in the position I am in today. So, it's just a situation. I put it together the way I wanted to. I made some mistakes, as the record will show, but I'm still proud of what I've done, and what I got to show for it.

"If you had been here with me and my brothers Joe and Bob and the government comes in bragging about how they were gonna move the Vickers off. The Vickers had it and we're gonna take it away from 'em. So we finally got that settled through that bill in Congress. If it hadn't been for my connection in politics, she's all gone. They even went so far as to tell us that they were gonna give us a reasonable length of time to remove our improvements and put the land back in it's natural state. Can you imagine that?

"I was sitting right there in Washington and Senator Gordon Allot, told me afterwards, he said, 'My god, Perk, when they said that, I looked over at you and I thought sure you were gonna have a heart attack.' He said, 'You finally got around to where you made a statement and I know you felt bad about it.' And I did apologize too. I said to this guy, I said, 'Let me tell you something! There's three of us Vickers together on that deal. My brother Joe was drafted into the Army when he was about eighteen when the war started. He served in the Army, he went to Africa and Sicily and France and he was captured in Germany. He was in the infantry and no doubt he was responsible for killing a lot of people on the way back and forth. My brother, Bob, was in the Japanese theater of war. He was in the heavy artillery. He did the same thing. I said when you notify us to move our families off, I said, well, old Perk will probably move, I'm a peace-loving man. But when you come up there to move my brothers off that land, you better come pretty well prepared.'

"When we got back to Allot's office, I apologized. He said, 'Well I could tell you was emotionally shook up.' He said, 'Now Perk, you go on back to Colorado and don't worry. I'll carry your bill in the Senate. You go back and do all the influence you can and you raise your family just like you're doing and don't pay no attention, we're gonna get that bill through.'

"Jesus Christ, I come home and I called a friend of mine in Amarillo and I said that bill's in the Senate now — the full subcommittee. And he said, 'Well, I'll make a call to Lyndon Johnson,' and I heard him tell Johnson, 'Now look, Lyndon, the Vickers Bill is in final approval with the subcommittee. If you don't recommend that bill and get it out of there in favor, I'll kick your ass all over Texas.' They was fraternity brothers. So he called Sam Rayburn from his office and said, 'Now, Sam, look. We got to get that bill through the Senate.'

"Sam Rayburn signed the bill. His name's on the deed. Well, I'm gonna tell you, that's why I tell people I put in a lot of time in politics, but it paid off in some respects 'cause I had the connections, I'm telling you. I keep telling my family, for Christ's sake, keep an interest in the political situation. It's a lot of trouble, but you got to do it. You meet a lot of good people in the process of doing it too.

"So then, I got ahold of Dr. J.A. Criss from Shreveport. We built that cabin over there for him. That number G. He was my good friend and a great friend of Russell Long. He told Russell, 'Keep moving on it. Keep working.' So if I hadn't had some political connections. Jesus Christ, you go back to Washington and tell them you're John Doe and you want to get a bill through, they'd laugh at you."

"I'm not sure there are any special congressional bills that deal with just one item anymore."

"As a matter of fact, the record will probably show that there's only been twice — including us — in the history of the United States that they got a record of. The Rockefellers got a special bill through there on some of the land up there in west Yellowstone. That's the only other time. You couldn't ever do it now. She's over with.

"See there, that's the Golden Quartz Mine you're looking at now. I still got that. The Golden Wonder is just on this side. I'll show it to you if we don't get rained out. If a guy just wanted to come out here and live and enjoy life, there ain't no place like it. Now, to make money, that's hard to do."

The narrow road wound up through an aspen grove. Perk shifted down into low gear to make the step climb.

"I built all these roads you see up and down this place. This road, we had to blast this. When I got that new patent I had to have a special authorization to use this road. This is on BLM land. This didn't come easy, either. Now this old road, we blasted it out here right down to the foot of Slumgullion and followed the river. They had a bridge right down here called the Dawn of Hope Bridge where the highway bridge is now. I don't know why they called it that. Then the road continued on down beside the lake. I helped build this in the '50s. I worked about two years on this damn road. Right here is the Belle of the East and the Belle of the West. They're tied together, both of them. Joel Swank bought that. It's on a part of an old placer. He sold that for a subdivision to a guy from Austin, Texas. Now we're coming to Belle of the East. That Belle of the East tunnel is right here."

We passed a car parked off the road in the trees. "See that car parked there. I know these guys. They're bow hunting up on that land. He's probably guiding. It's not easy to make a living here. That guy right there, he probably don't have a dime invested, except he just come in with his horses and stuff. Over there's Red Mountain. See, all those mines that are connected to the Golden Fleece and the Black Crook and all them mines did in fact produce some valuable minerals. The first one was the Golden Fleece right over there by that gulch. See where that outcropping is? That's where they found the first ore.

"You know it hadn't been too many years ago, a man by the name of Bud Vernon was County Assessor. That was during the '50s. He and a guy by the name of Chris Samplin, they found out that back in the old days some guy had stole some of that gold from the Golden Fleece and buried it under a tree. Said maybe a ton. In sacks. They went up there and they located it. He didn't have any right to it, but nobody else did either. They shipped that ore and it run about ten or eleven ounces.

"This is the Belle of the East right there. That goes back in there quite a ways. They shipped a lot of ore out of there. Matter of fact, the Belle of the East and the Belle of the West underneath are connected. In that Belle of the West you can go up that stope and you come out this tunnel. There's a lot of underground work went into that down there. They got a patent on a placer now, they called it the Malta Placer."

"Now, you couldn't dig any on a placer claim, right?"

"That's right. Surface work only. It's been subdivided now. All that land on that Malta Placer."

"And that's different from hard rock mining because there's no digging."

"That's right. No underground work. See up there on that hill behind the ranch? Our cookout place is up there on top. You've never been up there, have you? Aw, you're gonna — when you see that you won't believe it. Now this is Dead Man's Creek right here. This road right here goes up to the Golden Wonder. It's closed now, but I'm gonna open it up one of these days. It would be a lot shorter to haul the ore down this road than it would be by the other."

"Where does the road from the Golden Wonder come out now?"

"Right down through our subdivision. Right through the Upper Ranch. We'll go up that way this evening."

We crossed the Dawn of Hope bridge over the Lake Fork and headed back toward the ranch.

"When I surveyed that land out to get that patent I should have extended it out to get that bench too. But I'll tell you what, that special bill was designed to direct the United States government to convey title to Vickers on 110 acres. So when I got the surveyor in I went around and said I want that, I want that, I want that — walked all around with him. We finally drafted it ready for approval and we got 159 acres. I was afraid when I saw that. 'Aw Jesus Christ that's gonna kick the whole thing out.' But we got by with that. We had to buy that, you understand. They didn't give us nothing. I had to appraise and buy it. But I used some honest-to-god political strings to get the appraisal in our favor. The lies I told and the double cross you won't believe.

"As a matter of fact, when we went for that appraisal, I hired a guy by the name of Ruff Dunn. He was an engineer from Telluride and Ouray. He was staying down at the Elkhorn. One Sunday morning a guy came in the bar there and was bragging, sitting around there, and he and Ol' Ruff got to visiting. Ruff knew we was waiting on an appraiser, but we had no idea who that was. Well, Ruff got to visiting with this guy — his name was Nye. It was Sunday and they couldn't buy whisky. Finally in the conversation Ol' Ruff found out the guy must be the appraiser we was waiting for. And Ruff said, 'Send me a bottle up to Room 13.' He got a couple of drinks in the guy and Ruff says, 'By the way, Mr. Nye, what are you doing here in Lake City?' And Mr. Nye said, 'Well, I'm sent in here to do some appraisals for a ranch up the valley. There's a family up there that's been living off that government land all their lives, paying nothing to the government. I'm gonna make 'em pay for it.' He told Dunn that.

"When Ruff told me that, I had our attorney Bob Knaus go up to the BLM offices with a letter from me and a letter from Ruff Dunn saying that this fella should not be allowed to survey that property. So we disqualified that guy. So we got a hold of another list of surveyors that they would accept, and they give me a guy in Phoenix who was a very well known appraiser. So by god, we picked him, a guy by the name of Mel Davis that was in the bank in Gunnison.

"So I talked to Mel and I said, 'I'll tell you what I'll do. Why don't you wine and dine that guy from Phoenix a little bit?' So we got him up here and took him up to Crystal Lodge and I had Roy Pray cook a special steak and we had a big dinner, and then had a drink or two. So Mel talked this appraiser into letting him do the appraising for him. In exchange for that I gave him nothing, except that mining car from Isolde Mine. I brought that down and gave him that mining car and it's still setting down there in his yard at his home site at Crested Butte. He's dead now and so is his wife. So sometimes you think you didn't gain much but you gained more than you think."

"A lot of ground work in that deal."

"I was an expert at that."

"Was your father a good dealer, too?"

"Oh, my dad was the best trader you ever saw in your life. If he hadn't been a good trader, we'd starved to death, surer than hell. When he sold that Cleveland Mine up there just this side of Pelican, that 40,000 bucks was a fortune at that time.

"You know, in the end, Ol' John Vickers was right about two things. One is that there's gold in these hills, but now the gold is the hills themselves. The second thing he was right about is that it's worth fighting for."

We stopped in front of the ranch office.

"This was a good day, Perk. I'll go downtown and pick up that newspaper article."

"Well, that woman at the newspaper office is waiting for you."

"What was her name?"

"Damned if I know. As I get older I don't remember names as well as I used to. You read that article, and we'll go up to the Golden Wonder this afternoon."

I did, and I learned that as much as anything else, the story of the Vickers family is the story of the Golden Wonder Mine.

Silver World, 8/7/98

THE GOLDEN WONDER MINE: THE TRADITION CONTINUES

"In the mountains above Vickers Ranch, Au Mining Inc. is carrying on a long tradition of mining in the San Juans at the Golden Wonder Mine. Au Mining has leased the Golden Wonder from LKA International since June of 1997, where the owners are attempting to make a living mining high-grade gold. With the last load of 200 tons shipped to the Montana smelter they use, Au Mining capped off a 500-ton year. They need about 2 ounces/ton to cover their expenses. The owners, from Arkansas and Montrose, met while working at the Camp Bird Mine in Ouray. They became familiar with the mine when working at the Ute-Ulay mill, which was being used to concentrate some of the ore from the Golden Wonder. It was there they became aware that the Golden Wonder held a treasure of high-grade ore. After being laid off at the Camp Bird Mine, the owners made a lease purchase agreement for the mining claim. Now using safer techniques they are mining Level 6, blasting and drilling up to break into Level 5 along the gold vein. Hand sorting the best ore to go to the smelter. The Golden Wonder is a small epithermal vein where ore was placed as a fluid. It produces high-grade gold and moderate silver and little other metal — rare in

the Lake City district — more typical of the ore around Cripple Creek. The host rock is rhyolite. A mountain idyll in August 1880 resulted in the chance discovery of the famed Golden Wonder Mine. On the 5th of that month, Tom Beam, a 35-year old part-time assayer and sawyer invited 18-year old McClelland "Clell" Fisher to go prospecting. Beam had operated sawmills in the vicinity of Horse Park and felt there was a good chance of locating iron deposits in the area. The Crooke Smelter was then in operation and in great need of iron ore for fluxing.

Unsuccessful in their search for iron ore in Horse Park, Beam and his young colleague crossed over to the west face of Gold Hill and sat down to rest in the midst of a large rock slide. The location of the men's idyll was high up Deadman's Gulch, so named for its proximity to the graves of the men killed by Alfred Packer a few years before.

It was while seated in the rock slide that Beam and Fisher reverted to their old prospecting habits and began breaking some of the quartz-like fragments. Breaking one large boulder they were surprised to find it sprinkled with bright, shiny flecks.

The elder Beam was more cautious, calmly suggesting the glistening material was nothing more than mica; Fisher was equally adamant, however, declaring that the shiny bits were gold.

Samples of the rock were duly packed back to Lake City and both men were astounded later that evening when Beam completed a quick assay confirming the samples contained gold valued at $35,000 per ton.

The following morning, August 6, 1880, Fisher and Beam rushed back to the large rock slide to formally stake the Golden Wonder and the Golden Mammoth claims. The claim was kept quiet until proper papers were filed by the two men claiming ownership in the lodes on a 50-50 basis.

News of the strike attracted statewide attention and began what was known as the "Gold Hill

Excitement. " *Visitors flocked to the barren hillside in the coming days and within a short time the upper portion of Deadman's Gulch was covered with claim stakes for would-be bonanzas.*

Fisher and Beam's fond hopes for striking a rich bonanza on Gold Hill were bolstered later in the summer as assays showed Golden Wonder ore valued at between $45,000 and $104,000 per ton.

Starting immediately after staking the claim, the owners began limited operations, sorting and sacking rocks from the slide, all the while searching for the elusive source of the gold-bearing rock.

Beam and Fisher soon realized they were undercapitalized to carry on extensive development of their Gold Hill properties. The gold-bearing vein remained a mystery and soft, shifting soils on the mountainside made it difficult to excavate an exploration tunnel.

The original locators received numerous offers to purchase the Golden Wonder and finally in January 1881, the two owners agreed to sell the property to a consortium of Denver investors headed by C. C. Alvord.

As original locators of the Golden Wonder and Golden Mammoth, Fisher and Beam received $110,000. The fortune changed the lives of the locators. Clell Fisher later died in 1908 in a fall from a painting scaffold on the Denver City Auditorium, which was being readied for the 1908 Democratic National Convention.

Beam, who had arrived in Lake City by wagon from Kansas in August 1875, was one of the founders of Lake City. Beam and his brother started the Lake City Lumber Company of Bluff Street. Among his best-known construction projects were the High Bridge of the Denver & Rio Grande Railroad on the Lake Fork north of town and the beamed ceiling of the Armory. He was also involved with the Vermont and Alabama Lodes on El Paso Creek and the Japan Mine in Telluride. He lived in Lake City and died in 1923.

The mother lode was never found. The mine closed in 1882 in costly litigation.

John Vickers, whose upper Lake Fork ranch was located in close proximity to Gold Hill, was always fascinated by the defunct Golden Wonder Mine. Vickers quietly began buying up unpatented mining claims — among them the San Francisco-4, Lone Jack, Pride of the West, Golden Age and Windy Point — surrounding the Golden Wonder prior to 1930.

The long-closed Golden Wonder was at the time owned by three elderly widows living in Chicago. Their Colorado interests were represented by W. R. Davies. Vickers entered into a negotiation with Davies around 1930 and worked out a deal to obtain a bond and lease on the mine. Under terms of the transaction, Vickers had a five-year lease. At the end of five years he had an option to buy the mine for $45,000.

The would-be mine magnate immediately enlisted the aid of his young sons, Ivan, Jack, Robert, Joe, Howard and Perk and began development work at the highest level. They reconfirmed the original vein and began removing low-grade ore with an estimated two to three ounces of gold per ton."

Silver World, 8/14/98

ELUSIVE RICHES, CONTENTIOUS LITIGATION FORM GOLDEN WONDER MINE'S HISTORY

"While several of the brothers pushed development work in the mine, it fell to Bob and Perk to load the ore onto horses and haul it down the mountain. (Now Perk watches as the white sacks of ore accumulate near the door of his office.) Each horse was alloted five sacks of ore, after which the pack animal was lead down Deadman's Gulch to Vickers Ranch. (Down the same

gulch Packer walked out the year the town was founded.)
The ore was then dumped into a bin and the empty sacks
returned up the mountain to repeat the process. Ore col-
lected over a period of time was then trucked out of Lake
City to one of the two smelting operations in Leadville
and Colorado Springs.

It was at this time, in the early 1930s, that the
Vickers began to work on the second level of the Wonder,
a 400-foot tunnel which was excavated into the moun-
tain 100 feet down the mountain from the first work-
ings. The vein was again located and ore continued to
be removed.

The elder Vickers was short on development funds,
however, and successfully sought capital from a group of
eastern investors, among them Walter Crysler and Fred
G. Corning. The new-found investors hired J.G. Neal, a
well-known mining engineer who had most recently
worked in South Africa to come to Lake City to supervise
three shifts at the Golden Wonder.

Among the 12 to 15 men who were hired to work on
the project — receiving 50 cents an hour, plus room and
board — were Rondo Wilson, Joe Hunt, Glen Hunt,
Harry Ramsey and the Carmen brothers.

In February, 1933, J.W. Vickers told the News-
Champion he had encountered an exceedingly rich body
of ore at a depth of 245 feet in the Wonder. According to
Vickers' account, the original gold vein — estimated at
14 inches in width averaging six feet of high grade at
$200 per ton — was rediscovered at the bottom on a
winze on the second level of the mine.

"It is all free gold and tellurium," Vickers was
quoted in the Gunnison newspaper. He continued by
noting that he was then working five men and predicted
that a full force would be employed once a compressor
was installed.

He estimated that old-time miners "had missed by two feet the vein which was within their reach at that time."

It was at this point of optimism that Vickers and his partners were surprised when Davies, the owners' representative, attempted to renig on the original lease-purchase agreement. Rebuffed by Vickers when he sought to become an equal partner in the increasingly promising enterprise, Davies took Vickers to court to break the contract.

Lengthy litigation — certainly not the first nor the last in the Wonder's eventful history — continued through 1934 when the Gunnison District Court ruled in Vickers' favor. In the meantime, however, Vickers' eastern financial backers had become leery and pulled out of the deal. The decision was appealed to the Colorado Supreme Court and was again ruled in Vickers' favor.

It was a hollow victory for the Vickers family, however. "Sure, the contract was upheld, but where were we going to come up with the $45,000 purchase price?" Perk Vickers asks.

It was at that time that they turned to several short term "saviors," the first of whom was J.S. Bache of the venerable New York-based banking firm. In return for a $48,000 first mortgage on the mine, Basche agreed to pay the purchase price, attorney's fees and other related costs, which the Vickers had incurred.

The mine entered a brief period of inactivity as the majority of the Vickers brothers entered World War II. At the war's end, however, renewed efforts were made to reactivate the mine. In 1943 the Basche heirs agreed to sell the mine for $25,000 to another interim savior, Roy Goldston, well-known owner of Child's Park on the upper Lake Fork.

Goldston, in turn, agreed to a five year lease/purchase ending in the early 1950s to resell the property back to the Vickers partnership. Development continued *in the later '50s as the Humphrey Gold Corp. of Denver opened up the third level of the mine and worked to connect the lowest with the upper two tunnels.*

In the early 1970s the Southern Union Gas Production Company acquired an option to purchase the mine for $500,000. Southern Union in turn leased the mine to Rocky Mountain Ventures of Denver, which did little in the way of development but did haul out an estimated 2,500 tons of good grade ore which had been stockpiled. Perk Vickers still refers to this period in the mine's history as a big mistake because no royalties were ever received from the ore which was being hauled away.

Lake City Mines obtained an option on the mine from Southern Union in the early 1980s. They signed a lease/purchase on the mine, agreeing to pay Southern Union $3,000 per month, with an option to buy the property for $300,000. The company also acquired a lease/purchase on the old Ute-Ulay property on Henson Creek.

At the time, gold was $650-700 per ounce and Lake City Mines sold stock in the operation and pushed development at the Golden Wonder and took steps to renovate the old Ute-Ulay mill to process ore taken at the mine.

The company pushed development on the 6th level of the mine and excavating a raise accessing the third level, all in hopes of encountering "economically significant mineralization." As development geared up in 1980, the mine employed ten men on a three shift, 24-hour per day basis.

In August, 1981, mine manager, Ken Davies, reported that a "promising vein" had been discovered as the sixth level tunnel reached a depth of 1087 feet. The vein varied in width from a few inches to approximately 5.5 feet with gold and silver values. Mine management was careful not to set an estimate on the newly discovered ore, however, instead preferring to wait for assay results.

In an interview with the Silver World *in 1981, Davis was enthusiastic about the prospects of the newly discovered vein. "The geologist has marked the vein down and we're going to follow it — follow it up a tree if necessary."*

In October 1981 it was announced that Lake City Mines had exercised its option to acquire the Wonder from the Southern Union and was negotiating for partners to join in a joint venture. It was also reported that the company had terminated the employment of 12 employees to increase operational efficiency.

No further development occurred at the mine through 1982. Ownership passed to LKA International in 1983 as the result of a joint venture agreement which was signed with Lake City Mines in October 1982. Under terms of the agreement, Seattle-based LKA paid $250,000 for a 12.5 percent interest in the mine and the promise to expend at least $750,000 during the first nine months of 1983.

Operations continued through the summer of 1983 with 24 employees, although the number of miners was reduced to 14 in September. In November it was abruptly announced that all operations at the Golden Wonder would cease; early in 1984 Lake City Mines petitioned for bankruptcy protection citing $2.3 million in liabilities and assets $350,000 greater than liabilities.

Prior to Au Mining leasing the property, the Golden Wonder was briefly operated by Jeff Stone and Mike Waddell in 1993 under a lease negotiated between LKA and Utah-based Gold Wonder Mining Company. They worked a two-foot pay streak and shipped over 100 tons of ore said to yield one-90 ounces of gold per ton. The Utah firm gave up its lease in 1993 and in 1997, Au Mining began operations on a discovery that began 120 years ago."

And so the cycle begins again, buoyed by that same hope and optimism that kept Beam and McClelland Fisher awake on that night in August more that 120 years ago.

Later that afternoon, I met Perk back at the office and we headed off to the Upper Ranch and the Golden Wonder.

"If you were having to make payments on all those cabins you own, there'd be no way you could make a profit."

"Yeah, our dude ranch operation just about breaks even. If it wasn't for those high-price lots we're selling, we couldn't do the things we do. You get about four good months. You let all those beautiful cabins set there empty for six or seven months out of the year. We're coming to the end of the Upper Ranch now. This is where John settled. Farther up. This is where I'm doing some bulldozing here — making a place for the hay. There's the cattle. We'll feed 'em up in here this winter."

"Who helps you with this place?"

"Oh, we got a couple of guys."

"Can you stay in the cabins in the winter?"

"We got six of 'em winterized. The rest of them we don't open up 'til summer. We start getting them ready in April. You can see we built a lot of roads out here."

Several picnic tables were arranged under a grove of aspen trees.

"This is where we have our breakfast cookout right here. You rent the horses and ride a long time and eat breakfast right over there. Scrambled eggs, bacon, biscuits, gravy, coffee. Everybody loves this spot. See that lake right there. That's the last pond I built. I call that Lake Emma Jean after my wife. There it sets. It's a nice lake. About two acres. If a man wanted to subdivide this entire ranch into five-acre tracts, he'd make all kinds of money. But you wouldn't have it anymore yourself. We cut that hay already. That hay on the upper ranch is all on the ground. When we get some good weather we'll finish baling it. These aspens are really pretty aren't they? Hard to beat aspen. That old equipment over there, that's our old bone yard there. Some of it we'll use and some of it we'll never use."

"Looks like that old International truck finally gave up."

"Yeah, that's the one we used to haul garbage when you was a kid. That thing hauled garbage for forty years."

"You got a lot of land up here for lots."

"Except for that federal land begins right over there."

"You know that strip of federal land dividing your place might turn out to be a blessing. That's a buffer zone."

"Oh hell, yeah! Nobody else is gonna get it. And we use it anyway — for a road."

"So this whole place is surrounded by BLM land."

"All around it."

"That gives you a pretty big back yard."

Perk smiled. "Goes all the way to Gunnison."

"If Beam was up here in Horse Park with a saw mill and that mine, why did he run off and leave it? Isn't that where your dad settled, in Horse Park?"

"Well he settled in the Upper Ranch, about a mile around the hill."

"Isn't that where Horse Park is?"

"Well, Horse Park's up ahead here, but the mine's over there. This road to the left goes to the Upper Ranch. We'll take a run up there and then go over to the Golden Wonder. But you see what it said in that article about what Beam did. They found that gold. They found a boulder they say was about the size of a Ford automobile. Just one boulder. In an outcropping. They busted that boulder up into little pieces — I got a couple of pieces in the safe. It was extremely rich. But when they shipped that boulder at that price of gold years ago they got $35,000 out of that boulder. They did a lot of exploration work around there, and they couldn't tell where it came from. There were tunnels every direction. This way and that way. That thing bounced around. At one time a guy by the name of Sowers had it. He was sure the whole mountain was covered with gold. He even kept people from coming up the hillside."

"So by the time your father had come along, they had run off and left that?"

"By the time my dad came along it had been bounced around from pillar to post and there was two old women folks in Chicago ended up with the mine. Meanwhile, my dad got some unpatented mining claims all around that Golden Wonder. He got the Lone Jack and the Pride of the West and Windy Point — about six of those claims altogether. He staked some of it. He bought some of it. All those years he kept doing the assessment work on the unpatented claims hoping that sooner or later he might be able to tie up that Golden Wonder.

"So in 1929 or 1930 he was successful in making that deal with those two women for the Golden Wonder. For $45,000. It was what they called bond/release. The bond was $45,000 and he either had to pay royalties for five years or, if at the end of the five years if he didn't have the $45,000, he had to give them right back to those folks. They started right there.

"The strange part of it was, Joe, in the beginning those other guys had run a tunnel in there about a couple of hundred feet on what looked like the vein. It was a little stringer. Didn't amount to a damn. Well, when my dad got that thing he goes up over the hill, just a little bit north with my brothers and, by god, they uncovered that gold. So they started producing it. They put up an ore bin out there so they could sort that ore and sack it. Whenever they got forty sacks, Bob, Joe and I had to go up with a pack string and haul it back down to the ranch where the barn is. Well, that went on for a while and then Dad said, 'Well I'm gonna run this #2 level in under this structure'. Which he did.

"Meanwhile, he'd gone to New York and got ahold of an acquaintance of his by the name of Donneley in Patterson, New Jersey. Donneley got him acquainted with some people in Broad Street. Broad Street is pretty close to Wall Street, I think. So they said they would finance the exploration work. So he come back and started doing the work. These two widow women who had leased it to my dad for five years had contacted a guy by the name of Blll Davis who lived in Littleton, Colorado, to represent them. So Davis would come in and see that Vickers was complying with everything he did. So my dad was doing everything he could, producing that little bit of ore to keep us from starving to death. Davis come in one day and said, 'Well, Mr. Vickers, I'll tell you what. The mine looks so good to me I'd like to go in with you on the deal.' But my dad said, 'Well, I don't need anybody. I got my family, I got my sons and we don't need you. We'll comply with all the rules.' Then Davis went back to Littleton and hired one of the best mining lawyers in Colorado and brought suit against my dad claiming that he had violated the lease.

"The lease had a lot of stipulations in there. You had to do this and you had to do that. All that stuff you know. And he claimed we had run a drift and it was supposed to be seven foot in the clear — so you wouldn't hit your head — and four foot wide and all that stuff. We sunk a shaft, which he called it an underground winze. There ain't a damn bit of difference. He had all kinds of complaints, so we went to court. When we got into court, the people that was putting up the money to work the mine said, 'Well Mr. Vickers, we didn't want to, but there is a lawsuit. If you can get it straightened out we'll continue to finance the operation.' Well, by god, to court she went. And first we had to go to district court, and Davis lost in district court. Damned if he didn't appeal it to the Colorado Supreme Court.

"Meanwhile, we couldn't ship any ore, so we stole some of that. Sold it for money to live on. But it wasn't really stealing. It belonged to us. Meanwhile, we kept right on working, sorting that ore. Had to have the money to live on and we felt sure we was gonna win that lawsuit. But we were afraid that five years was gonna be used up before the lawsuit would be over and we knew we had to have $45,000 in our hand to put it in the court so they could pay the owners if we won the lawsuit. So Dad got a guy by the name of J.S. Basche, one of those big guys in

Wall Street — he's still there, too — to say that he would put up that money. And he said in the agreement that if we won the lawsuit he'd pay the owners $45,000 and he'd be reimbursed for the attorney fees and stuff. So he goes to work. We won the lawsuit and give the owners the money, and Basche ended up with a first mortgage for $82,000 on the mine. After all that experience, he got a first mortgage on us — and we had experience. And my brother, Ivan said, 'To hell with the mine, I'm quitting.' He went and got married. So did Jack, and they both moved away. They lived up here and lived like slaves all those years trying to make some money and at the end, end up with a big mortgage on them.

"So anyway, that went on for years. My brothers went into the service and I went to Texas and I worked for Roy Goldston in Tyler, Texas. And the mine set there. My dad stayed here, with my brothers all in the service. I had to leave Mr. Goldston in Tyler, Texas, and come home and help my mother and dad. Anyway this guy, Goldston, he was just like a second dad to me. He was very wealthy and he always said he would help me any way he could.

"So, my dad and I got to talking about it and said, by god, maybe we can somehow get that Golden Wonder back in our hands, free and clear, you know. So we started corresponding with Basche. The senior Basche had died and they got to searching in the file to see what there was. They knew Vickers wanted it. They wanted to see why Vickers wanted it.

"They got to looking through the files and there was a letter from J.S. Basche and Company that said something like this, 'If Vickers and his family ever decide they want that mine, I'd like for them to have first opportunity to get the mine.' So we started negotiating.

"Now we're coming up to the Upper Ranch now. This is one of our ponds. We got nine fish ponds here. Were you ever up here at all?"

"Never was."

"Well, all the time you were fooling around the ranch didn't you come up here to the Upper Ranch?"

"I was afraid to. Didn't want to be someplace I shouldn't be."

"We'll head over to the Golden Wonder now. So, as I was saying, we finally was successful in getting Basche to write us saying that they would give us a chance to buy that mortgage back for $25,000 cash. We were right in the middle of a war and there was no way to get $25,000. And I remembered Mr. Goldston said, 'If I can ever help you and your family let me know.' So I called him and he said, 'Well, I'm gonna be in Alamosa, Colorado one of these days and I'll give you a call and you can come over and spend the day with me and visit.' And I spent the night with him.

"By god, I come home with a letter that said he agreed that he would put up the 25,000 bucks. But, in the letter of intent, we had to deed it back to him. He bought it in his name. So finally that went on for about six or eight years or so, and we paid the taxes, and we were just sitting there wondering what the hell we was gonna' do. Finally, I made another trip to Tyler and I talked to Roy Goldston and he agreed that he would give me five years, my brother and I, and if we could pay back the money he had in it over five years with no interest, he'd give us the mine. That's how we got the mine."

"So you worked it and sold the ore."

"Yep. I worked it and sold it and got screwed in a lot of ways. But, when we got the mine back, I made a deal with Southern Union Production out of Dallas for $500,000. They had an agreement where they had to do so much work and if it didn't produce the ore and stuff they would give me back the mine, just like I had on so many other deals. But the fine print wasn't the way I wanted it. Those bastards. At the end of four or five years I had to give them the mine. But they owe me $500,000. Then they sold it to another company called LKA

International and these guys here have got a piece of it. These guys that's up here at the mine now are buying it from LKA. They're paying me my royalties just like they said they would. So, I'll get $500,000 sooner or later. I'll always have it coming."

"So, after Prohibition came in and shut the saloons down, your dad moved up here?"

"Right. He locked the door and come up here to the Upper Ranch and started raising cattle. Raising big horses. Draft horses. Started raising cattle and sheep. And every two years had another child. Ended up with eight children. That's a lot of children.

"After my dad got a dose of that cyanide he was sick a long time. That went on clear up to 1912 'til we got the mine. When we got the mine, Jack, Ivan, Dad and I stayed up there for four years. We lived up there. We had a little house. Didn't have no car, no truck. This road wasn't even here. I built this road in 1945. I had to make a road. Just cleaned up the trees.

"Did I ever show you? We had a story in *Sports Illustrated* called, "Turn Left at the Porcupine." The senior editor at *Sports Illustrated* came here. He spent three trips to get that story. Had nine pages of Vickers' Ranch on it. He was staying here and he had his own Jeep. We was always visiting, but didn't have time to take him around and all. I didn't think anything significant was happening to have a publisher here. And, I was telling him how to get up there — go to the Upper Ranch, you know, and take several switchbacks. And, you get to this one switchback you see a porcupine hanging in a tree. My brother had killed a porcupine and he had hung it in a tree so it would attract coyotes or bobcats. Left it hanging in a tree. I said, 'When you get to the tree with the porcupine in it, turn left.' And he made that the title of the story."

"So when you got the deed to the place, you got the easement for this road at the same time, even though this road is on government land?"

"I'll tell you about that road. After we finally got that subdivision ready for approval, I had to do something about that road. I had an engineer who worked for the U.S. government as a mineral surveyor, survey out that road to the upper ranch, and this, too. Well, we got it all done and signed the agreement. About a year or two later, one of those government guys come in and said he got to check our road and look at the road and see if it's where it's supposed to be and all that. And he said, 'This road here is much wider than it is supposed to be.' And I said, 'What do you mean, supposed to be?' And he said, 'It's only supposed to be thirty feet.' I said, 'You better look at it, we're supposed to have a sixty foot right-of-way.' And he said, 'No, this road's thirty feet.' I said, 'Well let's go down to the office and look at the contract signed by your government.'

"What I had done, I had that mineral engineer make it sixty feet and they got that right through their office and they didn't know the difference. They said, 'Well, by god, you're the only place we know in the state of Colorado where we've approved a sixty foot right-of-way.' And I said, 'Well, we're not gonna change it any, it won't make any difference anyway. We're not gonna make a sixty foot right-of-way.'

"Well, anyhow. Can you imagine that? Now sometimes here in our conversation, it might sound like we did things that were a little bit crooked. But you had to watch out for yourself to some degree, too. It was in the contract. If they was so damn smart, they would have noticed that. There wasn't any way they could change that."

Perk stopped the car at the entrance to the mine road. A cable strung between two metal posts blocked the road. A hundred feet beyond the chain, a small yellow dump was piled beside an unimposing tunnel entrance that had been boarded with what looked like scrap lumber. 'So this is the Golden Wonder,' I thought.

"There's the Golden Wonder, down at the end of that road. I didn't bring my key to that gate. They got a cable across there. No use going down to that mine. You can see the road there. That's where we had a cabin. We lived there, my brothers and I, for at least three or four winters. Summer and winter. We didn't have any water. We had a pipeline up there to that spring on top, and it was fine in the summertime. In the wintertime we had to drain it. We melted snow to make coffee with. We walked down to the ranch every Friday night or Saturday afternoon and come back up Sunday afternoon, bringing our groceries. It's about a mile straight down the hill. You can get there in about fifteen minutes. If you're running.

"This is what we call Gold Hill where we are now. See that blower over there? See that piece of equipment there? Got an engine that runs that blower — that fan. When we were putting in that tunnel down there, we didn't have any air so we had to run that blower in there to have air to keep working. Once we got that tunnel in 1,000 feet and run a stope upraise to connect with the tunnel above, it was just like a chimney. Might near blow your hat off, the wind would go through there so fast."

"Mining takes a lot of equipment, doesn't it?"

"Oh yeah. You can't just go get a shovel and get off. I ought to take that air fan down to the museum. I doubt we'll ever run another tunnel in there."

"Beautiful spot in here. All these aspens."

"Can't beat it. We got a salt lick right out there. See how the elk have eaten the bark off of all those aspen? We got to bring up another block. The elk come up here to eat that salt, and you can catch one pretty easy. You can take that road right up to the top of the mountain. You come up over the ridge and you're still on our property. On that side it's all BLM. Except for these few patented mining claims."

"A lot of elk in here now?"

"More elk than I've seen. More elk than there's ever been."

"So they come down here in the winter?"

"Oh, they stay here on these south hills all winter. Summer they stay in the high country. Timberline. They will be in here during hunting season, too. There are two elk seasons — separated by a few days. The permit is for one or the other. Otherwise, you would have everybody out there at once. Bow season comes first. I hate that. Every year we see an elk staggering around with an arrow sticking out of it. It's a shame. It should come later. The arrow wounds don't bleed out much. You can't track an elk on this land. Should wait 'til it snows, so you can see the blood on the snow."

"Well, I'll tell you I wouldn't get a lick of work done working at a mine here. I'd be looking at the scenery all day."

"Those are beautiful red spruce timber there. That's a beautiful tree there. That's an old son-of-a-bitch. I'll bet that tree's 1,000 years old. You'd be surprised how many people come up here just to look around. Hard to beat.

"Look. There's a deer or two. A doe and her fawn. Just looking. That fawn, he says why don't we get the hell out of here. We wouldn't kill a doe under any consideration."

"When does the season start?"

"Well this year we're not gonna have any. We had a severe drought. We didn't want one. The coyotes are killing all of our deer. We got to do something with those coyotes. Like those Bascos."

"This is where you come hunting?"

"We hunt from here clear to Waterdog Lake, about three and a half miles north of here. I'll go up by the Upper Ranch and show you how to get there. A couple of thousand acres of good hay meadow. See that slusher there? That's for getting the ore out of the mine. Fill it up and pull it out when you don't have a railroad car to get it on a mucking machine. That's Cannibal Plateau up there. That's good elk hunting all the way up to timberline.

"See, when I built this road, I was just learning to run a bulldozer. A lot of people said I'd swear to god you had an engineer. Once in a while we'd bring the dozer up to get the snow off the road. Now if you go up that road another mile you come to another park called Alden's Park. If you go north for another mile you come to Vickers Lake. We keep 'em well stocked. We got them restricted to three fish a day. That's all a person can eat. Now if they catch 'em with flies they can put 'em back if they want to."

"I didn't know any of this was up here."

"That's what you get for staying down there on the flat ground."

"Pretty aspen up here. I heard they're harvesting them heavy in the Gunnison area."

"Well, the government claims they're gonna die anyway. May be. They claim once they use up all that nutrient that's in the soil, they'll die. That's why there are so many open parks on the mountainside. I don't know how many more years before they all disappear. It may never happen. They got a lot of 'em to go."

"The history of the Golden Wonder spans the whole century."

"In that mining report that engineer said that the Golden Wonder was the best mineral in the whole valley. I've forgotten just what he said. He has better terminology than I'll ever have, of course. He was a great man. He lived in Charleston, West Virginia. He's dead now. No matter how great you are or how good you are or how wealthy you get, you're gonna die same as the rest of us."

"But I figure you come back. I was looking at one of those maps and saw where there was a Wise Brothers Market downtown. Down there near where the old medical center used to be. Well the buildings changed hands a lot. So I figure I've already been here once. And I'll be back next time. Now that I've got it located."

"We got a lot of cattle in here."

"You have to run them out in the winter or do they come down on their own?"

"Oh they come home in the wintertime. Just like the horses. You can take those horses clear to Rose's Cabin, and they'll damn near beat you home."

"When does your snow come? Thanksgiving?"

"Oh, you never know. Most generally that's about right. But, one Labor Day we had thirty-six inches of snow down at the ranch. I had to get the bulldozer, by god, to get the people across the bridge. That's the worst I've ever seen. It never stopped snowing it seemed like. Then, after that we had a good long fall. Just had to get it out of its system. The weather has a lot to do with this business we've got."

"Well, you get the tourists pretty much concentrated in the summer."

"Oh yeah. It's a big gamble. If you was to come into Lake City now and buy a business, or buy a piece of land to start a business, you're just wasting your time and money. You'd go broke surer than hell. You would. You couldn't make it."

"So, these guys are still up here working this mine?"

"Yeah, they have been working two years now. They sold damn near two million dollars worth of ore this year. I get five percent of the net proceeds. I'm happy with that."

"And they still owe you $500,000."

"But the $500,000 applies to the royalties. If I get enough money — $500,000 — it will be their property. But sooner or later, if they get that, it's only thirty acres back on that side of the mountain. It don't really mean that much to us. You know?"

"After we finished talking yesterday, I went back up Henson Creek and sat there by that mill."

"How far up?"

"Thirteen miles. I was right up there by the mill."

"Where they was repairing?"

"Yeah. And I sat there waiting for the sun to come out so I could take a picture. You think that sun would come out?"

"Hell, no, it wouldn't."

"That would be a good picture for the cover of the book. 'Cause that links it with the past."

"Well, I got a big picture of that mill in the office. Now this is that Park Placer. That twenty acres that's right here. I bought that from some people in Grand Rapids, Michigan. That god-damned property was divided into thirty-five different parcels. So I had to probate at least three or four foreign wills. Two of them in England, in Spain. That all costs money. But you had to do it."

"You need a lawyer in the family!"

"I wanted to be a lawyer to start with, but I didn't have enough brains or time to go to school."

"You need a lawyer around the clock."

"We've been getting by fine lately without a lawyer. Now, up this road, we're going up to where we have our cook out.

"It's pretty up here. I like these open aspen parks."

"You go around this next corner you're liable to lose your breath. That mountain up ahead. That's Roundtop."

He stopped the jeep on a small patch of level ground beside a picnic table.

"Look at that view there," he said. "That's Lake San Cristabol down there. We have the cookouts here every Wednesday night from the first of June. Now what you do, just get out and walk down here a couple of hundred yards and take a big look."

Perk was right. The view does take your breath away. From the cookout area, the view spread down and out over 180 degrees and 10,000 square miles of mountain wilderness. To the south, the mountains of the Continental Divide formed a jagged horizon and below them, the reflective blue of Lake San Cristabol. To the west, Grassy Peak, Sunshine Peak and the bare, rusty-rose of Red Cloud Peak formed a 14,000-foot high mass. To the north, beyond the Lake City valley and townsite, beyond Henson Creek Canyon, the sawtoothed, Swiss-like Uncompahgre Range punched up into the cloudless sky.

"Well, I can see why you have your cookouts here."

"You know, Joe, one night up here in July we had 191 folks. We had so many people up here you could hardly find a place to park your car."

"That's forty cars."

"Well, we bring a truck with a lot of people on it. Throw a few bales of hay on the truck. 'You're on a hay ride folks! This is, by god, a hay ride!' Right on the other side of this table you're on federal land. A little strip of federal land comes in from that direction."

I looked around at the vista again to make sure that what I had just seen was real.

"Perk, I tell you, if I lived here I'd spend all my time right up here."

"Well, we're lucky to have this. The people who really appreciate this say, 'We really appreciate you sharing this with us.' That's fine. But we're making money sharing this with them 'cause they're staying in the cabins. But, then we let many people come up here to the cookout that don't even live at the ranch. They love it. We've had a lot of people come every time. Never miss. Never miss. Hell, on our correspondence, when we're confirming the reservations from one year to the next, they'll say, 'Now we want to know for sure if you change the Wednesday night cookout, just let us know.'"

Perk walked over to the picnic table and sat down. He sat there for a minute, not saying anything, just looking out over the majestic scene.

"You know, Joe, I come up here a lot of times and just sit here by myself. Lots of times. I come up here after I get the hunters scattered out over the hills. Just sit around here and look at that view and say to my self, 'Perk, you're a lucky man. This is about as close to heaven as you'll ever get, right here.' I'm a strong believer in that."